THE THIRD FORCE IN CANADA

THE THIRD FORCE IN CANADA

The Cooperative Commonwealth Federation
1932-1948

By

DEAN E. McHENRY

UNIVERSITY OF CALIFORNIA PRESS

Berkeley and Los Angeles

1950

UNIVERSITY OF CALIFORNIA PRESS
BERKELEY AND LOS ANGELES
CALIFORNIA

◇

CAMBRIDGE UNIVERSITY PRESS
LONDON, ENGLAND

Preface

IN THESE YEARS *of postwar disillusionment, of an uneasy local prosperity in a world where hunger and privation seem the rule, and of "we or they" attitudes, free men ought to be searching for solutions to their problems in the light of the fullest possible information concerning social and political experiments. The present work aims to tell the story of a new Canadian political party, built in part on the pattern of the British Labour Party, yet adapted to the needs and aspirations of North America. The Cooperative Commonwealth Federation (CCF) is to this continent what the "third force" is to Europe—a middle way between the extremes of reaction and revolution. It is testing, in a country very like our own, the compatibility of the politics of democracy and the economics of socialism.*

This study is the writer's second in a series on Labour parties functioning within the British Commonwealth of Nations. The first, on the Labour Party of the United Kingdom, was published under the titles: The Labour Party in Transition, 1931–1938 *(London: Routledge, 1938), and* His Majesty's Opposition: Structure and Problems of the British Labour Party, 1931–1938 *(Berkeley: University of California Press, 1940). The third, now in preparation, will cover New Zealand under Labour rule.*

Heavy obligations have been incurred in the preparation of this book. The project was commenced in 1941–1942 under a research grant of the University of California. The necessary field work in Canada was made possible through a grant-in-aid from the Social Science

[v]

Research Council. *Some additional perspective has been gained through residence in New Zealand during 1946– 1947, and I am grateful to the foundation which made it possible.*

My gratitude to leaders of the CCF is greater than can be acknowledged by any conventional expression. From the first day I appeared in Ottawa in the summer of 1942, everything I requested was provided, every question was answered fully and frankly. They trusted me with irre- placeable records and confidential documents, and wel- comed me to convention and council sessions.

At Ottawa my greatest obligations are to M. J. Cold- well, David Lewis, A. M. Nicholson, and Stanley Knowles. In the Maritimes I wish to thank Fred M. Young, Lloyd Shaw, and Clarie Gillis. In Quebec I owe most to F. R. Scott and Stanley Allen. My chief Ontario informants were George Grube, Charles Millard, and Bert Leavens. In Manitoba I wish to thank Lloyd Stinson and Don Swailes. Those who assisted most in Saskatchewan include T. C. Douglas, Clarence Fines, C. C. Williams, and Fred C. Williams. For aid in Alberta thanks are due to Elmer Roper, H. D. Ainlay, and William Irvine. In British Co- lumbia I was assisted by Frank McKenzie, Mrs. Grace MacInnis, Mrs. Dorothy Steeves, and Bert Gargrave.

Both in the collection of material and in the prepara- tion of the manuscript I have enjoyed the counsel and help of my friend, Dr. Hugh MacLean, and the research assistance of Frederick C. Engelmann, now a graduate student at Yale University. Finally, I wish to thank the personnel of the University of California Press, particu- larly Mr. W. H. Alexander, who was himself a pioneer of the movement with which this book is concerned.

D. E. MCH.

Contents

CHAPTER I

Looking Backward

THE ORIGIN of the Canadian two-party system, like that of similar alignments in Anglo-American countries, is difficult to explain. In part, the system and the party names were borrowed from Great Britain. In part, the practical inclination of the Canadians called for a party arrangement that would produce the power to govern. In part, the Canadian line-up flowed from the group alliances formed in 1867 at the time of Confederation.

The debt of Canada to Great Britain in the field of political parties is surprisingly great on the surface. The Canadian parties took the nomenclature of the United Kingdom parties; but, as Alexander Brady has pointed out, they do not resemble the British parties in composition and principles.[1]

Even if the comparison between British and Canadian parties is made in the classic period of British parliamentary government, before the rise of the Labour Party, Canadian parties are found to adhere less consistently to principles and policies. Despite these departures from the British system, however, the Canadian parties function very much like the British in the formation, support, and criticism of a government. These are carried on in Canada in the tradition of the British parliamentary system.

Students of comparative politics are now placing emphasis upon the necessity of fixing on the government of the day the responsibility for the power to govern, rather

[1] Alexander Brady, *Canada* (New York: Scribner's, 1932), p. 83.

than upon perfecting a plan to provide exactly proportionate representation.[2] The multiparty system inherently
brings instability to parliamentary government. The operation of government under the French Republic from
1875 to 1940 may be contrasted with that of the United
Kingdom over the same period. The French multiparty
system may have reflected more accurately the shifts in
public opinion, but it has lacked the element of stability
which is a top-ranking asset of the British system.

The story of the formation of Canadian parties has
been best told by Professor Underhill.[3] By the time the
Dominion was born, in 1867, Sir John A. Macdonald had
welded together the various groups supporting the union.
The Conservative Party, which he headed, continued to
get support during the years that followed by fostering
expansionism through the construction of the Canadian
Pacific Railway, by a policy of protective tariff, and by
constant reëmphasis of the advantages of British Imperial
ties. The opposition, later known as the Liberal Party,
rallied its followers through the years by stress on provincial rights, low tariff, and Canadian nationalism.

The attention given to issues does not mean that the
history of Canadian parties can be considered mainly in
terms of principles and policies. It has been as much a
struggle of great party leaders—Macdonald, Blake, Laurier, Borden, King—attracting to their parties supporters,
who in turn passed on traditional affiliations to their de-
scendants. The cleavage of Canadian parties has also followed geographic and ethnic lines. Most of Canada's

[2] See, for example, Ferdinand A. Hermens, *Democracy or Anarchy? A Study of Proportional Representation* (University of Notre Dame: Review of Politics, 1941), *passim*.
[3] Frank H. Underhill, "The Development of National Political Parties in Canada," *Canadian Historical Review,* 16 (December, 1945): 367–387.

population is spread over a relatively narrow strip along the boundary shared with the United States. The country is divided by natural barriers: mountains, lakes, great rivers, bays, and straits. The several geographic sections— the Maritimes, Ontario-Quebec, the prairies, and British Columbia—have distinctive economic interests that are often reflected in politics. The French-speaking population, never assimilated by the English-speaking majority, has remained a complicated and mercurial factor in Canadian politics.

Upon analysis, the similarities of the Conservative and Liberal parties appear more potent than their differences. As in the United States, the original principles and policies have often become obscured. The tweedledum, tweedledee nature of major parties has repeatedly caused much consternation in the ranks of the party out of office in searching for campaign issues. The Conservative Party has faced a dilemma on several occasions in the last two decades. Under R. B. Bennett and John Bracken, it has appeared to forsake its traditional role and strike out on a "progressive" line. The Liberals, on the other hand, have increasingly appeared as the true conservatives, forcing the Conservatives to choose either the "wallpaper" role of ultraconservatism, or the more adventurous "new deal," or "progressive," part.

The rise of the Cooperative Commonwealth Federation (CCF) has intensified the search of the Conservatives for a program sufficiently attractive to the common man to win his vote. It has impelled the Liberal party to refocus its attention on social legislation.

If the CCF continues to gain strength, four developments in the party system appear possible: (1) the new party might continue as one in a field of three; (2) it might

displace either the Conservative or the Liberal party;
(3) it might cause coalition and eventual union of the
two old parties; or (4) the CCF might itself enter a coalition and lose its identity within an old party. The strong
stand taken by the CCF against participation in coalition
governments is a present safeguard against the last-named
possibility. Canada's two-party tradition and the determination of the Conservatives and Liberals to curb the
CCF movement indicate that the old parties are likely to
form provincial coalition governments, as they have in
British Columbia and Manitoba. If in a future election
no party secures a majority in the federal House of Commons, the old parties are likely to be driven into a national coalition, and perhaps ultimately to union of the
parties.

AGRARIAN FERMENT

The CCF of today is a lineal descendant of the recurring
farmers' movements that have spread over Canada since
Confederation. These farmers' movements have had both
economic and political aspects. They have flourished especially during periods of economic depression.

Canadian agriculture has long stressed production of
wheat and other commodities destined, in an important
proportion, for European export. As settlement of the
Dominion spread westward, the older farm areas of the
Maritimes, Quebec, and Ontario gradually shifted to general farming aimed mainly at supplying the Canadian
market. The new lands of the West were utilized for the
production of grains, primarily wheat. Depending upon
a fluctuating world market and subject to the hazards of
fickle weather conditions, the western farmers became
the great exponents of aggressive action. It was in the
prairie provinces—Manitoba, Saskatchewan, Alberta—

that the greatest farmers' cooperative enterprises and the most active farmers' movements developed.

The Grange in Canada.—The National Grange, Patrons of Husbandry, was organized in the United States in December, 1867. It spread rapidly over the country. The Grange was, and is, an organization which seeks to protect and advance farmers economically and also attempts to dignify the agriculturalist and to carry educational and cultural influences to the farm.[4] The attractiveness of the Grange to farmers developed in part from its secret-order atmosphere. The ritual used in the seven degrees was regarded as full of symbolism and beauty. Another source of strength of the Grange was its admission of women on a basis of substantial equality with men.

The Grange entered Canada in a hesitant and temporary way as early as August, 1872. The first subordinate grange, as the local units were called, was organized in that year in the Province of Quebec; but it died shortly afterward. In 1874, however, the movement reached out into Ontario, where it was to have the fullest development. Shortly thereafter, at a convention called at London, Ontario, a provisional Dominion Grange was established. This organization was formally incorporated by a federal statute law enacted in 1877. Despite considerable initial success at organizing, the Grange soon declined to a very modest role. In its heyday in 1878, there were subordinate granges in the Maritime Provinces, in Quebec, and a few in the West. The Ontario section of the movement was by far the most active and successful. Wood reports that the Dominion Grange membership

[4] Solon J. Buck, *The Granger Movement* (Cambridge: Harvard University Press, 1913), p. 302.

The Third Force in Canada

declined from its highest level of 31,000 members in 1879 to only 12,500 members in 1884.[5]

The Grange was instrumental in establishing several business and cooperative enterprises in Canada. In the beginning, subordinate granges concentrated on trading with merchants who agreed to limit their profits. The Grange also entered the field of cooperative purchasing and distribution. Its chief instrument was the Grange Wholesale Supply Company, which flourished between 1880 and 1890. A successful salt manufacturing concern was established in the same decade and remained in business as late as World War I. Grange ventures in insurance, finance, and colonization were not successful, and indeed their failure may have hastened the granges' demise.

Unlike the Grange in the United States, the Dominion Grange refrained from engaging in partisan politics. Individual Grange leaders, upon occasion, ran for federal and provincial offices. Primary stress was placed, however, upon the support of policies deemed of value to the farm population. The tariff was the principal issue with which the Grange was concerned. In the early days of the Grange in Canada, the members supported the idea of a protective tariff. By the 1890's the Grange began to regard the tariff as a bonus for industry which was paid for primarily by the farmers. The farm representatives were particularly concerned over the high tariff and resultant high prices of "coal oil" (kerosene) and binder twine.

In 1886 an interesting attempt was made on the part of trade union leaders to sound out the Dominion Grange with respect to questions of public policy. Wood has sum-

[5] Louis A. Wood, *A History of Farmers' Movements in Canada* (Toronto: Ryerson, 1924), pp. 60, 68.

marized the answers which the Grange gave to a questionnaire submitted at the time by the Secretary of the Trades and Labour Congress.[6] The labor and farm movements found common ground in their support of cooperatives, public ownership of utilities, and a few other matters. They found themselves at odds upon most other questions, including proportional representation, the eight-hour day, and several other reforms proposed by labor but opposed by grangers.

The Patrons of Industry.—Like the Grange, the order of Patrons of Industry entered Canada from below the border. It spread from Michigan into Ontario as early as 1889. After some preliminary organizational developments, the Canadian branch of the movement split off from the American, and the Grand Association of Patrons of Industry of Ontario was launched. From the first, the Patrons were more aggressive than the Grange in matters of politics. They came out squarely in opposition to the protective tariff and against combinations and monopolies. By February, 1892, the Patrons had 30,000 members in Ontario and Quebec. The maximum membership was reached in 1894, when 50,000 members were reported.[7] The decline of the Patrons after that date was gradual. In its period of activity, the order supported woman's suffrage, prohibition, the initiative and referendum, the single tax, and other reforms. Its economic undertakings were relatively minor.

In March, 1893, at Toronto, an attempt was made to bring together representatives of the various farm and labor organizations, but no lasting union was effected. The Patrons made some progress in the Province of Mani-

---

[6] *Ibid.*, pp. 103–104.
[7] *Ibid.*, p. 115.

toba in the 1890's, but little success was won in either the Maritime Provinces or Quebec.

The achievements of the Patrons of Industry in the field of politics were greater than those of the Grange. The Patrons went into politics soon after the order was founded in Canada, and enjoyed considerable success, especially in Ontario. In 1893 the order resolved to support Patron candidates for provincial and federal office, and the next year 17 seats were won in the Ontario legislative assembly. The legislative group, under the leadership of Joseph L. Haycock, occupied itself in the legislative assembly with relatively minor issues. Modest success came to Patron candidates in Manitoba also in 1896.

The Patron political platform was framed at an 1895 meeting at Toronto. It included planks for low tariff, statements of opposition to railroad subsidies and to corporations, and attacks upon privileges of public officials. In the federal election of 1896, 29 seats were contested, but only 3 Patron M.P.'s were elected. A by-election the following year produced one more. On the whole, the record of the order in politics was not impressive. The emphasis on tariff matters made the program of the Patrons appear similar to that of the Liberals. Reviewing the record of the Patrons of Industry in politics, one is impressed with the negative nature of the policies advocated. The Patrons stood against the protective tariff, against trusts and monopolies, against civil service retirement, against the military, against the pomp of the Governor-General and Lieutenant-Governors. Their program lacked any noticeable positive aspect.

The Grain Growers' Association.—The development first of Manitoba and later of Saskatchewan and Alberta into great grain producing areas posed many severe economic problems. The principal crop was spring wheat. Transportation facilities were poor and each fall were strained to the limit in the effort to get the grain from farm to railroad and through the Great Lakes before snow and ice made transportation impossible. Elevators were constructed to store and load grain. The farmers soon developed many grievances against the grain elevator companies. Some relief was found just before the turn of the century in the development and multiplication of simple loading platforms and flat warehouses.

Then came the "blockade of 1901." The western prairie produced a very heavy crop of wheat, reported to total 60,000,000 bushels. The railroads were unprepared to handle so heavy a volume, and approximately one-half the wheat remained in the hands of the farmers at the time the Lakes froze. The farmers were indignant, and vigorous attacks were made upon the Canadian Pacific Railway. The first of the grain growers' associations was formed in the winter of 1901–02.

The next year's crop was also a heavy one and the railroads again were unable to handle the crop satisfactorily. Farmers not only attacked the railroad but also alleged that the grading of grain was juggled by the elevator companies, that blending was resorted to, to the detriment of the farmer, and that there were many other abuses in the handling and marketing of their crops.

The major economic instrument of the grain growers' movement was the Grain Growers' Grain Company, which was established in January, 1906. It was a cooperative company owned by farmers. Its original purpose was to buy grain on a commission basis, and to sell the grain from the vantage point of a seat which it hoped to acquire on the Winnipeg Produce and Grain Exchange. The company had trouble in obtaining a charter that would permit it to conduct its business as it wished. Failing to obtain a federal charter, it incorporated under Manitoba provincial law. It purchased its seat on the Winnipeg Exchange and proceeded to buy grain as planned. The first attack upon the company was made by the Grain Exchange itself. Objecting to the dividend sharing principle of the company, the Exchange denied it trading privileges. The company narrowly escaped being caught with its grain unmarketed as winter set in; only the timely assistance of the Scottish Cooperative Wholesale Society saved it in the initial months of its operation. The intervention of the government of Manitoba in the end forced the Exchange to restore to the company its trading privileges.

The Grain Growers' Grain Company developed, in several years thereafter, great economic power. By its operation it was able to solve some of the most difficult problems of farmers in the West. It became the bulwark of the farmers' movement and was able to finance publications and services in various parts of Canada.

Playing the roles of founder and defender of the company were the several provincial grain growers' associations. The first was the Territorial Grain Growers' Association, launched in the winter of 1901–02. It was followed in 1903 by the Manitoba G.G.A. In 1905, with the formation from the North-West Territories of the provinces of Alberta and Saskatchewan, reorganization of the farmers' groups took place. In Alberta, the Society of Equity and the Farmers' Association of Alberta were merged into the United Farmers of Alberta, or U.F.A. The Manitoba and Saskatchewan G.G.A.'s continued. In

1909, the G.G.A.'s, the U.F.A., and the Grange formed the joint Canadian Council of Agriculture. The Council was for more than ten years the united front of the farmers' movement of Canada and the leading spokesman for organized agriculture.

The grain elevator problem was not solved by the success of the Grain Growers' Grain Company. Under the leadership of E. A. Partridge, the farmers' organizations of the prairie provinces began, in 1907, to agitate for public ownership of elevators. The original proposal was that the Dominion and the provinces should divide ownership and operation. After rejecting several more modest proposals made by the provincial and federal governments, the farmers secured the enactment of provincial ownership legislation. In Manitoba, the plan adopted was that of a province-wide public enterprise managed by a commission under government control. The Saskatchewan law, enacted in 1911, provided for cooperative local participation in financing and management. Alberta followed the Saskatchewan plan in establishing a cooperative elevator company. The Manitoba elevator enterprise was launched on an ambitious basis but did not receive the farmers' support. State operation was abandoned and the elevators were leased to the Grain Growers' Grain Company. The Saskatchewan and Alberta schemes proved successful and profitable economic ventures.

The United Farmers' Movements.—The next phase in the development of farmers' organizations in the Dominion may be called the "United Farmers' era." It was in the decade 1910–1919 that most of the provinces developed a new type of organization, generally known as the United Farmers. These organizations flourished in

Ontario, in Alberta, in Manitoba, in Saskatchewan. They were less important in Quebec, New Brunswick, Nova Scotia, and British Columbia.

The United Farmers of Ontario (U.F.O.) was a successor to the Farmers' Association of Ontario (F.A.O.), launched in 1902 under the inspiration of Goldwin Smith. The F.A.O. was organized on the basis of federal parliamentary constituencies, but it was never very influential in politics. It stood for government ownership of utilities, the initiative and referendum, reduced railroad rates, and lower tariffs. In 1907 the F.A.O. was merged with the Grange. Although the union of the two groups brought a period of renewed activity to the Grange, the combination soon lost its strength.

A concerted demand for a farmers' organization of a new type led to the creation, in 1914, of the United Farmers of Ontario. The U.F.O.'s early policy declarations were concerned with the issues of the war. It adopted a policy toward conscription which was very much like that to be advocated later by the CCF in World War II. Conscription of man power was opposed unless wealth were conscripted too. In 1919 the Association entered provincial politics and won a resounding victory in the general election held in October of that year. Since it had won a majority in the provincial legislature, the leader of the U.F.O. group, E. C. Drury, was chosen premier, and his government held office until June, 1923. The government was composed of representatives of both labor and the U.F.O. Holding a strong majority in the legislature, the government proceeded to bring Ontario up to date in social legislation, to extend rural electrification under the provincially owned hydroelectric system, and to achieve other modest reforms.

Early in the new farmer-labor emergence, however, Premier Drury and J. J. Morrison, secretary of the U.F.O., began to clash on questions of tactics. Drury favored a broad farmer-labor, or "progressive," party; Morrison maintained that the U.F.O. should be retained as the political instrument solely of the farmers.[8] Drury was charged by his U.F.O. critics with playing into the hands of the Liberals. The internal dissension was an important contributing factor to the defeat of the government in the election of 1923. Shortly after its defeat, the U.F.O. voted to abandon its venture in politics.

In Alberta, the United Farmers' Organization remained out of politics until the close of World War I. Early in 1919 the U.F.A. convention decided upon political action. At first it operated through a separate political association; but soon the political association was dissolved, and the U.F.A. under the presidency of H. W. Wood entered the political arena fully and openly. In the Alberta provincial election of 1921 the U.F.A. won 42 of the 61 seats in the legislature. The first farmers' premier was Herbert Greenfield. The U.F.A. was the most consistent adherent of the "economic class idea" of organizing the farmers to defend and promote agrarian interests. The U.F.A. controlled the government of Alberta, chiefly under the leadership of J. E. Brownlee, a lawyer, from 1921 until its defeat at the hands of the Social Credit forces in 1935.

In Saskatchewan, the Grain Growers' Association phase of organization lasted longer. Farmers' representatives were included in the wartime Liberal government of the province. In 1921 the farmers' representatives retired

---

[8] J. J. Morrison, "Parties and Platforms," *Canadian Forum*, 5 (August, 1925): 330–331; also, "Political Future of the U.F.O.," *Canadian Forum*, 7 (February, 1927): 138–140.

from the Liberal government, and the Saskatchewan association decided to enter the provincial election campaign. In the 1923 election the farmers elected a group of 16 members to the legislative assembly; these constituted the official opposition under the leadership of J. A. Maharg. The United Farmers of Canada (Saskatchewan Section) was launched in the middle 'twenties. Soon after the CCF was started, the U. F. of C. withdrew from political activities.

Manitoba farmers, organized under the name of United Farmers of Manitoba, entered the 1920 provincial election campaign without thorough organization, but were able, nevertheless, to elect 14 members of the legislature. This was the largest group in a house divided into four parties. Another provincial election was held in 1922. At this time the U.F.M. appeared before the electorate with an elaborate platform and numerous candidates; 27 of the 55 seats were won by the U.F.M., and it became a member of the Progressive Coalition. The new majority in the House persuaded President John Bracken of the Manitoba College of Agriculture to accept the premiership, thus beginning a long series of coalition governments in the province, and launching on his political career the man who was to serve as national Conservative leader from 1942 to 1948.

The United Farmers of British Columbia, launched in 1917, never attained the importance of similar organizations in the prairie provinces and Ontario. The U.F.B.C. may, however, have been partly responsible for the election of three "progressive" M.P.'s in the election of 1921.

Although United Farmers organizations were established in both Nova Scotia and New Brunswick, in neither of these provinces did the movement exert the

lasting influence that it did in central Canada. The United
Farmers of Nova Scotia managed to elect 7 M.L.A.'s in
the provincial election of 1920. The U.F.N.B. entered
candidates in the 1920 provincial election and also managed to procure the election of 7. The United Farmers of
Quebec was organized in 1919. Although it entered an
ambitious slate of candidates at the next election, it did
not achieve the election of any.

The National Progressive Party.—The Canadian Council of Agriculture developed, in the course of World War
I, a declaration of policy for the organized farmers of the
Dominion. Its platform was known first as "National
Policy" and later as "New National Policy." It was
especially upon the issue of the tariff that the farmer
representatives broke with the wartime Conservative
government. After the war, the Council of Agriculture,
concerned with the election of M.P.'s favorable to the
New National Policy, summoned a conference, which
met in January, 1920, at Winnipeg. In addition to the
strong farmers' organizations of the prairie provinces,
delegates came also from the U.F.O., the U.F.N.B., and
the Canadian Council of Agriculture, the convening
body. Following the conference, a National Progressive
Party caucus was organized in the House of Commons at
Ottawa. Eleven M.P.'s adhered to the new party. T. A.
Crerar was elected leader of the group.[9]

In the federal general election of 1921 the Progressives
put in the field 150 candidates, of whom 64 were elected.
The Conservative group of M.P.'s was reduced to 50 in
number; the Liberals, with 117 seats, constituted the

[9] With respect to previous party affiliation, 5 were Liberal Unionists, 2
U.F.O., 1 U.F.A., 1 Liberal, and 2 were independents. They represented
the following provinces: 6 Saskatchewan, 2 Ontario, 1 Manitoba, 1 New
Brunswick, 1 Alberta.

largest group but did not possess a clear majority. Failing to secure the participation of the Progressives in his cabinet, Prime Minister Mackenzie King had difficulty in maintaining the confidence of the House. The Liberal government strengthened its position, however, by reversing its tariff policy and by granting concessions to the West.

The Progressive group in Parliament did not remain intact. Its first leader, Mr. Crerar, resigned in 1922 over his advocacy of cooperation with the Liberals. Robert Forke as chosen to succeed Crerar. But the Progressive group was lacking in leadership and program. The Progressives declined in strength rather rapidly. In the 1925 general election they won only 25 federal seats. In 1926 they won 31 seats, but by this time the group had split several ways.

The main reason for the failure of the Progressive Party was, according to William Irvine, one of the M.P.'s composing it, that it was based upon an emotional wave and lacked organization and education on which to build a persistent movement.[10] Like other farmers' organizations, the Progressives offered a somewhat negative program. There was little agreement upon an affirmative national policy. The Progressive Party, like most other Dominion-wide organizations, had to contend with the geographic separation of the several sections of the Dominion. Improvement of economic conditions in the middle 'twenties diminished the demand of farmers for radical change.

One of the basic difficulties encountered by the Progressives was lack of discipline in their Parliamentary group. Rank-and-file M.P.'s were irritated over attempts to bind

[10] "Report of Organizer" (Edmonton: Alberta Provincial C.C.F., 1941), p. 9.

their freedom of action through the caucus method. Like the British Labour parliamentary group in 1929–1931, the Canadian Progressive M.P.'s resented the controls that would have been necessary to make them a cohesive group.

This National Progressive Party of 1920 left to future leftist political movements in the Dominion an example of considerable success in parliamentary elections and a model for financing party politics on a democratic basis. The story of the Progressives is a story of failure, but there were enduring lessons of value to be learned from the history of the era.

RISE OF THE LABOR MOVEMENT

Canadian trade union history begins before Confederation with the organization of local unions among printers, shoe workers, and other craftsmen. These local bodies were formed in Ontario, Quebec, and the Maritime Provinces. Until the decade of the 'seventies, however, there was no concerted effort to bring these scattered unions together into a central organization.

In 1860 the tendency to organize international unions began. The pattern of an international union is that of an organization started in the United States but with Canadian locals affiliated. Among the early international unions were the International Molders' Union of America, the International Typographical Union, and various railroad organizations.[11]

Trade Union Organization.—In 1881, the Knights of Labor, which had spread so successfully through the United States, was organized in Canada. The Knights provided for industrial organizations of the same type as

[11] Canada, Department of Labour, *30th Annual Report on Labour Organization in Canada, 1940* (Ottawa: King's Printer, 1941), p. 12.

those open to farmers through the Grange. The Knights of Labor was not, properly speaking, a trade union. It placed its stress upon education and agitation for the replacement of the competitive system with a cooperative one.[12] In Canada, the Knights reached their greatest influence and membership in 1888 and declined sharply after that time.

In the meantime, trade unionists of Toronto had taken the lead in forming a central body for Canadian labor. The local unions had formed in 1871 a "trades assembly," along the lines of the modern central council. Two years later the Toronto group invited other Ontario trade unions to send delegates to a conference. At this meeting the Canadian Labour Union was organized. This embryonic central organization held conferences annually for the next five years, but after that had only sporadic bursts of life.

In 1883 the Toronto trade unions, now using the name "Trades and Labour Council," invited representatives of Canadian trade unions and Knights to another conference in Toronto. The delegates assembled formed the Dominion Trades and Labour Congress. In 1893 this body took the name "Trades and Labour Congress of Canada." The Congress has had a continuous existence since that time, and during the past fifty years has been the most influential central organization of Canadian unionism.

Concurrent developments in the United States, however, brought a new element of disunity into the Canadian labor movement. In 1881, conferences were held by trade unions in the United States with a view to forming

---

[12] John R. Commons and others, *History of Labour in the United States* (4 vols.; New York: Macmillan, 1921), 2: 198, 335, 495.

a central labor organization. The effort resulted in the launching of what is now known as the American Federation of Labor. Almost at once, the new A. F. of L. came into conflict with the Knights of Labor over jurisdiction and policies. This conflict was carried into Canada, with the result that in 1902 the Trades and Labour Congress voted to exclude various Dominion and independent unions which claimed jurisdiction conflicting with that of craft unions.

Having thus been eliminated from the central body, the all-Canadian unions organized themselves into a rival amalgamation which, in the last stage of several metamorphoses of name, was known as the All-Canadian Congress of Labour. The essential conflict between the two central bodies turned originally on the international versus the national scope of organization. The international unions were affiliated with the A. F. of L. and with the Trades and Labour Congress. The national (wholly Canadian) unions belonged to the All-Canadian Congress of Labour. These latter came to favor somewhat the industrial over the craft type of organization.

With the split in the American labor movement in the middle 'thirties there came a new cleavage in Canadian unionism. In 1935 some of the larger A. F. of L. unions formed a committee for industrial organization to encourage the unionization of workers in mass production industries on an industrial union basis. After the A. F. of L. called a halt to this organizing campaign, the unions which had sponsored it withdrew and formed what is now known as the Congress of Industrial Organizations. Although the C.I.O. was launched in the United States in October, 1936, the international unions in Canada with C.I.O. affiliation in the United States remained for a time within the Trades and Labour Congress of Canada. By 1939, however, the split in the American labor movement was duplicated in Canada. Upon the demand of William Green, president of the A. F. of L., the Trades and Labour Congress of Canada expelled the C.I.O. unions. Most of the C.I.O. unions in Canada then proceeded to join with the national unions of the All-Canadian group to form a new federation called the Canadian Congress of Labour. The C.C.L. today includes unions of two types: the national unions limited wholly to Canada, and the Canadian divisions of C.I.O. international organizations of the industrial type.

At various periods in Canadian history, unions and groups outside of the main currents of the labor movement have flourished. On the left wing, the Industrial Workers of the World grew to considerable strength during and just after World War I. Dissatisfied with the conservative policies of the Trades and Labour Congress, I.W.W.'s formed, in 1918–1919, The One Big Union, an omnibus organization covering workers in all trades and industries. I.W.W. elements were strongest in this period in Winnipeg, Calgary, and Vancouver. In the last two months of World War I, the I.W.W. and alleged ancillary groups were declared unlawful by an executive order promulgated by the Governor-General-in-council in the recess of Parliament. As in the United States, the I.W.W. objective was the promotion of industrial unionism, and its greatest support came from migrant workers of farm and forest. The legal status of the I.W.W. was reëstablished in Canada in 1922. Its One Big Union attained its largest membership in 1920, but despite decline it is still in existence and has demonstrated surprising strength in the western provinces even in the last decade.

The separate organization of Roman Catholic workers, especially in Quebec, followed upon an encyclical of Pope Leo XIII promulgated in 1891. As additional Catholic syndicates were organized, a demand for a central body arose. Beginning in 1918, representatives of the national Catholic unions met annually to discuss common problems. In 1921 a permanent organization was formed, called the Conference of Catholic Workers of Canada. The syndicates which were members of the Conference were organized on a craft basis. The influence of the Church is very strong, and the movement frequently demonstrates its hostility toward both industrial unionism and radicalism.

A fourth central labor organization in Canada is the Canadian Federation of Labour. It split off from the All-Canadian Congress of Labour in 1936, after a dispute between the Congress president and a portion of the executive.[13]

Trade Union Law.—The early trade unions of Canada were organized without benefit of defined legal status. Like the British trade unions of the time, labor bodies were liable to prosecution for conspiracy. Following the example of the British act of 1871, the Canadian parliament enacted the Federal Trade Unions Act of 1872, providing legal status for the trade unions that registered. This feature (legal status) had not been included in the United Kingdom act.

Following the federal legislation, the various provinces, except Ontario and Prince Edward Island, enacted legislation covering trade unions.[14]

---

[13] Descriptions of this split may be found in the Canadian Department of Labour's *Labour Gazette*, 35 (October, 1936): 858 and (November, 1936) 977; and in *The Canadian Unionist*, 10 (October, 1936): 112.

[14] Leon Lalande, "The Status of Organized Labour," *Canadian Bar Review*, 19 (November, 1941): 638–681.

After the enactment of the National Labor Relations Act in the United States, most of the Canadian provinces adopted laws guaranteeing rights of collective bargaining. National legislation now prohibits employers within the jurisdiction of the federal government from dismissing employees solely because of trade union membership.[15]

Trade Unions and Politics.—Proposals for political action by Canadian trade unions have been influenced largely by the example of the British Labour Party, but until 1940 the tactics actually followed were those employed by unions in the United States. As early as 1887 the Trades and Labour Congress was committed to an expressed belief in the necessity for direct labor representation in parliamentary and local offices. There followed a period of sporadic local activity in general and by-elections, but little sustained political action was taken by the unions. In 1900 the Trades and Labour Congress agreed in principle to the formation of a separate labor party. In 1906 the Congress granted the provincial organizations autonomy in the matter of establishing provincial labor parties. This policy resulted in the formation of a number of local groups but produced no unified national party. Finally, in 1921, the Canadian Labour Party was established with the approval of the Congress. In the federal election of 1921 the Canadian Labour Party put up 30 labor candidates. Only 2, including J. S. Woodsworth, were elected. Only slight success was obtained in the various coalitions entered into with the farmers' movements of this period. The Drury government of Ontario was a farmer-labor government

---

[15] Criminal Code, Sec. 502A, 1939. The text of Sec. 502A can be found in J. L. Cohen, *Collective Bargaining in Canada* (Toronto: Steel Workers Organizing Committee, 1941), p. 16.

(1919–1923), with 11 of the members of the legislative assembly elected under the Labour label. As might have been expected, the Labour representatives in Parliament and in the provincial legislatures were elected mainly from urban centers.

Considered as a whole, the record of the Canadian Labour Party and its local branches and affiliates was a disappointing one. Organized at the end of World War I when unrest was great and economic conditions poor, the Labour Party was unable to maintain its initial success in the period of the relatively prosperous 1920's. By 1932, on the eve of the launching of the CCF, the labor parties enjoyed some local and provincial strength but had been, since about 1927, without a central organization.

BIRTH OF THE CCF

The Cooperative Commonwealth Federation represents a merger of the political activities of the farm and labor movements of Canada. It was launched in 1932, a year of depression marking also the lowest ebb of farm-labor political fortunes.

Chronologically, the first step in the launching of the CCF was the formation, in 1931, of the League for Social Reconstruction. The League was composed of intellectuals, largely from the faculties of Canadian universities. It commenced at once the task of social and economic planning and the publication of pamphlets and books for popular education in those fields. The role played by the L.S.R. in the CCF has been similar to that of the Fabian Society in the British Labour Party.

The second move toward unifying the scattered farmer and labor parties, groups, and factions was taken in May, 1932, when four labor M.P.'s—J. S. Woodsworth,

William Irvine, A. A. Heaps, and Angus MacInnis—
and a few others met in Ottawa to plan the formation
of a "Commonwealth Party." J. S. Woodsworth was
chosen president, and organizing responsibilities were
allocated: for Ontario, to Agnes Macphail; for Saskatchewan, to M. J. Coldwell; and for Alberta, to Robert
Gardiner.[10]

The time having arrived for action, the leaders of this
new venture in politics decided to utilize the forthcoming annual meeting of the Western Conference of Labour Political Parties. This Conference, containing
representatives of the various labor parties of the four
western provinces, had resolved in 1931 to consider a
union with farmer groups for joint political action. It
was the meeting of the Western Conference at Calgary at
the end of July, 1932, which was, by the addition of
farmers' representatives, transformed into the body that
launched the CCF.

Invitations to the Calgary meeting were issued by the
Western Conference of Labour Political Parties, of which
C. M. Fines of Regina was president. They were sent
both to groups and to individuals interested in "a new
social order."[17]

The joint meeting was called to order by Fines on
August 1, and E. J. Garland, M.P., was selected as chairman. The chairmen of the convention committees were
N. F. Priestley, credentials; M. J. Coldwell, resolutions;
and W. H. Alexander, publicity.

[10] *The First 10 years—1932–42, Commemorating the 10th Anniversary of
the C.C.F.* . . . (Ottawa: C.C.F., 1942), p. 7.
[17] The details concerning the Calgary Conference are available in the
original minutes, entitled "Conference resulting in the formation of the
Cooperative Commonwealth Federation held in the Labour Temple,
Calgary, Alberta, August 1, 1932."

Delegates representing groups from four provinces and one national organization were seated:

Alberta: United Farmers of Alberta; Canadian Labour Party; Dominion Labour Party.
British Columbia: Socialist Party of Canada.
Manitoba: Independent Labour Party.
Saskatchewan: United Farmers of Canada (Saskatchewan Section); Independent Labour Party; Cooperative Labour Party.
National: Canadian Brotherhood of Railway Employees.

The basic resolution presented at the Calgary meeting was a broad one previously adopted by the Western Conference. Offered by M. J. Coldwell, it included the following matters:

1) Formation of a national federation of organizations interested in a "cooperative commonwealth."
2) Correlation of political activities of the member organizations.
3) A program calling for socialization.
4) Organization of (a) a provincial council in each province, composed of representatives of member organizations, and (b) a Dominion council composed of national officers and delegates from provincial councils.
5) Financing through affiliation fees.
6) The name "Cooperative Commonwealth Federation (Farmer-Labour-Socialist)."

Evidently the name Cooperative Commonwealth Federation was the product of several minds working toward a mutual adjustment. Among other names proposed were; Canadian Commonwealth Federation (by J. S. Woodsworth); Socialist Party of Canada (by Mrs. Louise Lucas); National Party (by C. M. Fines); United Workers Commonwealth (by Rice Sheppard); United Socialist Federation (by John Queen); National Workers Political

Federation (by W. H. Alexander). The adoption of a
name stating a goal in attractive words rather than describing the composition of the party (as labor, workers,
farmers) or setting forth an aspiration in doctrinaire terms
(as socialist) was a happy inspiration. The name chosen
had the virtue of being couched in three words of favorable connotation which were positive rather than negative, and capable of meaningful abbreviation. The name
was left general, to acquire meaning as the movement
developed character and leadership.

On the organizational front, sound decisions were
made. It was anticipated that the groups represented at
the conference should be the nucleus, "foundation members," of the Federation. Provincial sections were given
power to admit other bodies. Thus the national organization would remain a federation of provincial bodies,
avoiding the direct control by member bodies exerted in
the British Labour Party.

For officers of the new party the convention chose the
venerable J. S. Woodsworth, M.P., president, and Norman F. Priestley, secretary. The following were elected
to the provisional national council.

Saskatchewan: George H. Williams, Mrs. Louise Lucas.
British Columbia: Angus MacInnis, M.P.
Manitoba: John Queen, M.L.A.
Alberta: William Irvine, M.P., Mrs. George Latham.
Ontario: A. R. Mosher.

No definitive policy declaration was produced by the
founding fathers at Calgary. General agreement prevailed with respect to broad principles and policies. Social
and economic planning of production, distribution, and
exchange was demanded. Public ownership of banking,
credit, utilities, and natural resources was favored. Se-

curity of tenure for the farmer on his land used for productive purposes and for the worker in his home was sought. Cooperatives were to be encouraged. Equal social and economic opportunities for all were to be provided. Social legislation and facilities, including especially measures relating to health and employment, were to be extended.[18]

The reception given by the press to the birth of the new party was, on the whole, a cold one. The major daily newspapers of Canada were somewhat sarcastic over the birth of another political party in the prairie provinces. An article in *Saturday Night* (Toronto), entitled "Asking Farmers to Abandon Profits," relates that "such innovations no longer excite the natives." After reviewing the list of political parties launched in western Canada at the rate of about one in seven years, the author concluded that "new political stripes do not transform human weaknesses and personal vanities." Thus was the lusty infant born in a Dominion shrouded by depression, amid expressions of hostility by the publicists of the old parties.

The first year of the CCF was distinguished by an enthusiastic organizing campaign throughout most of the country. Great emphasis was placed upon securing adherents to the new party in Ontario and in the Maritime Provinces.

The first CCF national convention, held at Regina in July, 1933, accomplished two major things: it adopted a general policy declaration, and it framed a constitution. The convention also provided an opportunity for the new party to review its record and evaluate its prospects.

The statement of principles and policies that was adopted in 1933 stood for nine years as the major program

---

[18] *The U.F.A.* (August, 1932), p. 3.

of the CCF, and is still considered valid by the party, being historically known as the "Regina Manifesto." Drafts of the platform had been discussed in the provisional National Council and in affiliated groups through much of the year since the Calgary meeting.[19] Since the 1933 Manifesto will be covered more fully in a subsequent chapter, only the broad outlines will be mentioned here.

1. Planning. A planned, socialized, economic order, to develop natural resources efficiently and to distribute national income equitably.
2. Finance. Socialization of all finance machinery—banking, currency, credit, and insurance.
3. Social Ownership. Socialization of utilities and other industries essential to social planning.
4. Agriculture. Security of the farmer on his farm, encouragement of cooperatives, achievement of fair prices.
5. External Trade. Abolition of protectionist policies. Control of exports and imports through public boards and licensing.
6. Cooperative Institutions. Encouragement both of producers' and consumers' cooperative enterprises.
7. Labor Code. A national act to protect workers against hazards of illness, accidents, old age, unemployment, and discrimination.
8. Socialized Health Services. Publicly organized health, hospital, and medical services.
9. British North America Act. Amendment of this Act, which defines the Canadian Constitution, to give the

---

[19] At the first meeting of the National Council, M. J. Coldwell was asked to submit a draft of a manifesto to N. F. Priestley and W. N. Smith ("Meeting of the provisional National Council, held at the close of the Calgary Conference, August 1, 1932," p. 2). Later the Council appointed Priestley and Smith to draft the manifesto based on the eight-point program adopted at the Calgary Conference (minutes of the provisional National Council, Calgary, Alberta, January 24–25, 1933, p. 4). The research committee of the League for Social Reconstruction also was asked to help.

Dominion government adequate powers to deal with problems national in scope; abolition of the Senate.

10. External Relations. A foreign policy to obtain economic cooperation, disarmament, and peace.
11. Taxation and Public Finance. Taxes for revenue and social purposes.
12. Freedom. Full guarantees of civil liberties.
13. Social Justice. Commission to humanize the administration of law, and to deal with crime and punishment.
14. Emergency Program. The Dominion government to deal with the unemployment situation by providing work or maintenance.

A final paragraph of the Regina Manifesto declares flatly: "No CCF Government will rest content until it has eradicated capitalism and put into operation the full program of socialized planning which will lead to the establishment in Canada of the Cooperative Commonwealth." That declaration still stands.

The constitution adopted in 1933 was a simple document. It declared as the object of the CCF: ". . . to coordinate the activities of member organizations in order to promote through political action and other appropriate means, the establishment in Canada of a Cooperative Commonwealth in which the principle regulating production, distribution, and exchange will be the supplying of human needs and not the making of profits." The membership was defined to consist of organizations accepting the CCF program and constitution. Provincial councils were to have the responsibility of directing CCF provincial affairs. The National Council was empowered to direct the national organization and carry out its policies between national conventions. Provision was made for affiliation fees, disciplinary action, and adoption of candidates.

This constitution, although amended frequently by subsequent national conventions, served admirably as an outline around which to build the new party. It provided latitude which would allow the provincial branches to develop in their own ways, yet assured unity in essentials affecting the movement as a whole. Judged on the basis of its capacity to permit adaptation to changed conditions, the constitution was highly successful. It permitted the transformation of the federation, within ten years, from a loose alliance of scattered local parties into a national political party. When necessity has arisen, the convention has not hesitated to amend the constitution to make it conform to the needs of a growing organism.

CHAPTER II

National Party Organization

PARTY organization is extraordinarily important to parties of the social-democratic type. Committed by program to the democratic process in governmental affairs, such parties ought to arrange party machinery in such a way that internal affairs will be conducted democratically. The British Labour Party is substantially democratic in the determination of tactics and the formulation of policy. The British Conservative Party, on the other hand, is virtually a dictatorship headed by the party leader. During the 1945 British election campaign, Winston Churchill attempted to convince the electorate that if Labour should form a government a small Labour Party group (the Executive) would give orders to cabinet ministers. He was a man in a glass house throwing stones. The charge gave the Labour Party an opportunity to explain its own organization and to show how autocratic are the powers of the Conservative leader.

When one is considering the organization of the CCF, a strong case may be made for taking the most elementary local organization first, since the broad democratic base of the party rests upon the poll (precinct) committees and the community CCF clubs. I shall first, however, describe the national organization, because the over-all picture can be made clearer that way. Throughout the discussion of the national party machinery, the reader should bear in mind that the CCF is one of the most democratic of political parties. National organization, at the top of the pyramid of party structure, is supported by provincial and local organizations, which in turn are thoroughly representative of the individual CCF membership. The CCF is still a young party, and has not yet suffered from the "oligarchical tendency" which so often afflicts political parties.[1] It has had able, enthusiastic leadership and has developed a strong democratic tradition.

THE NATIONAL CONVENTION

The Canadian party convention has drawn more from the model of the American convention than from the British party conference. It resembles the American in that the convention selects the national party leader; it resembles neither in that the Canadian major party conventions are held at irregular intervals. Before World War I, Canadian party leaders were selected, as in most parliamentary countries, by the party caucus in Parliament. The first leader selected by the convention method was W. L. Mackenzie King, who was chosen by the 1919 Liberal convention. Although Arthur Meighen was chosen Conservative leader in 1920 without reference to a convention, Conservative leaders following him have all been selected by party convention.[2]

The CCF adopted the convention plan in part because of its utility in a young movement not yet widely represented in provincial and national legislatures. The convention method of selecting was also in harmony with the emerging Canadian political practices of the preceding

[1] See Robert Michels, *Political Parties: A Sociological Study of the Oligarchical Tendencies of Modern Democracy* (New York: Hearst's International, 1915), pp. 54 ff.

[2] John W. Lederle, *The National Organization of the Liberal and Conservative Parties in Canada* (unpublished Ph.D. dissertation, Ann Arbor: University of Michigan, 1942).

twenty-five years. The first CCF conventions were held annually, except that none was held in 1935. In 1938, however, the constitution was amended to provide for biennial rather than annual meetings. The constitutional provisions regarding the convention are rather simple. The convention is held at a time and place selected by the National Council. National conventions have been held as follows: 1933, Regina; 1934, Winnipeg; 1936, Toronto; 1937, Winnipeg; 1938, Edmonton; 1940, Winnipeg; 1942, Toronto; 1944, Montreal; 1946, Regina; 1948, Winnipeg.

Basis of Representation.—The basis of representation in the national convention, as established in the 1946 constitution, is as follows:

Federal constituencies: One delegate for 50 to 500 members; one additional delegate for every additional 500 members.

Affiliated groups: One delegate for each 500 members, with a maximum of ten delegates from the locals of any one union or other organization in the province.

National Council: Members are, *ex officio,* delegates.

Youth Movement: One delegate from every provincial section of the CCYM (Cooperative Commonwealth Youth Movement). Constituency delegates are elected by the federal constituency organizations, or, when this is not possible, are appointed by the provincial council.

The CCF convention is a convocation of small size, as compared with the huge conventions of the American parties. Credentials committee reports in the last several meetings have shown the number of delegates to range from 63 (1937) to 208 (1944). Travel distances play a large part in representation at the convention. In 1944, when the convention was held in Montreal, 81 delegates were from Ontario and 37 from Quebec; the four provinces of the West sent 68 delegates. In 1946, the Regina convention drew only 45 from Ontario and 18 from Quebec, while 99 attended from the four western provinces. In order to equalize somewhat the financial burdens of convention attendance, a registration fee of $10 per delegate is charged, and the fund created is used to pay part of the travel expenses. In 1946 the sum of $1,767.50 was available for the purpose; it was distributed in such a way that about two-thirds of the basic rail fare of those from other than adjoining provinces was cared for.

In 1944 the national convention at Montreal was attended by 208 voting delegates; in 1946 at Regina there were 179; in 1948 at Winnipeg the total was 207. They represented the provinces as follows:

	1944	*1946*	*1948*
British Columbia	13	20	18
Alberta	13	15	13
Saskatchewan	30	47	40
Manitoba	12	17	14
Ontario	81	45	56
Quebec	37	18	9
New Brunswick	7	5	5
Prince Edward Island	2	3	1
Nova Scotia	8	9	6
At large	0	0	45

Although 40 places for voting delegates were allocated to affiliated trade unions, actually only 19 of the places reserved for unions were filled at the 1944 convention, and only 9 in 1946, a year of many strikes. Both in 1944 and 1946, special arrangements were made in order to stimulate the meager Quebec organization.

Convention Procedure.—Convention procedure has become fairly well established. The national chairman calls the meeting to order. An address of welcome may be given by a local CCF leader and by the mayor of the city. A chairman and a vice-chairman (one English- and one French-speaking) are elected, normally by acclamation. Beginning in 1942, the national secretary, on behalf of the National Council, moves that certain delegates be declared elected. The same procedure is followed in the election of convention committees. In order to expedite convention business, four committees—credentials, resolutions, order of business, and constitution—are chosen in advance by the National Council and the action is ratified by the convention; earlier conventions had also a publicity committee. Fraternal greetings are received from other labor and socialist groups in various countries. In 1946 the British Labour Party sent a fraternal delegate.

The keynote speech of the CCF convention is the national president's address. As given by M. J. Coldwell, the present leader, this address provides a review of the accomplishments of the movement over the years, and of the CCF solutions for the problems faced by the Dominion. The details concerning the CCF developments during the past two years are then presented in the Report of the National Council and Executive, which is read by the national secretary. It contains a review of national and provincial elections, of organizational progress, and of problems facing the movement. The biennial financial statement is presented by the national treasurer. Unlike other organizations, the CCF publishes a full statement of its receipts and disbursements. The financial statement is then subjected to discussion in closed session. After its acceptance, the national treasurer presents the budget for the next year or two-year period. On motion of the treasurer the various recommendations on ways and means are voted upon.

As the national convention has increased in size through the years, it has had difficulty in considering all the resolutions and other matters that properly come before it. One recent development, paralleled in provincial conventions, is to divide the delegates into panels for the more detailed consideration of various problems. In 1944, one afternoon of the convention was taken up with meetings of panels on the following subjects: CCF newspapers, trade unions, financing of the movement, relations of provincial sections, federal candidates, research and literature, farmer activity, returned men, and racial discrimination. These panels presented reports to the convention in plenary session and often the reports included resolutions on which the convention voted. Similar panels were planned for the 1946 convention, but were canceled in order to allow more time for discussion of the problems and accomplishments of the CCF government in Saskatchewan. Unable even with the panel device to consider every resolution, the convention refers many matters to the National Council for action. Most of the proposals so referred are carried or carried as amended.

In recent conventions, the National Council has assumed a larger and larger role of leadership. Meeting two days in advance of the convention, the Council plans in some detail the agenda and procedure of the larger body. The Council both appoints and instructs the resolutions committee. It is now the accepted practice for that committee to classify resolutions submitted by various party bodies according to relative importance, to control the order in which they reach the floor, to consolidate, to introduce substitutes, and to recommend concurrence or nonconcurrence to the convention. Because far more resolutions are proposed than can possibly be considered, the committee's control over the convention's selection for consideration is great. Of course, the convention has power to reject the committee's recommendations regarding procedure and action if it chooses.

Although there has been a rule since 1937 requiring that proposed resolutions be submitted well in advance of the convention date, large numbers are submitted too late for inclusion in the printed program; in 1946, for example, 127 resolutions were submitted on time and 33 arrived after the deadline. In addition, provision is made for dealing with emergency resolutions, responsibility for which rests with the resolutions committee.

In the later stages of the convention, election of national officers for the coming two-year period takes place. In recent years the tendency to reëlect the top officers has been so strong that contests have been limited mainly to election of members of the National Council, of whom ten are selected by the convention.

Appraising the Convention.—Appraising the CCF national convention is a difficult task. From one point of view, it is a very drab assemblage. On the floor and in committee the delegates are desperately serious. There are no decorations in the convention hall, no music, no songs, no display of enthusiasm. Although delegates from particular provinces tend to group themselves together on the convention floor, no placards proclaim which delegation is which. To this observer it appears that much time and energy is wasted debating questions of policy that have already been settled repeatedly and adopting, on the spur of the moment, resolutions that may subsequently be used by opponents to embarrass the party. The whole field of policy resolutions might be clarified through a careful codification of all policy resolutions of the past, together with the Regina Manifesto and the several election manifestoes. The initiator of a resolution might then be required to show precisely how he intended to fit his proposal into past policy declarations. If it were possible to do this, it would provide the CCF (and its opponents) with a comprehensive and up-to-date statement of policy. Such a scheme might release time for the convention to devote itself to the acute organizational problems of the movement. One feature of earlier conventions might well be restored: province-by-province reports on electoral and organizational progress and a frank interchange on provincial and national problems.

On the other hand, many good things can be said about the convention. It is thoroughly representative of the movement. Its deliberations are carried on in an atmosphere conducive to thoughtful discussion. It has come part way along the path of "guided democracy" in which leaders offer solutions and the convention rejects or accepts. So long as the number of delegates remains around two hundred and the CCF is in power only in a single province, existing procedures may suffice.

If the convention grows to great size and CCF responsibilities of office multiply, the pattern of the convention must be altered. The delegates will require fuller reports from the parliamentary caucus and from the provincial leaders. Some form of the panel system would appear to be essential if adequate consideration is to be given to all the diverse problems of the movement. A series of panels might indeed take on much of the work now performed by the resolutions committee, thus constituting the specialized agencies through which detailed consideration is given to proposed resolutions. Real thought and effort ought to be given to arousing enthusiasm among delegates and visitors. Without employment of the colossal clowning and showmanship of the American party conventions, some concession might be made to the inherent human attraction to be found in pleasing colors and sounds. Even a church appeals to its people in part through community singing, organ music, and ritual. Where are the songs of the socialist movement, the music of Canada and the old country, the orators under whose spell thousands plunge into a campaign?

THE NATIONAL COUNCIL

During the interim between national conventions, the National Council directs the tactics and policies of the CCF. The constitution admonishes the Council to consult provincial councils before deciding major questions of policy.

The National Council is composed of a maximum of fifty-six members. These are the president, chairman, two vice-chairmen, and ten representatives elected by the national convention. Each of the ten provinces is represented on the National Council by the provincial president, the provincial leader, and two representatives who are elected by provincial conventions. Both the secretary and the treasurer, chosen by the Council, are *ex officio* members of the Council. Since 1942, one representative of the Cooperative Commonwealth Youth Movement, chosen by the CCYM national convention or council, has a seat on the Council. Vacancies in the National Council which occur between conventions are filled by action of the National Council or provincial council concerned. Since a 1942 amendment to the constitution, the National Council has been required to meet at least twice each year; previously it had met only once a year.

Directly following a national convention, usually the next day, the new National Council meets. One of its first actions is to appoint a national secretary and a national treasurer. If, as frequently happens, those appointed have been elected to the Council by the convention, then the Council's next task is to fill the vacancies created by their elevation to offices that carry *ex officio* membership on the Council. Then the Council elects six of its members to serve on the National Executive. Generally a distinct effort is made to achieve a geographic balance in the Executive and also to secure personnel that is about one-half M.P.'s and one-half geographically accessible (Ontario and Quebec) non-M.P.'s.

In order to secure truly national representation, the Council recently has undertaken to pay the traveling expenses to Council meetings of one of the members elected by each province. Although this involves a considerable outlay, it is necessary to make certain that the voice of the provinces will be heard and that management of the national party will not be exclusively in the hands of Ottawa and eastern elements.

The new constitution adopted in 1946 altered slightly the basis of representation in the National Council by raising from six to ten the number of Council members elected by the national convention. Occasionally the equal representation of each province appears somewhat ridiculous in view of the vast disparity in party organizational strength and total population among the provinces. On the other hand, election to the National Council may inspire a member from a province with a weak party organization to exert himself to strengthen it.

It is occasionally suggested that the Council be given authority to ratify the choice of federal candidates as

made by constituency nominating conventions and provincial organizations. This power to approve and disap-
prove, possessed now by the Ontario CCF and long used
by the British Labour Party executive, is a very potent
weapon. If it is ever granted to the Council, it will materially strengthen the influence of the national CCF organization. In practice, an important share of responsibility
for management of the party's affairs is delegated by the
National Council to the National Executive. The Executive consists of the president, chairman, vice-chairmen,
secretary, treasurer, and six other members chosen by the
National Council.

National Council meetings average about three a year.
They are held in various cities, but rarely east of Montreal
or west of Calgary or Edmonton. Most National Council
sessions convene over two or three days of a week end.
National Executive meetings are normally held in Ottawa. Sessions of the Executive extend over one or two
days. Because the size of the Executive is small, it is possible to assemble that body on shorter notice and with
much less expense than the unwieldy National Council.
Therefore, the Executive meetings are used to deal with
both routine and emergency questions, while the Council
normally includes in its agenda only matters of major
importance.

National Council proceedings are considered semicon-
fidential. No stenographic report is taken, but minutes
of the important votes and actions are kept up to date.

THE NATIONAL OFFICE

At the time the CCF was launched in Calgary, in 1932,
Norman F. Priestley, vice-president of the U.F.A., was
selected secretary. From his Alberta office he communi-

cated on behalf of the movement with the various economic and political groups whose affiliation to the CCF
was sought. There was no staff in the major political party
sense. Responsibilities for publicity were assigned to
Professor W. H. Alexander of the University of Alberta.
Funds were raised by appeals to private persons. The
policy manifesto was drafted by M. J. Coldwell, W. N.
Smith, and others. Organizational responsibilities in
western Canada were undertaken by William Irvine,
M.P., E. J. Garland, M.P., and Angus MacInnis, M.P.[3]

As the party grew in strength and responsibility, the
necessity for specialized organizational talent was recognized. M. J. Coldwell of Saskatchewan was selected as
national secretary, and the national office was moved to
Regina in October, 1934. The modest basis on which the
party was operating as late as 1935 is indicated by the
report of the secretary to the National Council that $80
per month was an irreducible minimum for office expenses.[4] Later in the same year, Coldwell reported to the
Council that arrangements had been made with the
Saskatchewan CCF Research Bureau in Regina for accommodations, stenographic services, and the like, for a
period of one year.[5] After Coldwell's election to the House
of Commons in October, 1935, it was necessary to reorganize the national office. E. J. Garland, who had lost his
seat in the House of Commons at that election, ultimately
took over the responsibility of managing the central
office, with the title of National Organizing Secretary;
but Coldwell, despite his own protests, continued to act

[3] Minutes of the meeting of the provisional National Council held at
the close of the Calgary conference, August 1, 1932, pp. 1–2.
[4] Minutes of the National Council, Ottawa, February 8–9, 1935, p. 3.
[5] Minutes of the National Council, Winnipeg, November 30, 1935, pp.
1–2.

as national secretary for several months. A review of Garland's first organizing efforts was given to the 1936 convention. Lacking assured funds, he moved from province to province, often relying upon contributions made as he proceeded. He once told of a socialist lawyer from England who drove him four thousand miles in the course of the organizing campaign.[6]

Following the 1936 convention, the national office was opened in Ottawa, where it has remained since that time. The National Council appointed David Lewis as national secretary in August, 1936, but he did not begin serving in his new position until early in 1937. In the meantime, M. J. Coldwell continued to act as secretary despite his heavy load of work in the House of Commons. Up to the time that David Lewis entered the office of national secretary, the CCF had been handicapped in its national office by the lack of a full-time secretary and of adequate office space, equipment, and staff. The late W. H. Dalton constituted the full-time staff, and upon his shoulders fell the responsibility for the multitude of detailed tasks that must be performed in a growing movement.[7]

A new era in the national office was inaugurated when David Lewis took over its management. During 1937 and most of 1938 he functioned on an honorary and spare-time basis; but from October 1, 1938, he took up the secretaryship on a full-time basis as a definite job. Upon the shoulders of this young lawyer, still in his twenties, hardly back in Canada from his Rhodes Scholarship years, fell the primary responsibility for constructing an organization and managing the diverse affairs of a new

[6] Minutes of the second session of the national convention, Toronto, August 3–5, 1936, p. 1.
[7] *The C.C.F. Marches On,* full report of the fourth national convention of the CCF, Winnipeg, July 27–28, 1937, pp. 15–16.

party. The first step after he entered the office as full-time secretary was to move the national headquarters into a small office building at 172 Wellington Street, facing the Houses of Parliament. There the functions of the national office expanded rapidly.

An impression of the activities of the central office, and of the sacrifices connected with its operation, may be obtained by reviewing the financial reports of the party. In the two-year period 1934–1936, office administration cost only $1,141. For 1936–37, administration expense was reported as $705.24; the national organizer, Mrs. E. J. Garland, received the magnificent salary of $1,200 per year! By 1937–38, administration expenses had risen to $1,185.20, but only $416 of this amount was for office assistance. As the financial strength of the movement increased, it was possible to offer more and more services. In 1938–39 the salary roll of the national office had increased to $3,787; for 1939–40 it was $3,912. The highest level so far reached, that for 1947–48, showed salary expenses of $27,942. The transformation of the national office in a decade may be shown by contrast. In 1933 the CCF national headquarters was a minor activity annexed to the U.F.A. vice-president's office. In 1948 the national office of the CCF was a beehive of activity in its own building in Ottawa, with several full-time employees. Nevertheless, though the financial position of the CCF has improved greatly, the salaries in the national office have remained low. As additional resources have become available, they have been used mainly to employ further assistance and provide more literature and organizing help for the movement. The present employees of the national office are David Lewis, national secretary; Donald MacDonald, education and information secretary;

Lorne Ingle, research secretary; Allan O'Brien, parliamentary secretary; Helen Peart, librarian, and several stenographers. A. M. Nicholson serves as national treasurer.

The functions of the national office are numerous. It serves as a secretariat to the national conventions, the National Council, and the National Executive. It keeps the records of these bodies and is primarily responsible for the execution of the decisions made by them. The office keeps in touch with the many phases of the movement through correspondence and travel. It publishes literature and the monthly membership bulletin, *Across Canada*. It plans the use of the radio on a national basis and makes recordings of speeches by national leaders for use by provincial organizations. It initiates special campaigns and helps weaker sections of the movement. The office also provides research services for the party. The results of its research work are made available to the CCF parliamentary group and to the movement generally. A large part of the work of the central office is parliamentary; the CCF M.P.'s are extremely active on the floor of the House of Commons and require much assistance and reference work.

AFFILIATIONS TO THE CCF

Not all the original parties to the federation formed at Calgary became active affiliates of the CCF. The United Farmers of Alberta, routed in the provincial elections of 1935, decided in January, 1939, to retire from politics. For some years, U.F.A. affiliation with the National Council had been less than complete; yet it had been difficult for the CCF to set up an organization in Alberta because of the presumed political functions of the U.F.A.

In 1938 it was reported to the National Council that neither the U.F.A. nor the Canadian Labour Party (Alberta) had been paying per capita dues to the national office. The Council decided to write off the arrears, but urged that dues be paid promptly thereafter. Then the National Council adopted another resolution, asking the U.F.A. to place its affiliation to the CCF upon a complete and unconditional basis and urging the Alberta Association of CCF Clubs and the U.F.A. to coordinate their political efforts. The 1939 U.F.A. decision to abandon political action simplified the Alberta organizational situation and made it possible to set up a regular provincial council and CCF branches.

The expected national affiliation of the Canadian Brotherhood of Railway Employees never materialized. In January, 1933, the National Council decided that the C.B.R.E. should be considered affiliated through the Ontario provincial CCF.[8] The same Council meeting decided to advise the United Farmers of Manitoba, who wished to affiliate, but not for political purposes, to route their application through member bodies in Manitoba. Presumably this meant the Independent Labour Party, since that was the only Manitoba group formally represented at Calgary.

The Provisional National Council was somewhat embarrassed by the request for affiliation of various political action organizations which used the words "cooperative commonwealth" in their names. Among these were the so-called Cooperative Commonwealth of British Columbia and the Cooperative Commonwealth Association of Alberta. In addition, a few other applications came from

---

[8] Minutes of the provisional National Council, Calgary, January 24-25, 1933, pp. 1-4. Some locals of C.B.R.E. affiliated with provincial parties, beginning in 1942.

various sections of the Dominion. The applications for affiliation of cooperative commonwealth groups were of special significance because general membership bodies were destined to become, before long, the basic units of the federation.

After the affiliation of the C.B.R.E. was transferred to a provincial basis, none of the affiliated members had more than provincial scope. This left the door open to the restructuralization of the national CCF into a national federation of provincial CCF branches. Since the first year of its life, the CCF has discouraged most applicants for national affiliation and has recommended the Ukrainian Labor organization (Winnipeg), Poale Zion, and others to seek local or provincial affiliation.

A strong desire persisted, however, to secure the formal affiliation of nation-wide economic groups of farmers and workers. The spread of the C.I.O. ferment from the United States to Canada encouraged CCF leaders to hope for a new recognition on the part of trade unionists of the need for political action. The National Council decided in 1937 to recommend to the national convention that "every effort be made by the National Council to facilitate the affiliation of economic groups, such as cooperatives, farm organizations, and trade unions as provided by the programme and constitution of the CCF."[9] The first fruits of this effort were gained when, in August, 1938, the United Mine Workers of America, District 26 (which covers Nova Scotia and New Brunswick), resolved to affiliate as a group with the CCF.[10]

The decision of the United Mine Workers to affiliate was approved by the locals of District 26, and the applica-

[9] Minutes of the National Council, Winnipeg, July 24–25, 1937, pp. 2–3.
[10] Report of the sixth national convention, Winnipeg, October 28–29, 1940, pp. 5–6.

tion was accepted by the National Council. Because this
section of the U.M.W. covered more than one province,
it was considered necessary that the affiliation be to the
national organization. The importance of the U.M.W.
affiliation can scarcely be overemphasized. It brought to
the party a considerable measure of financial strength at
a very critical period. In the biennium 1940–1942, for
example, the contribution of Nova Scotia, mostly from
the U.M.W., exceeded $1,800, the largest contribution
made by any province to the national CCF in that period.
The U.M.W. affiliation was advantageous also because it
brought organizational strength to the CCF in the Maritime Provinces, which had been one of the weakest links
in the federative chain. Soon after U.M.W. affiliation, the
CCF captured three seats in the Nova Scotia legislature,
and in 1940 one Nova Scotia seat in the Dominion House
of Commons.

The U.M.W. affiliation posed, however, some per-
plexing questions concerning the future of the federal
structure. Leaders of the CCF were well acquainted with
the preponderant control exercised over the British
Labour Party by the trade unions. The Labour Party in
the United Kingdom has always given its affiliated bodies
direct representation in its national organization. When
policies or tactics are being decided in the national convention of the Labour Party, a few leaders of the trade
unions are able, by the use of block proxies, to dominate
the convention. When the time for convention voting
comes in the Labour Party, the delegate representing a
local party with 1,000 individual active members has just
one-tenth the influence of a trade union leader casting
proxy votes for 10,000 of his fellow unionists, who may be
completely inactive in party affairs except for the annual

payment of a small political fee. The CCF has been hard pressed in its desire to secure the advantages of trade union affiliation in the form of financial and organizational strength without accepting the bitter pill of external domination. Much attention has been given in the last seven years to working out the details of trade union affiliation. As late as February, 1942, the exact basis of representation in the national convention had not been determined. In reply to an inquiry from the Steel Workers Local in Sydney, Nova Scotia, the Executive stated that "direct union affiliation necessarily carries with it direct representation at party conventions on a basis still to be worked out."[11]

Later in 1942 the National Executive gave attention to this very task. The Executive recognized that the primary responsibility for trade union affiliation would rest with the provincial councils because most affiliations would be handled on a provincial basis. The Executive laid down the following premises: (a) The final decisions concerning affiliation should be in the hands of provincial authorities, but the importance of uniformity and equal treatment must be recognized. (b) Trade unions should affiliate with the appropriate provincial council. (c) Arrangements made in this experimental period should be tentative only and should be subject to change with changing conditions. (d) The same arrangements offered to trade unions should be considered available to farmers' organizations should they wish to affiliate.[12]

The detailed provisions covering trade union affiliation laid down by the Executive may be summarized as follows.

[11] Minutes of the National Executive, Ottawa, February 2, 1942, p. 1.
[12] Minutes of the National Executive, Ottawa, September 19–20, 1942, p. 2.

1) The numbers on which dues and representation are calculated shall be the numbers on which the union bases dues to the congress with which it is affiliated (T. and L. C., or C.C.L.).

2) Representation at provincial conventions shall be based upon the average paid-up membership affiliated with the CCF three months before the convention call.

3) Per capita dues of the union to the CCF shall be 2 cents per member per month. Of this amount, 1 cent goes to the national office and 1 cent to the provincial office.

4) The basis of representation at provincial conventions shall be one delegate for each one hundred union members, with a minimum of one delegate.

5) The affiliated trade union shall decide how representatives in provincial conventions shall be elected as among local unions, but delegates shall be chosen by the local unions so far as possible.

6) Affiliated local unions shall be entitled to representation in all constituency meetings and conventions on the basis of one delegate for each one hundred union members.

7) Members of an affiliated local union may become individual active members of local CCF constituency organizations by: (*a*) individual application, including a declaration that he belongs to no other political party, and (*b*) payment of a fee equal to that portion of an ordinary annual membership-at-large fee which goes to a local constituency.

Having qualified for membership in the constituency party, the trade unionist is entitled to all the rights and privileges, including voting.

The crucial question concerning the basis of representation in the national party if and when Dominion-wide unions affiliate remains unsettled. The evils of direct union representation found in the national affairs of the British Labour Party can be avoided by not permitting proxy voting in the national convention, by continued stress upon the importance of provincial and local affiliation rather than national, and by the denial of direct representation of trade union affiliates in the National Council and National Executive. The new constitution adopted in 1946 settled the basis of representation for affiliated bodies in the national convention at one delegate for each five hundred members, with a maximum of ten delegates from a single union in any province.

NATIONAL PARTY FINANCE

From its humble beginning in 1932, the national CCF has relied primarily upon affiliation fees and contributions from affiliated bodies. The increasing financial strength of the movement is shown by the annual and biennial reports[13] of receipts and disbursements:

Years	Receipts	Expenditures
1933–34	$ 1,475.28	$ 1,312.26
1934–35	1,745.50	1,435.22
1935–36	2,832.36	2,244.80
1936–37	2,217.38	2,694.56
1937–38	3,442.93	3,266.48
1938–39	9,157.45	8,157.34
1939–40	11,547.45	11,544.77
1940–1942	16,497.99*	17,164.92*
1942–43	17,172.81	12,727.62
1943–44	28,320.92	33,355.08
1944–45	35,928.88	34,535.16
1945–46	38,166.46	29,820.57
1946–47	37,846.40	43,034.74
1947–48	49,507.80	49,959.27

The original plan for financing the CCF placed primary reliance upon the affiliation fee of $25 required of

[13] These figures were obtained from the minutes of National Council meetings and national conventions, 1933–1948. An asterisk indicates figures for the biennium 1940–1942.

each member organization. To this was added the re-
quirement that provincial organizations must pay dues
of 10 cents per member per year. As the individual membership developed and the provincial organizations became the major units in the federation, membership dues
became increasingly important as a source of revenue for
the national party.

Another source of revenue that loomed large in the
early days of the party was the contribution of federal
M.P.'s. In the financial statement for 1934–35, CCF M.P.'s
were credited with contributions of $250, which repre-
sented $50 each. In the biennium 1934–1936, it appears
that the M.P.'s continued their contributions at the rate
of $50 per year. A total of $590 was donated by M.P.'s in
1937–38, at which time there were seven CCF members
of the House of Commons. In 1938–39, the same number
of federal members gave $295.15; in 1939–40, their dona-
tions totaled $100. In the biennium 1940–1942, federal
M.P.'s donated $2,227.25; during most of this period
there were only eight CCF M.P.'s. In 1945–46, M.P.'s
gave $3,249.50 to the national office and $6,295 to provincial CCF organizations. The sacrifices made by the
federal M.P.'s in order to build a party organization constitute an epic story of self-denial and applied zeal.
Federal M.P.'s are paid only $4,000 per year, plus a flat
tax-free expense allowance of $2,000. On this sum many
support families and maintain two residences. All of
them travel widely over the country to aid in party organization, and all of them have willingly assessed themselves by these heavy contributions to the party. Similar
contributions are made to provincial councils by CCF
members of legislative assemblies out of their meager
"sessional indemnities" (legislative salaries).

In recent years, the national party's receipts from provincial fees, dues, and contributions has accounted for the major part of its total national revenues. Formerly, as we have already noted, this came to the national office on the basis of a $25 affiliation fee for each provincial organization and dues of 10 cents per member per year, paid through the purchase of annual membership cards. The national office published the membership cards and distributed them to the provincial organization. Later, a system of "quotas" was worked out by provinces, and the income was carried in the financial statements as "provincial contributions." Quotas were revised by the National Council in September, 1945; in terms of monthly obligations the new quotas were as follows: Alberta, $300; British Columbia, $480; Manitoba, $300; New Brunswick, $50; Nova Scotia, $130 (including U.M.W.); Ontario, $500; Quebec, $100; Saskatchewan, $500; total, $2,360. The provincial parties often failed to achieve their quotas. In 1943–44, for example, only Alberta, Ontario, and Saskatchewan managed to reach their quotas, although British Columbia and Manitoba made very creditable records. In 1944–45, British Columbia, Nova Scotia, and Saskatchewan achieved their quotas, and both Alberta and Ontario came reasonably close.

The whole basis of national party financing was altered by the adoption in 1946 of the national membership fee; beginning at the end of the next membership years in the several provinces, a national fee of $1 per member was to be collected by the provincial organizations and transmitted to the national office. For 1947–48 the membership fee produced a revenue of nearly $37,000. The former quota system was abolished. In addition to the benefits of the stable income from the fee, the new plan places the national office in direct contact with the individual member for the first time. The national party now also supplies directly to all members a monthly publication, *Across Canada.*

Except for the low salaries paid and the rather small staff employed, the expenses of the national CCF reveal nothing out of the ordinary. No salary items appeared in the financial statements until 1936. From then until a full-time national secretary took office in 1937, the salaries were for a national organizer and part-time assistance. During the past ten years, however, they have become the largest single item in the expenditure column. In each fiscal period since 1940, the salaries have constituted about one-half the total expenses.

The party has been daring in its adoption of financial plans. At the 1937 convention it adopted a budget calling for the expenditure of $19,000 in the next fiscal year. The report to the 1938 convention showed, however, that the total amount expended was only $3,266.48. The proposed budget of 1943–44 called for expenditures of $35,250, which was approximately twice the amount of income of the previous fiscal year. Actual expenditures for that year were $33,355.08. Substantial progress has been made over the years by stating frankly the needs of the movement and making energetic efforts to raise the money to meet those needs.

FINANCIAL PROBLEMS

The development of the CCF has, however, been handicapped greatly by the absence of adequate financial support. To an outside observer it appears that substantial progress has been made, but those who are close to the national office see many phases of its work left undone.

If the finances of the CCF are compared with those of major political parties, both in Canada and abroad, the smallness of CCF financial support is most striking. This is compensated for, however, by vast contributions of enthusiastic, voluntary, organizational work by individual rank-and-file members in the various provinces. During the last four years another compensating factor has been the extensive support given to CCF candidates and policies by trade unions. Labor support is forthcoming not so much in terms of financial contributions as in terms of publicity in labor journals and that effective device of practical politics—passing the "lowdown" along by word of mouth.

The second unique factor in CCF financing is the absence of large donations from individuals and business interests. Direct contributions to the national party by individuals have never loomed large. Even in the enthusiasm generated by the successes of the party from 1942 to the present time, direct donations to the national office have never exceeded 15 per cent of the total annual income.

One of the principal barriers to the launching of a new party in Canada is the election deposit required of candidates for the House of Commons. The idea of the deposit is to head off irresponsible candidates, but the qualifications for the refund of the deposit are so severe as to discourage a new party which does not possess some financial resources. In Canadian federal elections the deposit of $200 is forfeited if the candidate fails to obtain a number of votes equal to one-half that cast for the successful candidate. This is very much more severe than the deposit stipulations in effect in the United Kingdom, where the polling of only one-eighth of the total votes is sufficient to secure a refund. Edward Porritt has called the Canadian election deposit rule "undemocratic in operation . . . without a parallel in the election codes of English speaking countries."[14] He traces the origin of the penalizing section to a blow aimed at the Liberals by the Conservatives in 1882. Its more recent effect, however, has been to discourage third-party movements, including the CCF.

The CCF has considered, from time to time, plans for the creation of a deposit insurance fund through which the risk of losing a deposit would be shared broadly by the various CCF groups distributed over the nation. No final arrangements have been made for this step, but either financing of election deposits by the national party or some insurance plan appears to be a prerequisite toward securing CCF candidates to contest elections in substantially all the constituencies of the country. The British Labour Party "Deposit Insurance Fund" has operated since 1929. The deposit there amounts to £150, but the risk of losing is much less than in Canada, as has already been explained. The Labour Party requires that a premium of £10 be paid on behalf of each candidate. If the candidate loses his deposit, the "Deposit Insurance Fund" repays him the £150 he has put up.

The CCF should also give its attention to the problem of financing by-elections. Up to the present, the party has conducted Dominion-wide campaigns to raise funds for each federal by-election contested. As the party matures and responsibilities for conducting provincial governments are incurred, some more regular basis for raising by-election funds will be needed. Here the model of the

---

[14] Edward Porritt, *Evolution of the Dominion of Canada, Its Government and Its Politics* (Yonkers: World Book Company, 1918), p. 342.

British Labour Party may again be followed to advantage. Its by-election insurance fund was established in 1932 to spread the financial burden of by-elections over the whole of the party's affiliated membership. The plan in the United Kingdom involves an assessment of all affiliated organizations for each by-election contested. The money is collected nationally and allocated to the constituency party conducting the campaign. Labour Party collections and grants for single by-elections have ranged in recent years from £225 to £500.

Next, there is the problem of general elections campaign funds. The CCF has fought only four federal general elections since its inauguration in 1932. The 1935 expenditures by the national office for campaign purposes appear to have been exceedingly small. A special Woodsworth radio fund was raised to secure access to the air by the party's national leader. Beginning in 1937, a special campaign fund was collected, but it appears to have been expended chiefly for augmented services by the national office. The item reappears in the 1938–39 financial statements as a "special national office fund," and in 1939–40 as a "special organizing fund." In the former year, $3,500 was raised; in the latter, $7,440 was available mainly for the campaign leading up to the election of March, 1940. From 1939 to 1942 the special organizing fund was continued, and relatively large amounts were raised in each of the years of this period.

In preparation for the federal general election which finally was held in June, 1945, the CCF began in 1943 to raise funds for the campaign. The national election fund raised for 1945 was $83,822.38, or more than ten times that of 1940. The money was obtained through provincial organizations; the device employed was that of setting

an objective for each province and then making a broad
appeal to individuals and party units to meet subquotas.
The actual receipts for the 1945 campaign funds[15] were as
follows: Saskatchewan, $42,491; British Columbia, $15,-
448.25; Alberta, $7,120; Manitoba, $6,812.50; Ontario,
$6,151; Maritimes, $684.63; Quebec, $100; sundry,
$5,015; total, $83,822.38. The strong showing of Saskatchewan is explained in terms of that province's enthusiasm over its first CCF government. The poor results
in Ontario were due in part to the necessity of fighting
a provincial and a federal election contest falling within a
week of each other. The fundamental weakness of the
CCF in Quebec and the Maritimes is quite obvious from
these figures.

More than one-half the 1945 campaign fund was spent
for publicity, including newspaper advertising, billboard
space, and campaign literature. Organizers' salaries and
expenses constituted the second largest item on the expenditure side. In third place were subsidies to areas in
which the CCF was weak organizationally; in order of
size of subsidy, the aided provinces were: Quebec, Prince
Edward Island, New Brunswick, and Yukon (Territory).
Fourth were the traveling expenses of national officers
and speakers. Total expenditures were low enough to
leave a balance of nearly $2,500 after all bills were paid.

Enough has been said to indicate that the money-
raising powers of the CCF have increased vastly since
1940. Financial resources of the national organization,
however, are still much below actual need. The movement needs a national newspaper, a fuller information
service, more pamphlets and posters. The parliamentary
group requires more research workers and other assist-

---

[15] Report of the 1946 CCF convention, p. 14.

ance. Weak provincial organizations need initial subsidies until they are able to stand on their own feet.
Overworked national officers—expecially the leader, the
secretary, and the treasurer—must have help, for they cannot fairly be asked to carry indefinitely the heavy burdens
that constantly threaten their health. In at least two fields,
agriculture and labor, full-time secretaries ought to be
working on affiliations and planning stratified electioneering.

THE CCF IN COMMONWEALTH AND INTERNATIONAL GROUPS

One of the many signs of the growing maturity of the
CCF is its recent acceptance by Labour parties of the
British Commonwealth as the labor party of Canada.
Recognition of this role for the CCF came gradually. It
began with the exchange of fraternal greetings between
the United Kingdom Labour Party and the CCF on the
occasions of their conferences and conventions. It now
extends to inclusion of the CCF as a full partner of the
Labour parties of Great Britain, Australia, New Zealand,
and the Union of South Africa. Canada was strongly
represented by CCF leaders Coldwell, Lewis, Scott, and
others at the conference of Commonwealth labor parties
held in London in 1944. Analysis of the addresses delivered there reveals a Canadian contribution far greater
than the electoral strength of the CCF would lead one to
expect.[16] The CCF proceeded to plan another Commonwealth conference in Canada in the fall of 1946, but this
was postponed until 1947 because of general elections

---

[16] See *Report of the Conference of British and Dominion Labour Parties
Held at London, September, 1944* (mimeographed; London: Labour
Party, 1944). On the broad implications of this problem see F. R. Scott,
"Socialism in the Commonwealth," *International Journal*, 1 (Winter,
1945–46): 22–30.

scheduled in both Australia and New Zealand in late
1946. Playing the role of host in September, 1947, height-
ened the prestige of the CCF in Canada and directed the
attention of Canadians to the fact that the Dominion was
politically out of step with other member nations of the
Commonwealth.

At the London conference one of the principal decisions reached was that an international organization of
democratic socialist and labor parties should be revived.
The CCF was organized too late to take part in the Second (Socialist) International, which the British Labour
Party joined in 1904, or the merger in 1923 of the "Berne
International" and the "Vienna International" to form
the Labour and Socialist International. The CCF did not
become a member of the L.S.I., which had its headquarters in Brussels. When, in May, 1946, an international
conference of socialist parties was held in Clacton Hall,
London, the CCF was represented, although by members
resident in Britain rather than by party officials. The Clacton conference decided not to reëstablish the socialist
international at that time. Two reasons for this decision
were given by the secretary of the British Labour Party's
international department.[17] First, previous internationals
of social-democratic parties, producing only "grandilo-
quent" manifestoes, had "irritated the parties in office
and disillusioned the parties in opposition." Second, the
socialist parties of central and eastern Europe do not feel
free to join an international under western, perhaps
mainly British, leadership. Unquestionably the main de-
terrent was concern lest the launching of a socialist international be misunderstood as an attempt to form a world

---

[17] Denis Healey, "First Postwar Socialist Conference Postpones New International," *CCF News* (B.C.), July 11, 1946.

front against Communism. The Clacton conference contented itself with formation of a liaison and information office in London, and resolved to meet again. The provisional name of the group is The International Socialist Conference; it maintains an office in London for the purposes just mentioned and also published a quarterly journal, *The Socialist World,* which ceased in 1949.

The urge to North American socialist unity is seen in the active participation of CCF leaders in the activities of the League for Industrial Democracy, the major social-democratic educational organization in the United States. In 1946, M. J. Coldwell, national leader of the CCF, was elected a vice-president of the League;[18] he, David Lewis, A. M. Nicholson, and several others have addressed audiences in the United States, carrying the story of the CCF to envious American progressives.

---

[18] *LID News Bulletin,* 11 (June, 1946): 2.

CHAPTER III

Provincial Organization

PROVINCIAL organization of the CCF, described in this chapter, varies considerably from province to province in detail but follows a rather standard general pattern. Some variety arises naturally from the democratic nature of the movement; different people discover diverse methods of doing things when left to decide for themselves. Perhaps more than any other factor, however, diversity in provincial structure and practices arises from the relative electoral strength of the CCF in the several provinces. Saskatchewan, with its huge membership and CCF government, requires an elaborate organization that would be ridiculous in Prince Edward Island, where the party is only getting started.

CCF provincial agencies, found in substantially the same form in each province, are the convention, council, executive, leader, and office. Wherever the CCF has made real progress with its organizing efforts, it attempts to maintain an organization in each federal constituency, provincial constituency, and poll (precinct).

EVOLUTION OF CCF PROVINCIAL STRUCTURE

In the beginning the CCF was merely a federal union of various local and provincial parties and groups. Within each province the "foundation bodies," or original parties to the federation, were in active charge of local organization. For British Columbia and Manitoba this meant that the Socialist Party of Canada and the Independent Labour Party, respectively, constituted the provincial CCF organizations. For Alberta and Saskatchewan the situation was more complicated, for in each of these provinces there were three original groups which were represented at the Calgary conference in 1932. Except through the Canadian Brotherhood of Railway Employees, Ontario was not represented among the groups at Calgary; neither Quebec nor the Maritime Provinces had any representatives there at all.

Their hopes stimulated by the prospect of creating a national progressive party, which might be able to meet the problems of the great depression, people began in 1932, 1933, and 1934 to form unofficial local units of the party. These were generally called "cooperative commonwealth" clubs or associations. Many federated on regional and provincial bases and began applying for affiliation to the national CCF. Although these applications proved highly embarrassing at the time, they served to indicate that the future organization of the CCF on a provincial basis would need to be based upon its own branches rather than on affiliated bodies. It is remarkable that within ten years the structure of the party was completely transformed and that the separate affiliation of the United Farmers and local labor parties had passed out of existence. This change-over took different forms in the several provinces and required from one year to ten years to complete.

British Columbia.—Organized around the turn of the century, the Socialist Party of Canada early gained considerable strength in British Columbia and succeeded in electing four M.L.A.'s in 1904. At the close of World War I, the party split, as did socialist parties all over the world, between those who advocated revolutionary methods and those who believed in social democracy. The former joined the Communist Party; the latter, in British Columbia, established the Federated Labour Party, in which both J. S. Woodsworth and Angus MacInnis participated. In 1932 the old name, Socialist Party of Canada, was restored and two delegates were sent from British Columbia to the Calgary convention at which the CCF was launched. Individuals who desired to participate in the CCF without affiliating with the Socialist Party formed "Reconstruction Party" clubs. This phase of the struggle for control over the CCF organization ended just after the 1933 election with the liquidation of the separate groups. In another sense, however, the rivalry between club and Socialist Party elements continued in the long contest for leadership waged between the Rev. Robert Connell, leader of clubs, and Ernest Winch, leader of Socialist Party elements. In 1937, Connell resigned the leadership of the CCF group in the legislative assembly and left the party. Although there have been subsequent splits in the B. C. section of the CCF, they have centered around personalities, policies, and tactics rather than original cleavage. Today the B. C. provincial organization is composed of both CCF clubs and constituency associations.

Alberta.—For ten years after its beginning in 1932, the CCF had a difficult organizational situation in Alberta. Since the United Farmers of Alberta was one of the pioneer groups affiliated with the CCF and enjoyed unusual prestige because it was the only affiliate actually in charge of a government,[1] it was not possible at an early period to launch the CCF in Alberta on a general membership

---

[1] Having routed the Liberals in 1921, and remaining in charge of provincial affairs until 1935.

basis. Until 1935 the responsibility for CCF politics was largely in the hands of the U.F.A. and the Canadian Labour Party (Alberta Section). After the election of 1935 there developed an insistent demand for a third unit in the Alberta CCF. Within a year, 87 CCF clubs were organized in various parts of the province.[2]

The Alberta club section of the CCF held a convention in Calgary in July, 1937, and adopted a resolution which declared it necessary that CCF clubs should proceed with the organization of every federal and provincial constituency in the province. Relations with the U.F.A. were at times obscure and at times strained. The U.F.A. was confronted with the problem of deciding whether or not to withdraw from political action, having been utterly routed at the 1935 provincial election, when Social Credit took over. It was the view of the "club section" that, irrespective of whether the U.F.A. withdrew from politics or continued to nominate provincial candidates under the U.F.A. banner, it was necessary for the CCF clubs to put forward their own candidates.[3]

In 1938 the National Council considered the unsatisfactory organizational situation in Alberta and adopted a resolution which provided that the U.F.A. affiliation for 1937–38 should be accepted, but reiterated its opinion "that it is against the spirit and intent of the CCF constitution for any body to affiliate federally and not provincially." The National Council then instructed the provincial council of Alberta to extend clubs throughout the province and to urge affiliates of the CCF in Alberta (U.F.A. and Canadian Labour Party) to assist in this work.[4]

---

[2] Report of the 1936 CCF convention, p. 5.
[3] Minutes of the convention of the Alberta club section of the CCF, July 6–7, 1937, pp. 1–2.
[4] Minutes of the National Council, Ottawa, February 26–27, 1938, p. 2.

The delicate situation continued into 1939. A Calgary central council of CCF clubs was established without taking into account the federal nature of the Alberta CCF organization. A committee of the National Executive authorized the national organizer to intervene if necessary in support of the provincial council.[5] Shortly afterward, E. J. Garland, national organizer, and E. E. Roper, provincial secretary, participated in a meeting at Calgary at which the differences between the provincial party and the Calgary group were resolved.

Another minor crisis occurred in 1941 when the Canadian Labour Party (Alberta Section) adopted a resolution declaring the CCF setup in Alberta cumbersome and asking that political organization in industrial constituencies where labor is organized be left "entirely in the hands of the Canadian Labour Party for municipal and provincial elections."[6]

At the same time the National Council had before it another resolution from the provincial council—a resolution that originated with the general membership section of the Alberta CCF. It asked that the Labour Party reconsider its resolution and support the abolition of the federal form of organization and the formation of a single Alberta section of the CCF by amalgamating the Labour Party and the general membership section. Apparently the CCF club element was willing to leave the field of municipal elections in urban constituencies to the Labour Party. The National Executive finally approved a statement drafted by the national secretary declaring that existing organization in Alberta was confusing and inefficient, rejecting the Canadian Labour Party proposal,

[5] Special meeting, Committee of the National Executive, May 15, 1939, p. 1.

[6] Minutes of the National Council, Ottawa, November 15–16, 1941.

and declaring for the unification of the CCF as a necessary step to an effective program. In this way national
support was given to the CCF general membership element in Alberta.

The two elements of the Alberta CCF finally met in
joint convention in January, 1942, and formed a unified
organization. The presiding officer at the convention was
Chester A. Ronning, chairman of the provincial council.
The resolution for unification was offered by E. E. Roper.
It provided that the two organizations, the Canadian
Labour Party (Alberta Section) and the general membership section of the CCF "do now combine to form a single
political party to be known as the Cooperative Commonwealth Federation—the Alberta Farmer-Labour Party."
The resolution was carried unanimously.[7]

Since 1942, the Alberta CCF organization has re-
sembled that of other provinces. Local units are known
as clubs. For electoral activities, members are divided
into poll (precinct) organizations, which in turn send
representatives to the provincial constituency association.
Federal constituency organization is based on that of the
provincial constituencies.

Saskatchewan.—Although the CCF had at the beginning three Saskatchewan affiliates, they were successfully
welded together into a single party in short order. The
initial steps toward unity of farmer-labor political movements were taken in Saskatchewan before the Calgary
conference. The first annual convention of the Saskatchewan Farmer-Labor Group was held in July, 1932, and
was attended by representatives of the United Farmers
of Canada and of the Independent Labour Party. The

[7] Minutes of the joint convention of the Canadian Labour Party (Alberta Section) and the Alberta general membership section of the CCF,
Edmonton, January 24, 1942, pp. 1–2.

question of leadership might easily have kept the two elements apart, had it not been for the statesmanlike attitudes of George H. Williams and M. J. Coldwell. The two were nominated for the post of political leader. Williams, leader of the U.F.C. group, withdrew. Coldwell, leader of the urban group, was elected. Despite the intense feelings developed in later years between supporters of these two men, Coldwell and Williams believed in unity and practiced it in their joint organizing efforts.

By July, 1934, the Farmer-Labor Group was willing to change its name to "Cooperative Commonwealth Federation, Saskatchewan Section," and the present organizational basis was established. The basic unit of organization is the provincial constituency, but most CCF members function through local clubs, and appropriate emphasis is given to poll and federal constituency activity.

Manitoba.—Manitoba was represented at Calgary by the Independent Labour Party only. The I.L.P. was launched after the 1919 general strike in Winnipeg, partly in order to avoid on the political front the ill effects of the trade union split on the industrial front. In 1910 the Manitoba Labour Party first put up its leader, Fred Dixon, as a candidate for M.L.A.; he finally secured election as an "independent progressive" in 1914. In the violent struggle that attended the 1919 strike, several key leaders of the group, including Dixon, John Queen, and J. S. Woodsworth, were arrested. Some of them were still serving jail sentences at the time they were notified of their election to the Manitoba legislative assembly in 1920. In the federal election of 1921, J. S. Woodsworth was elected by Winnipeg North Centre under the Canadian Labour Party label. The I.L.P. continued to be the principal political instrument of the organized workers in provincial affairs, including as it did elements from both the older Trades and Labour Congress unions and the militant new "One Big Union" of the left.[8]

Supplementing the I.L.P., in 1933 and 1934, there were organized three other elements of the emerging party, the "farmers' section," "social reconstruction clubs," and the CCYM. They secured representation on the provincial council. In 1935 the farm and reconstruction groups merged into a CCF club section. A new constitution was adopted in 1936, forming a single party, the provincial CCF with affiliated club, I.L.P., and other units. A representative of Manitoba reported to the national CCF convention that the provincial party still operated on a federated basis "different from other provinces"; the provincial council in 1936 had seven members from the I.L.P., seven from club units, and three from the CCYM.[9] Tensions developed between I.L.P. and club sections, and the I.L.P. appeared ready to withdraw, but the timely intervention of the National Council prevented a final break.

By 1942 the I.L.P. had but four branches in operation, of which only three were active. Although the I.L.P. provincial board was still in existence, its activities were almost nil. I.L.P. representation in the provincial convention and council was reduced somewhat in proportion to the relative unimportance of the I.L.P. branches as compared with the 40 or 50 CCF local units in Manitoba. The name I.L.P. has persisted in Winnipeg municipal politics. In the municipal elections of 1940 and 1942 the candidates for alderman were designated in their literature as CCF-I.L.P. As in other provinces, the cleavage

[8] See J. S. Woodsworth, "The Labor Movement in the West," *Canadian Forum*, 2 (April, 1922): 585–587.

[9] Report of the 1936 CCF convention, 1st session, p. 4.

between new CCF local units and the older federated
groups eventually was bridged by the absorption of the
older body.

In February, 1943, the I.L.P. finally voted to discon-
tinue the use of its name and to consider the former
branches of the I.L.P. as units in the CCF. This action
was explained as necessary because of confusion created
in the public mind and the assumption by many that the
I.L.P. and the CCF constituted two separate parties. The
resolution read as follows:

> In view of the fact that the CCF, of which we are a part, is
> working as a national party for the same policies as those ad-
> vocated by the Independent Labour Party, *be it resolved:*
> That the branches of the I.L.P. discontinue the use of the
> name Independent Labour Party and be known hereafter as
> units of the Cooperative Commonwealth Federation.[10]

Today the Manitoba CCF has a structure similar to
that in other provinces. Members are required to belong
to the appropriate provincial constituency association,
except in Winnipeg, where they are organized according
to federal constituencies. Local units are under the jurisdiction of the constituency associations.

Ontario.—At the launching of the CCF, it was anticipated that the United Farmers of Ontario would affiliate
with the party and lead its organizing effort in rural Ontario. But the U.F.O. never did so, for it was disillusioned
over its experience in politics from 1919 to 1923 and did
not again return to the political field with its former enthusiasm. In 1943 the identity of the U.F.O. was finally
obscured through its merger with another farm organization. Although the CCF National Council voted in
January, 1933, that the Canadian Brotherhood of Rail-

---

[10] *Manitoba Commonwealth,* February 19, 1943, p. 1.

way Employees should be considered affiliated provincially to the Ontario CCF, no formal affiliation took place until locals of the C.B.R.E. began to come in during 1942. The new Ontario section of the CCF allegedly fell under Communist influence, and the national leader in 1934 abolished the section and sponsored the organization of a wholly new provincial body.

Early meetings of the National Council and National Executive record much concern over the organization of the CCF in Ontario. Since the party lacked any affiliated organizations in the province, organizational efforts from the beginning centered around the establishment of CCF clubs. These local groups have remained the primary units in the Ontario CCF organization. There were many early disappointments in the launching of the CCF in Ontario. The first provincial election held after the formation of the CCF resulted in the election of only one legislator under the CCF label and one under the U.F.O. label. Very ambitious plans were made for the federal general election held in 1935. Graham Spry, later an assistant to Sir Stafford Cripps, reported to the National Council after the election that the CCF had run 50 candidates in Ontario, for whom nearly 130,000 votes were polled. But not one CCF candidate was elected and $10,000 in election deposits was forfeited.[11]

In spite of this defeat, however, the Ontario CCF was in a healthy, though modest, condition. It had 5,000 paid-up members; it was publishing a weekly newspaper; its youth movement had 25 units, and new CCF groups were being established at a satisfactory rate. The 1936 convention was informed that Ontario had 197 affiliated units.[12]

[11] Minutes of the National Council, Winnipeg, November 30, 1935.
[12] Report of the 1936 CCF convention, 1st session.

Even at this early time, Spry recognized and reported that the Ontario CCF was largely a labor movement with its greatest strength in districts where old-country Britishers predominated. The absence of rural support in Ontario was as conspicuous then as it is now. The prosperous, mixed-farming agriculturist of Ontario leans toward capitalism today.

Quebec.—The CCF has made little impression on the Province of Quebec. The province was not represented at Calgary in 1932; ten years later it had only a rudimentary CCF organization. The first CCF clubs were established in Montreal, mostly in English-speaking sections and in areas populated mainly by immigrants from continental Europe. As late as 1942 the provincial convention was informed that there were only 7 CCF units in Quebec and that some 60 members-at-large were affiliated with the provincial office.

Maritimes.—All through the 1930's there were sporadic attempts to get the CCF under way in Nova Scotia, New Brunswick, and Prince Edward Island. A few local clubs were organized, first in New Brunswick and Nova Scotia and later in P. E. I. The modest success so far achieved in the Maritimes has been concentrated mainly in Nova Scotia, among the coal miners and steelworkers of Cape Breton Island, long accustomed to industrial organization. Since 1940 a moderately effective provincial organization has been in operation in Nova Scotia; even more recently, in New Brunswick and P. E. I.

CONSTITUTIONS AND CONVENTIONS

Each of the provincial branches of the CCF has a written constitution of its own choosing. These constitutions establish the fundamental law, the organic rules under which party affairs are conducted. Typically, they begin with an article on name, followed by one on object and on membership. Thereafter is set forth the structure of the party, its agencies, and their composition and powers. The procedure for choosing party candidates for public office is put down in some detail.

The usual length of the constitution is from 3,000 to 3,500 words. Saskatchewan's exceeds 5,000 words; it contains many minute provisions that other provinces have considered unnecessary. Most of the provincial parties print their constitutions in a handy leaflet of vest pocket size. Saskatchewan publishes annually a "Members' Handbook," which contains both the constitution and a directory of information concerning provincial and national CCF officers and committees, and CCF M.L.A.'s and M.P.'s.

The constitutional amending process in the CCF provincial branches requires a two-thirds vote of the delegates to a provincial convention. Some of the provincial constitutions require that amendments originate with either the provincial council or a constituency convention. The number of proposed constitutional amendments dealt with by provincial conventions is often very large. In the 1946 British Columbia convention, for example, 41 amendments were proposed, of which 6 were adopted by the convention. The 1945 Ontario convention, although it had adopted a new constitution only a year earlier, still had 26 amendments before it, of which 3 were carried.

The annual convention is the highest authority in the provincial CCF. The powers of the convention are very great, and so are its responsibilities. It determines provincial policy, amends the constitution, selects the political leader, elects the provincial council, and receives annual reports and financial statements from party officials and agencies. Provincial conventions are also very important in stimulating enthusiasm, receiving the faithful, securing publicity for the movement, and renewing the acquaintances upon which intraparty collaboration is largely based.

In two provinces, constitutional provisions require conventions to be held in certain months: Saskatchewan in July, and Manitoba in October. British Columbia requires its convention to be held before the national convention, but permits the executive to set the date. In Alberta, Ontario, and Nova Scotia, convention dates are fixed by the provincial council. In practice, B. C. prefers April, Ontario April or November, and Alberta November. Provincial conventions generally attract, in addition to the regular delegates, the national secretary, chairman, treasurer, and occasionally the national leader.

Composition of the provincial convention is determined by the constitution. The basis of representation varies with the nature of local party organization. In provinces in which the provincial constituency is the basic unit or organization, either a flat number of delegates (Saskatchewan gives 10) is assigned to each constituency, or a ratio of delegates to individual party members is worked out (as in Manitoba, which allocates one delegate for each 10 members). Where CCF clubs remain as local units, as in British Columbia and Ontario, delegates are allocated among clubs in proportion to their numbers of members. Since 1942, trade union affiliation has become common, and each provincial party has worked out a scheme of representation in provincial convention for affiliated unionists. The ratio is one delegate for each 100 affiliated trade union members in Saskatchewan, British Columbia, and Ontario; one for each 25 in Alberta; and one for each 500 in Nova Scotia.

In addition to the delegates specially selected to represent sections of the party at conventions, there are other delegates who serve in conventions on an *ex officio* basis. Each provincial CCF provides that members of the provincial council shall be convention delegates; only British Columbia denies them the vote. Alberta and Saskatchewan also include as delegates all CCF M.P.'s and M.L.A.'s elected from within the province.

This rather generous representation of party membership and affiliates produces a potentially large number of delegates, but since not all of them attend, the delegations are manageable. The total number of voting delegates reported by credentials committees at recent conventions were: British Columbia (1946), 135 and (1948) 98; Ontario (1944), 464 and (1945) 203; Saskatchewan (1945), 400. In addition, there are considerable numbers of alternates and visitors.

Convention procedure is fairly well standardized. The various affiliated bodies are required to send in advance any resolutions or constitutional amendments which they wish to propose. The convention elects its own officers and committees. Among committees commonly found useful at CCF provincial conventions are those on agenda, credentials, and resolutions. Recently, under the lead of British Columbia and Saskatchewan, there has been a tendency to divide the conventions into sections or panels, in order to permit specialization in considering resolutions, reports, and recommendations. In 1945 and 1946, B. C. had sections on organizational, constitutional, provincial, and national and foreign affairs. At the

Saskatchewan convention of 1946, resolutions were considered by panels on agriculture and cooperatives; reconstruction, national and international; municipal affairs, resources, and highways; health, welfare, and education; and labor, legal, and taxation problems.

The volume of work before a provincial convention is often so great that many resolutions and other matters cannot be reached by adjournment time. Even when four days are taken for the convention, many matters not considered are referred to the newly elected provincial council, or to committees, for disposition. Convention proceedings are reported through the provincial CCF newspapers and occasionally in mimeographed or printed reports. Saskatchewan and Ontario CCF's print reports and proposed resolutions received in advance of the convention in a "delegates' handbook" or "agenda." Only B. C. publishes an adequate report of convention proceedings. The B. C. *Report of the 1947 Provincial Convention* is not a verbatim report, but it does contain all reports made to the convention and a careful record of actions taken.

An important part of the work of every provincial convention is the selection of provincial officers for the coming year, and the election of provincial representatives on the National Council.

Councils, Executives, and Secretaries

The provincial body comparable to the National Council is called, in all provinces except one, the provincial council; Alberta alone uses the name provincial board. It is a rather large body, ranging from a dozen or so in the less thoroughly organized provinces to more than fifty in Saskatchewan, British Columbia, and Manitoba. Invariably the council has a few *ex officio* members, such as the president, vice-presidents, political leader, secretary, and treasurer. Most of the provinces provide that some members of the council shall be elected by the convention; Ontario chooses the majority of its council members in this manner. Another category of council members is chosen by constituencies, provincial or federal; the four western provinces use this method for selecting most of their council members. The CCYM is assigned from one to three council posts in most provincial organizations.

Like the National Council, the provincial councils are usually required to meet a minimum number of times in a year. The number of meetings appears to be controlled mainly by the size of the council; Ontario, with a council of modest size, requires five meetings a year; British Columbia, Saskatchewan, and Manitoba, all with large councils, require from two to four meetings a year.

In general, the provincial council is given broad responsibility for conducting the affairs of the party between conventions. Each provincial constitution lists powers and duties of the council. These commonly include passing on applications for membership or affiliation, enforcing discipline, and appointing the provincial secretary and occasionally other officers.

The provincial executive directs the business of the provincial branch council meetings. Executives are small bodies in all provinces, having from seven to fifteen members each. Generally they are composed of the officers of the provincial section (president, vice-presidents, secretary, treasurer) and a fixed number selected by and from the provincial council. Saskatchewan, Ontario, and Alberta make the political leader an *ex officio* member of the executive. In British Columbia alone the nonofficer members of the executive are selected by the convention. Saskatchewan delegates authority even beyond the executive. When the executive is not in session or cannot be called, decisions may be made by a board of strategy composed of the president and two others elected by and from the provincial executive. Recognizing that large bodies are not well suited to handling employment matters, Saskatchewan alone vests power to appoint the provincial secretary in the executive rather than in the council.

The minimum staff for any CCF provincial organization is a full-time provincial secretary. The four western provinces and Ontario have supported such full-time officers for several years. Quebec and the Maritimes have made a number of starts but have yet to achieve real stability in the management of their provincial offices. The national CCF has, very properly, considered a full-time secretary in each province an imperative necessity. Year after year the National Council has voted subsidies to provincial branches in Quebec, Nova Scotia, New Brunswick, and Prince Edward Island, in order that they might employ provincial secretaries. Although national officers do not interfere in a provincial branch's selection of a secretary, there is evidence that subsidies have been withheld until qualified persons were found for the post. As previously stated, the appointment of a provincial secretary is usually made by the provincial council; only Saskatchewan has placed the power of selection in the hands of the provincial executive.

The provincial secretary is the director-general of the provincial office. Operating under the general oversight of the council and executive, he manages the office staff, serves the CCF M.L.A.'s, and keeps in touch with local party units and with the national office. In provinces where the CCF is not yet strong he often edits the provincial newspaper and functions also as field organizer. It is obvious that the provincial secretaryship is a post of key importance and that the selection of a secretary is a most crucial matter. The typical provincial secretary is a young man in his thirties or early forties. They come from a variety of backgrounds, but at least three of the present incumbents previously were trade union leaders.

Most of the active provincial offices are in the provincial capitals; hence CCF provincial news comes from Edmonton, Regina, Winnipeg, and Toronto. There can be little doubt that this is desirable, in view of the inevitable preoccupation with provincial politics and the necessity of serving the CCF M.L.A.'s, if there are any. Special situations have caused CCF branches in British Columbia, Quebec, and the three Maritime Provinces to maintain headquarters in some city other than the provincial capital. Vancouver is so obviously the hub of the West Coast labor movement that Victoria, the provincial political capital, was overlooked. CCF strength in Quebec has never amounted to much; yet, if and when a start is made, the most likely point for a foothold is in the Montreal area, and for this and other reasons the provincial office is in Montreal. In New Brunswick and Prince Edward Island, headquarters have been established mainly for the convenience of provincial officers. The situation in Nova Scotia is a confused one; the movement got its start among the miners on Cape Breton Island, and its leadership and electoral strength have been mainly concentrated there. The provincial convention insisted that the provincial office remain on Cape Breton Island, alternately at Glace Bay and at Sydney. However, the division of organizing efforts between the mainland and Cape

Breton Island was ended in 1945, when the provincial headquarters was finally established in Halifax, the provincial capital.

The provincial office that functions under the secretary may have an extensive staff, as in Ontario, British Columbia, and Saskatchewan, or no employees other than the secretary, as in New Brunswick and P. E. I. The larger CCF organizations often have one or more organizers, an editor of the CCF provincial newspaper, a financial secretary, and several office workers. The typical provincial office is quartered in an office building: the Ontario CCF like the national CCF has acquired its own building, which it has named "Woodsworth House."

RELATIONS WITH THE LEGISLATIVE GROUP

The relationship between the political party and the public officials elected under its auspices is crucially important in a democratic polity. In Canada and its provinces, as in other states under the parliamentary system, each party has two great divisions. First, there is the party machinery, which bends its efforts to achieving the election of the greatest possible numbers of M.P.'s and M.L.A.'s. The other division is the parliamentary party or group, composed of the legislators elected under a given party label; these occupy a relatively autonomous position. During the election campaign the party machine labors long and hard to win parliamentary seats. After the election the party organization becomes in large measure the servant of the results of its efforts, namely, the party group in the legislative body.

In the CCF, the legislative group or caucus is less independent of party organizational control than are many parliamentary parties. There are several reasons for this.

First, the Canadian practice is for the party convention to select the political leader. This method of selection is now universally employed by the CCF on both national and provincial levels. Only in Saskatchewan has convention supremacy in this field been challenged. After M. J. Coldwell, designated as political leader by the convention of the farmer-labor group, failed to win election to the legislative assembly in 1934, George H. Williams was selected by the CCF M.L.A.'s as their leader; and consequently he also became leader of the opposition in the provincial legislature. In both 1935 and 1936, proposals were made to the Saskatchewan CCF convention to change the method of selecting the leader by empowering either the CCF M.L.A.'s or the legislative group plus the provincial council to select. Through the years 1936 to 1941, Williams served both as political leader and as a provincial president. A question of principle was involved, even though it was obscured in the factional struggle for control. Williams went to active service in the army early in 1941. At the provincial convention of 1941, T. C. Douglas, M.P., was elected president over Williams. Since Douglas was not a member of the legislative assembly, he could not function as political leader, so the CCF M.L.A.'s designated as their leader J. H. Brockelbank, who thereby became leader of the opposition. The 1942 convention finally decided to separate the offices of provincial president and political leader, and then proceeded to elect Douglas leader. While the posts of leader and president are separate in all provinces, they are combined in the national CCF, in which Coldwell is both national leader and national president.

Second, the CCF is an extremely democratic party, and its machinery is devised to make the voice of the rank and file heard in Ottawa and the provincial capitals. The party persists in regarding elective representatives as servants of the people, and has, in some provinces, elaborate disciplinary devices for ensuring service. In Saskatchewan, for example, an M.L.A. can be "recalled" by a process involving the filing of a recall petition signed by 100 members, the convening of a special constituency convention, and a two-thirds vote to remove. Candidates are required to sign a "recall agreement" stating they will resign if recalled. Although this contract might not be legally enforceable, the procedure does tighten the sinews of obligation that bind an M.L.A. to the party. The recall is frequently proposed for adoption in other provinces. British Columbia's CCF constitution makes members elected to public office responsible to the provincial executive between conventions; on questions of "policy, tactics, and contentious matters" the executive's decision is binding.

Not only do the CCF provincial organizations keep a considerable measure of control over legislative groups, but some of them take precautions against the exercise of undue influence by holders of public office in the party machinery. The separation of the offices of leader and president has already been mentioned. British Columbia's CCF provincial executive may include no more than three M.P.'s or M.L.A.'s among its eleven members. Ontario's CCF limits the number of M.P.'s and M.L.A.'s on the provincial council to one-third of the council, less two. Saskatchewan's CCF forbids either an M.P. or an M.L.A. to hold the office of provincial president or vice-president.

The desirability of having the parliamentary groups keep in touch with the provincial organization is recognized, too. Alberta, Ontario, and Saskatchewan make the leader an *ex officio* member of both the provincial council and the provincial executive. British Columbia designates one place on both bodies for a representative of the M.L.A.'s. In addition to the provincial leader, the Saskatchewan CCF makes one M.P. and two M.L.A.'s provincial councilors *ex officio*. Only in Saskatchewan is the CCF required by its constitution to have a legislative advisory committee, which has the task of assisting the legislative group in preparing legislation to carry out CCF policies; the committee also advises the CCF premier-designate on the selection of cabinet ministers.

MEMBERS AND AFFILIATES

Membership in the CCF is a provincial matter. In all provincial sections, however, membership is open to persons who subscribe to the principles and program of the CCF, who agree to adhere to its constitution, and who are not members of any other party. These requirements are drawn with a view to barring from membership those who are unwilling to cut their ties with other parties. They provide a measure of protection against infiltration of old-party and Communist agents, by compelling them to perjure themselves if they would gain admission to the CCF. The power to reject persons for membership is usually vested in the provincial council or executive. A member may be suspended or expelled, although such drastic action often requires an extraordinary majority in council. It is common practice for provincial sections of the CCF to require members to be affiliated with the appropriate local unit of the party.

The provincial individual membership fee, above and beyond the national membership fee of $1, ranges from

$1 to $2 per year. Those who advocate retention of the $1 fee, as in Saskatchewan, argue that a higher fee is a barrier to building a mass membership. The Saskatchewan CCF is the only section that has built a large membership, 31,858 as of May 31, 1944 (in an election year), but reduced to about 17,500 as of May 31, 1946. Those who prefer the higher fee, as in Ontario, place primary emphasis on the financial needs of the growing movement. Adoption of the national membership plan by the 1946 convention will mean the addition of the full $1 to existing provincial membership fees, except those paid under the family membership plans. The provincial fee is split about equally between the provincial office and constituency organizations.

Beginning in 1942, a considerable number of trade unions affiliated with the provincial sections of the CCF. The general rules laid down by the National Executive have been followed in the several provincial branches. The affiliated union must affiliate the same number of members as it does to the congress (C.C.L. or T. and L. C.) to which it is affiliated. Per capita dues are 2 cents per member per month, of which 1 cent goes to the national and 1 cent to the provincial office. Affiliated unions are represented in provincial and constituency conventions usually on the basis of one delegate per 100 members. Trade union delegates to party conventions must be individual members of the CCF in Saskatchewan, but Ontario accepts as delegates nonmembers who accept the CCF program and who support no other party. The only other variation in trade union affiliation is in the ratio of delegates to affiliated members; in place of the usual one per 100, Alberta uses one per 25 and Nova Scotia has one per 500. These differences are necessary in order to keep the representation something like proportionate. Nova Scotia's CCF would be dominated by a single union if the Alberta ratio were used; few Alberta unions would be enticed into affiliation by the meager representation allowed under the Nova Scotia plan.

LOCAL ORGANIZATION

For contesting federal and provincial elections, the most essential local divisions of the CCF are those in the polls (precincts), provincial constituencies, and federal constituencies. When the party is in battle formation, its workers man positions in these three key organizational units. Poll organizations are small, even in areas where the CCF has a large membership and there is a natural desire for a larger party unit for social and educational purposes. Most of the provincial branches of the CCF have made the provincial constituency the basic unit of organization; only Ontario uses the federal constituency for this purpose. Nearly all provincial constituencies are single-member districts; that is, they elect only one M.L.A. from the division. In areas that elect two or more provincial legislators from a single district, as in Vancouver, Edmonton, Calgary, and Winnipeg, party organization takes a somewhat different form. The magnitude of the organizing task confronting provincial offices may be indicated in part by listing the numbers of constituencies which are basic units of organization: British Columbia, 41; Alberta, 49; Saskatchewan, 49; Manitoba, 46; Ontario (federal), 82; Quebec, 91; New Brunswick, 17; Prince Edward Island, 15; Nova Scotia, 30.

In most places, however, the poll is too small and the constituency too large for an effective social and educational program, and therefore there has been a strong tendency to organize neighborhood or community CCF clubs. Sometimes called "locals" or "units," these CCF clubs provide the initial contact and the binding tie to the movement for a large proportion of party members. The typical club meets once or twice a month in a home or rented hall for a combined business meeting and study session. Whist parties and dances may be held as infrequently as once a month or as often as twice a week. Occasionally clubs resort to bazaars, rummage sales, and other money-raising activities. British Columbia experimented from 1943 with "industrial clubs," organized in factories and shops rather than in residential areas, but decided in 1946 not to set up any new units of this type.

Rivaling the club type of organization, in some provinces, is the constituency CCF association. It is especially suitable in urban areas where transportation facilities are good and members can easily reach a central headquarters. It is not so well suited to rural areas where constituencies are geographically large and the long and severe winter makes transportation difficult. Where the constituency association prevails, it has a number of advantages. It often has enough financial strength to maintain a headquarters with recreational and educational facilities. It may serve a large enough area to develop an attractive CCYM program, attract speakers of prominence, operate an adequate political literature service, or conduct a good discussion series. On the other hand, the constituency association is condemned in terms of the "curse of bigness" and monopoly. One British Columbia club proposed to the 1946 provincial convention the resolution:

WHEREAS the Constituency association form of organization tends towards centralization and bureaucratic control of the movement;

Therefore be it resolved that Article 3 of the Constitution be deleted and that the areas at present developed in this form be allowed a period of one year in which to realign themselves within the terms of the amended constitution.[13]

The methods used for mobilizing local units for an election campaign vary from province to province. If the prevailing local body is the provincial constituency association, then the organization is ready-made for a provincial election. In Ontario, where the federal constituency is the basic unit, party machinery is already suited to a federal election. Elsewhere, special organizational devices are necessary. British Columbia uses "district executives" or councils to coordinate the electoral work of clubs, and appoints a federal "coordinator" to manage party organization in each federal constituency during campaigns. Alberta provides for a federal constituency board made up principally of officers of provincial constituencies within the federal constituency. Saskatchewan maintains both federal and provincial constituency organizations with their own executives. Ontario simply provides that there shall be constituency associations in each district.

The amount of activity on the constituency association level ranges from the multiple functions of a CCF club in some urban areas to an election spurt once in three or four years in others. Saskatchewan, the best-organized province, places great stress on the annual provincial constituency conventions. They are held in June and July. Conventions are composed of constituency officers, candidates, or M.L.A.'s, and three delegates from each poll. The conventions elect their officers and executives for the coming year, and each selects ten delegates (twenty from double-membered constituencies) to the annual

[13] Report of the 1946 provincial convention, British Columbia and Yukon Section, p. 9.

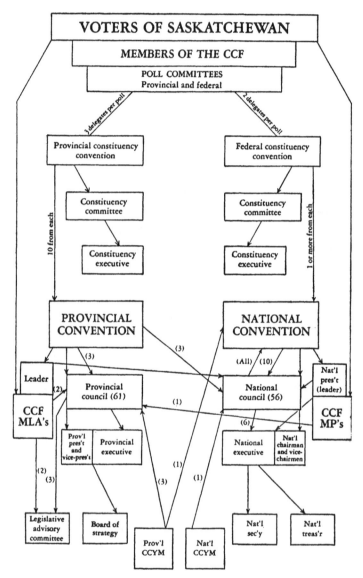

VOTERS OF SASKATCHEWAN

MEMBERS OF THE CCF

POLL COMMITTEES
Provincial and federal

3 delegates per poll

2 delegates per poll

Provincial constituency
convention

Federal constituency
convention

Constituency
committee

Constituency
committee

Constituency
executive

Constituency
executive

10 from each

1 or more from each

**PROVINCIAL
CONVENTION**

**NATIONAL
CONVENTION**

(3)

(3)

(All) (10)

Nat'l
pres't
(leader)

Leader

(2)

Provincial
council (61)

(1)

National
council (56)

CCF
MLA's

(6)

CCF
MP's

Prov'l
pres't
and
vice-pres't

Provincial
executive

National
executive

Nat'l
chairman
and vice-
chairmen

(2)
(3)

(1)

(1)

(3)

Legislative
advisory
committee

Board of
strategy

Prov'l
CCYM

Nat'l
CCYM

Nat'l
sec'y

Nat'l
treas'r

(For explanation of diagram see facing page)

provincial convention. Almost invariably the constituency annual convention is followed by a public meeting at which the speaker is some provincial or federal CCF leader. Federal constituency conventions are called when an election is imminent. The elaborate Saskatchewan CCF organization may be seen in graphic form in the accompanying diagram.

PROVINCIAL CCF FINANCES

The story of CCF financing is one of ingenuity and persistence. As the British Labour Party built its organization on the hard work and shillings and pence of the working class, so has the CCF been constructed by the volunteer labor and hard-won dollars and cents of devoted supporters. Some of this story has been told under the heading of national finances, but there it was mainly in terms of quotas set for the provinces and of doing very much on very little. But the money, or most of it, is actually raised in the provinces, locally.

The three provincial CCF organizations of greatest financial strength are those of Saskatchewan, British Columbia, and Ontario. In the year ending May 31, 1945,

---

CCF PARTY ORGANIZATION

This diagram shows the major party agencies through which an individual member of the Saskatchewan CCF is represented in provincial and federal affairs. The Saskatchewan provincial organization is the most elaborate and most effective in the CCF. Forty-nine provincial constituency conventions are held, and there are an equal number of constituency committees and executives. Now that the reapportionment of representation in the House of Commons has gone into effect, Saskatchewan has twenty M.P.'s and therefore the same number of federal constituency conventions, committees, and executives. This diagram was adapted in part from one in *CCF Members' Handbook for Saskatchewan* (Regina: Saskatchewan CCF, 1946), pp. 32–33.

the Saskatchewan CCF raised a gross total of $151,057.99, of which $107,108.07 was in "Victory Fund" receipts. For the year ending December 31, 1945, the British Columbia CCF had revenues, excluding those for its newspaper, of $98,836.97, of which $78,048.50 was for a "Victory Fund," federal and provincial. In the year ending March 31, 1945, the Ontario CCF had receipts totaling $69,296.27, which included $37,027.39 in "Victory Fund" income. It should be noted that 1944 and 1945 were years of great money-raising activity in the CCF in preparation for the federal general election finally held in June, 1945. The Saskatchewan total may be inflated because of activities surrounding the provincial election of 1944. The British Columbia total is proportionately more abnormal than the other two because it is for the full year 1945, which included both federal and provincial election campaigns.

Excluding "Victory Fund" revenues and newspaper operations, the major receipts of the three provincial sections of the CCF for the fiscal year indicated were derived as follows:

British Columbia (1945)	*Per cent*	*Saskatchewan* (1944–45)	*Per cent*
Membership fees	42	Memberships	42
Donations, miscellaneous	21	Literature	27
Ways and means committee	19	Radio fund contributions	22
Budget committee	13	Club donations	2

Ontario (1944–45)	*Per cent*
Membership fees	60
Literature sales	18
Club dues	12
Union dues	5

British Columbia raises money in a variety of novel ways. Its ways and means committee managed to net around $2,500 a year in both 1944 and 1945 through luncheons, a bazaar, raffles, and drawings. Exclusion of the "Victory Fund" is necessary in order not to dwarf the ordinary finances and distort the whole picture. It must be remembered, however, that some special fund-raising campaign is under way nearly every year. The leading source of income for the CCF is gifts from individuals.

How are these large sums of money spent? Excluding newspapers and national portions of special funds, leading expenditures for the same fiscal years were:

British Columbia	*Per cent*	*Saskatchewan*	*Per cent*
Salaries	40	Radio expense	16
National office	24	Salaries	16
Printing and stationery	6	Field organization, provincial election	15
Rent	5	Literature purchase	9
Postage and excise	3	Advertising and publicity	9
		National office	7

Ontario	*Per cent*
Salaries	22
National office	20
Organizers' salaries	12
Literature purchase	12
Organizers' expenses	12

Again it must be borne in mind that election campaigns occurred in these periods. The emphasis placed on radio by the Saskatchewan CCF is obvious in both revenues and expenditures.[14]

---

[14] These financial data are from the report of the 1946 provincial convention, British Columbia and Yukon section, pp. 11–20; delegates' handbook, 10th annual Saskatchewan provincial convention, 1945, pp. 9–10; CCF (Ontario Section), report of the annual provincial convention, 1945, appendix.

Outsiders and newcomers to the CCF often express disdain or impatience over the progress made by the party. Whether considered in terms of votes obtained or in finances raised, the relative advance ought to be a major criterion. The amounts of money received by the British Columbia, Saskatchewan, and Ontario sections in 1944–45 are some ten times the size of their budgets in 1941–42! In the earlier year, the British Columbia CCF received $7,594, Saskatchewan $13,605 (at the time probably the highest provincial budget in CCF history), and Ontario $6,780. Alberta and Manitoba, while not yet ranking with the big three, have demonstrated considerable money-raising capacity. Nova Scotia still requires some outside help, but if United Mine Workers affiliation fees were retained in the Maritimes, it might be able to stand alone. The other three provinces are definitely in the poor relations category.[15]

THE PROVINCIAL CCF PRESS

One of the principal handicaps of the CCF is lack of support from the press of Canada. Not only is the daily press no help to the new party; it is overwhelmingly hostile and often viciously unfair in its attacks. The only daily paper in the Dominion that supports the CCF is the Glace Bay *Gazette,* published on far-off Cape Breton Island. Only a handful of dailies and a group of weeklies, somewhat larger, report news objectively and are editorially fair to the CCF.

Consequently, one of the most essential early steps of the CCF in each province has been to establish a newspaper as an organ of the movement. There are now six

[15] Newfoundland, the tenth province to join the Canadian confederation, as of March 31, 1949, probably will require much aid from the CCF national organization.

newspapers of importance in the CCF; they range from weeklies to monthlies; from four pages to twelve pages, with an occasional larger edition. On the whole they are well written and attractively printed. Their news coverage is good on local and provincial matters, and fair on national affairs. Feature articles and overseas dispatches,

Province	Newspaper	Frequency of publication	Pages	Width in columns	Ownership
B. C.	CCF News	Weekly	6	6	Federationist Publishing Co.
Alta.	People's Weekly	Weekly	8	5	Alberta CCF
Sask.	Saskatchewan Commonwealth	Weekly	12	5	CCF Publishing & Printing Co.
Man.	Manitoba Commonwealth	Fortnightly	8	5	Manitoba CCF
Ont.	CCF News	Fortnightly	8	5	Ontario CCF
N.B. N.S. P.E.I.	Maritime Commonwealth	Bimonthly	4	5	Halifax District CCF

many through the Cooperative Press Association, help to broaden horizons by presenting stories on developments in other countries. Editorially each paper reflects the views of its owner or controlling board, which invariably follow the CCF party line. Possibly the papers would be more interesting if they permitted more controversy, but the youthful movement contents itself in that regard with the safety valve of a "letters to the editor" section.

The principal characteristics of six newspapers may be exhibited as in the table on this page. Quebec has a French-language newspaper, *Le Canada Nouveau,* which it published from 1943 to 1945 and which has recently been revived. Recently, too, the New Brunswick CCF has launched a newspaper, named *True Democracy.* The

Saskatchewan Commonwealth is published by a company that has assets of $67,000 including a printing plant.

The several provincial newspapers have been aided considerably by the establishment in 1944 of the Co-operative Press Association. This ambitious project was launched on a financial shoestring, but soon was recognized as a great asset of the movement. Aided in its first year by a grant of $200 from the national office, and by another $500 in the second year, the C.P.A. is financed mainly by quota assessments on the CCF papers using the service. Its budget for 1946–47 was estimated at $3,880, to be raised mainly by a monthly fee paid by each paper, and ranging from $10 to $20. The service includes regular dispatches from Ottawa, Great Britain, New Zealand, and Scandinavia, as well as syndicated labor news from the United States.

SELECTION OF CANDIDATES

The nominating convention is universally used by the CCF as a means of selecting candidates for legislative and parliamentary office. Usually it is a convention of delegates. The basis of representation varies a good deal, even within provinces. British Columbia provides for either a delegate or a unit membership convention; if the delegate convention is used, then the ratio is one delegate for ten members or fraction thereof. Saskatchewan characteristically prescribes in detail that the provincial nominating convention shall be composed of three delegates from each poll, and the federal nominating convention of two. Alberta allows two delegates for the first ten members in a poll, one for each ten thereafter, and one for every twenty-five affiliated trade unionists. Ontario permits each constituency to choose whether it will nominate by

membership convention, delegate convention, or referendum. Only in Ontario and Manitoba is the candidate
selected by a nominating convention subject to further
review; Ontario candidates must be endorsed by the provincial council, and Manitoba candidates by the provincial executive.

A nominating convention is generally held in an audi-
torium in a central location in the constituency. Only
duly accredited delegates are permitted to speak and vote,
but visitors are welcomed. The names of the aspirants
for the nomination are placed before the convention by
delegates. Usually the aspirants are themselves present
and are given an opportunity to speak. After the speeches,
the delegates vote and the results are announced. Often a
public meeting follows, featuring addresses by a prominent CCF leader and the newly selected candidate.
Satisfaction with the convention system of nominating
appears to be general. Two proposals for modification
have been made recently. In Saskatchewan it has been
suggested that membership rather than delegate conventions be permitted in the urban constituencies of Regina,
Moose Jaw, and Saskatoon. In national CCF circles the
idea of providing for National Executive or National
Council approval of federal candidates is being considered. The latter procedure would represent a great step
toward centralization, but it may be that a national body
should pass judgment on the qualifications of men and
women who stand for the office of M. P.[16]

---

[16] The irresponsible conduct on the floor of the House of Commons, in
the opening days of the parliamentary session of 1949, of a newly elected
member from Vancouver must have caused most of the present parliamentary CCF representatives to desire something of that kind. Pressure
was undoubtedly exerted, and the incident was closed when the member
apologized to the Speaker of the House.

EDUCATIONAL AND YOUTH ACTIVITIES

In addition to the discussion groups and addresses that are common features of the educational programs of most parties, some of the CCF provincial sections have embarked upon more ambitious projects. British Columbia and Saskatchewan operate summer camps which combine recreational and educational activities. A British Columbia CCF summer school has been held for fifteen years at Camp Woodsworth on Gabriola Island near Nanaimo. In recent years the camp has operated over a period of four weeks; about two hundred persons attended for some part of each summer. The Saskatchewan section also operates a summer camp at Crystal Lake near Canora; it met for the twelfth successive year in 1948.

Most of the provincial CCF organizations have developed schools or lecture series of significant educational value. Beginning in 1944, the Ontario CCF presented a series of lectures on party policies and program; the addresses of the first series, given by such men as Frank Scott, T. C. Douglas, M. J. Coldwell, and David Lewis, were of such quality that in printed form they are regarded as an authoritative statement of party policy.[17] The Saskatchewan CCF regularly holds one or two winter schools in early January; they provide an opportunity of bringing together the people from the constituencies to explore some of the complex problems of policy and tactics which lie in the months ahead. British Columbia in 1942 conducted a leadership training course in which students, in eight weekly sessions, learned how to prepare and give talks, conduct discussion groups, preside at a

[17] *Planning for Freedom: Sixteen Lectures on the CCF, Its Policies and Program* (Toronto: Ontario C.C.F., 1944). The second series was distributed in mimeographed form.

public meeting, organize a group, and write publicity. In the summer of 1946 the British Columbia Section opened its Boag Labor College with a two weeks short course. Successful camps, schools, and short courses have also been conducted from time to time in Alberta, Quebec, and Nova Scotia.

The work of the CCF among young people is of extraordinary importance. The voting returns from the armed forces during the war indicated clearly that younger men and women find the CCF more palatable politically than the older people do. It is obvious that if youth can be won and held today, victory in a few years may be assured. The organization of young people for political purposes is, however, a difficult matter. The British Labour Party has made a great effort to build up its League of Youth, but without conspicuous success. On the one hand, it is notoriously hard to interest young persons in weighty matters of state. On the other, the ones who do become interested are apt to fall into the clutches of the Communists, who manage to appear mysterious and somewhat glamorous with their dark talk about "real action."

Through the difficult years of the war it was largely Saskatchewan that kept the torch of the CCYM burning. For years the *Saskatchewan Commonwealth* has set aside one page for the use of the CCYM. Dr. Carlyle King of Saskatoon has given much time and talent to the youth movement. The CCYM has been given an honored place in the provincial convention and on the provincial council, and has been included in the preparation of literature and the planning of broadcasts. It is not surprising that more than two-thirds of all CCYM members as of January, 1946, were in Saskatchewan.

Since the end of the war there has been a revival of interest in the youth movement. During much of her term as national president of the CCYM (1944–1946), Mrs. Doris French worked in Ottawa near the center of party activity, and she has been able to see the role of youth in the movement and to work more closely with the national counselor, Mrs. Grace MacInnis, than her predecessors have done. Besides a considerable gain in membership and in number of active units, the CCYM acquired organizational strength through the appointment in 1946 of a full-time national secretary who works out of Woodsworth House, Ottawa.

In 1946, also, the Cooperative Commonwealth University Federation (CCUF) was launched. Unlike the CCYM, the CCUF has no formal affiliation with the CCF although it does consist of university groups which support the program and policies of that party.

CHAPTER IV

Friends and Foes of the CCF

THE CCF was originally projected as a federal union of parties, trade unions, and farmers' organizations. This united front was expected to attract the affiliation of trade unions and united farmers' groups. In the first ten years of its existence, the CCF was able to secure the formal affiliation on the farm front of only the United Farmers of Alberta, and this connection was presumably to be dissolved as the U.F.A. withdrew from politics. No trade union affiliated with the CCF in the first seven years of its existence.

THE TRADE UNION MOVEMENT

Finally, in 1938, the United Mine Workers, District 26, voted to affiliate with the party nationally. Although no other unions followed suit immediately, by 1942 a steady stream of local unions were applying for affiliation with the provincial parties in Ontario, Alberta, Saskatchewan, Manitoba, and Nova Scotia. This record of affiliation with the party was accelerated by the increasingly favorable attitudes of the two major labor congresses.

As described in an earlier chapter, the older body is the Trades and Labour Congress, which today is composed mainly of international unions affiliated with the A. F. of L. in the United States. The Trades and Labour Congress is the exponent of craft unionism in Canada. Most of the unions affiliated with it are composed of skilled craftsmen. Until 1939 the T. and L. C. included in its membership many unions which in the United States were affiliated with the C.I.O.

In 1939, however, two events led to the expulsion of the C.I.O. unions from the T. and L. C. First, the Houston convention of the A. F. of L. demonstrated a hostility toward the continued collaboration of Canadian A. F. of L. and C.I.O. unions in the T. and L. C. Second, the C.I.O. was transformed from a committee to a congress at a Pittsburgh convention. The executive of the T. and L. C. ordered the suspension of the Canadian C.I.O. unions, and the convention approved this action by a vote of 231 to 98.[1]

At the time the suspension was confirmed, the T. and L. C. reported that fewer than 22,500 unionists (for whom the congress per capita tax had been paid in 1938) were involved. Of that number the U.M.W. accounted for 15,000, the Amalgamated Clothing Workers for 4,000, and the Steel Workers Organizing Committee for 1,120. Today, however, the Steel Workers have the second largest membership of any union in Canada.

There was already in existence a rival congress, which after 1930 called itself the All-Canadian Congress of Labour. It was composed of "national" unions with membership limited to the Dominion alone. After the expulsion of the C.I.O. unions, the All-Canadian Congress group invited them to unite in a new central body.[2] They accepted and the federation took the name Canadian Congress of Labour.

---

[1] Trades and Labour Congress, *Report of the Proceedings of the 55th Annual Convention, London* [Ontario], *1939*, pp. 156–157.

[2] The first convention proceedings were entitled: The Canadian Congress of Labour, *Proceedings of the 10th Regular Convention, All-Canadian Congress of Labour, and the First Convention, Canadian Congress of Labour, Toronto, Ontario, September 9–12, 1940.*

Thus it came about that the C.C.L. embraced vigorous elements of the new unionism—steelworkers, automobile workers, rubber workers, and the like. It includes also the U.M.W., which withdrew from the C.I.O. in the United States but remained with the C.C.L. in Canada. One important step taken by the first convention of the new congress was to provide that jurisdictional and other disputes between member unions should be settled by the C.C.L. and not, as is done by the T. and L. C., referred to a body in the United States.

Trades and Labour Congress.—The typical political activity of the T. and L. C. is the annual presentation of its program of legislative requests to the government. When this is laid before the national government, it draws unionists from all the provinces of Canada to Ottawa and generally commands the presence of the Prime Minister, the Minister of Labour, and most of the other cabinet members who are available. The presentation is made in respectful terms and the program is left for the Prime Minister and his colleagues to consider.

This approach to politics has proved singularly ineffective. The rigidity of the party system in Canada makes it virtually impossible for the trade unionists effectively to lobby individual M.P.'s or M.L.A.'s who belong to the majority party group. The omnipotence of the ministry in the parliamentary system reduces nearly to nil the possibility of securing without government support the adoption of a private member's bill.

The T. and L. C. has not been immune to the trend toward more political action. In its 1942 convention it was confronted with several resolutions concerning that point. The resolutions committee offered a rather feeble substitute resolution in which the history of labor po-

litical organization was reviewed, and it was then resolved to leave autonomy "in the hands of established
labor political parties, and that this congress continue to
act as legislative mouthpiece for Organized Labor in
Canada independent of any political organization."[3] In
the discussion of this resolution many delegates urged
either affiliation with the CCF or study of the CCF program, but there was also expressed a great deal of hostility toward affiliation with any political party. The
official resolution was finally adopted.[4]

In its 1943 convention, the T. and L. C. was again confronted with several resolutions demanding political action. The resolutions committee's substitute resolution
this time called for the new device of local political action
committees. The resolution as adopted was as follows:

Resolved, that this convention calls upon its affiliated unions
to take all necessary steps in the community and provinces of
the Dominion to create Trade Union Committees for political action, so as to enable the trade unions to play a more
direct and appropriate role in influencing and shaping the
great movement for independent political action and thereby
secure trade union representation on all governing bodies;
we further recommend that labor unions support candidates
who favor the policies of the trade union movement as represented by this congress.[5]

The 1944 T. and L. C. convention decided to establish
a political action committee, but after its personnel was
appointed and an initial statement made, it was clear that
the CCF could expect little aid from T. and L. C. circles,

[3] Trades and Labour Congress, *Report of the Proceedings of the 58th Annual Convention, Winnipeg, 1942,* pp. 228–229.
[4] *Ibid.,* p. 337.
[5] Trades and Labour Congress, *Report of the Proceedings of the 59th Annual Convention, Quebec, 1943,* p. 346.

and perhaps some obstruction. The committee determined to stay out of partisan politics and to prevail upon the government, irrespective of party, "... to enact legislation tending to fuller, freer and happier lives for the workers and people of Canada as a whole."[6] Later statements were thinly veiled endorsements of the Liberal side in the 1945 election. In June, 1945, for example, the committee reviewed the wartime pledges of the government and concluded:

> Those who made those pledges must be given an opportunity to redeem them. They are charged with that responsibility. They must be given the opportunity of keeping faith with the people and establish [*sic*] a peacetime economy that will assure a free, full, and happy life.
> There is a danger that a new group, put in power at this time, would institute policies that might have no relation whatever to the pledges that an overwhelming number of people of this country have put their faith in."[7]

In seeking to provide an explanation for this stand, CCF leaders stress two factors. The first is the traditional caution of the T. and L. C. regarding politics, borrowed from its big brother, the A. F. of L. The second is the alleged growing influence of the Communists within the T. and L. C. Despite these barriers, the CCF has made some progress by dealing directly with local T. and L. C. unions. Approximately one-half of the local unions affiliated with the CCF in Ontario, Alberta, and Saskatchewan are T. and L. C. unions. Of the 34 Ontario CCF legislators elected in 1943, 10 were members of T. and L. C. unions and 9 of C.C.L. unions.

Canadian Congress of Labour.—Prominent leaders of

---

[6] Trades and Labour Congress *Journal*, 24 (May, 1945): 19.
[7] *Ibid.* (June, 1945), p. 44.

the C.C.L. had long been identified with the CCF. Charles Millard, Canadian national director of the United Steelworkers of America, has served as a member of both national and provincial councils of the CCF and was elected CCF legislator in the Ontario elections of 1943 and 1948. A. R. Mosher, president of the C.C.L., had represented the Canadian Brotherhood of Railway Employees at the 1932 Calgary conference. Although the C.B.R.E. did not affiliate with the CCF, Mosher has long been considered friendly toward the party.

Progress toward C.C.L. support of the CCF was made when the 1942 convention of the labor body adopted a resolution commending the work of the CCF representatives in Parliament and other legislative bodies and urging chartered and affiliated unions to study the CCF program.[8]

At the 1943 convention in Montreal the C.C.L. took a most far-reaching step toward political action. Combining the thoughts contained in several resolutions submitted by various affiliated unions, the resolutions committee proposed and secured the adoption of the following resolution:

WHEREAS, It is becoming increasingly apparent that organized labour, if it is to play its part in improving the welfare and economic status of the workers, must take political as well as economic action, due to the inevitable and ever-enlarging control that governments are exercising over all aspects of economic life and industry in this country; and

WHEREAS, In the opinion of this Congress, the policy and programme of the Co-operative Commonwealth Federation more adequately expresses the viewpoint of organized labour than any other party:

[8] Canadian Congress of Labour, *Proceedings of the 3rd Annual Convention, Ottawa, Ontario, September 14–19, 1942*, pp. 51, 160.

Be it therefore resolved, That this Convention of the Canadian Congress of Labour endorse the Co-operative Commonwealth Federation as the political arm of labour in Canada, and recommend to all affiliated and chartered unions that they affiliate with the Co-operative Commonwealth Federation.[9]

The resolution was strongly supported by delegates from steelworkers, miners, and members of the executive board. It was opposed by some who took the Labor-Progressive point of view and by others who were sharply critical of the CCF's failure to provide what they regarded as adequate direct representation of the unions. This resolution was very important in securing the affiliation of C.C.L. union locals in 1943–1944.

In addition to endorsement of the CCF as the political arm of labor, the C.C.L. proceeded to establish its own political action committee, of nine members, one of whom, to serve as chairman, was C. H. Millard, the most prominent CCF trade unionist in the Dominion. At least six of the nine committeemen represent unions which in the United States have participated actively in the C.I.O. political action work. However, the C.C.L. political action committee concentrated during its first two years on educating local unions, doing liaison work between the C.C.L. and the CCF and publishing a few leaflets stressing the need for working-class political action. Local labor councils have established political action committees in some districts. In a few centers, C.C.L. and T. and L. C. local unions are working harmoniously on joint political action programs. The work of the C.C.L. P.A.C. has been a disappointment to CCF enthusiasts

---

[9] Canadian Congress of Labour, *Proceedings of the 4th Annual Convention, Montreal, Quebec, September 13–17, 1943,* pp. 53–56.

who expected it to raise large sums of money and put many organizers in the field, as was done by the C.I.O. P.A.C. in the United States.

AGRICULTURAL GROUPS

Canadian farmers' organizations have for the most part withdrawn, in the last twenty years, from active participation in party politics. At the close of the last war, the U.F.O. and the U.F.A. formed governments in their provinces and functioned much like political parties. Today, both of these organizations have withdrawn entirely from politics and the Ontario group recently lost its identity in the Ontario Federation of Agriculture.

The most influential agricultural organization is now the Canadian Federation of Agriculture and its affiliated bodies. The Federation was started in 1935 as a national organization of certain farm commodity groups. Today its affiliated bodies are primarily provincial chambers and federations. The following are affiliates: British Columbia Chamber of Agriculture, Alberta Federation of Agriculture, Saskatchewan Cooperative Confederation, Manitoba Federation of Agriculture, Ontario Federation of Agriculture, Maritime Chamber of Agriculture, Canadian Dairy Farmers Federation, La Coopérative Fédérée de Québec.

The Federation of Agriculture has been nonpolitical with respect to partisan politics; nevertheless it has put forward forcibly its legislative program. In 1943, for example, it urged the adoption of a Dominion Health Plan. The chief political weapon of the Federation appears to be lobbying. Organization of the provincial bodies varies considerably. The Ontario Federation maintains its principal functioning units at the local committee level.

Judging from its record during the past few years, the Federation is likely to continue concentrating upon economic rather than political problems. Preoccupation with demands for higher farm prices may cause it to neglect the broad social problems that confront the country as a whole, as the farm bloc in the United States has done.

THE COOPERATIVE MOVEMENT

Consumers' cooperatives got started in the Dominion of Canada at a relatively late period. There was a good deal of interest between 1900 and 1914 in societies based upon the Rochdale plan. After 1936, interest grew rapidly and the number of cooperative enterprises launched was very large indeed.

In 1930 the Canadian federal government surveyed Canadian cooperatives and found a total of 1,173 societies doing an aggregate business of nearly $23,000,000.[10] By 1943 the figures on cooperative endeavor showed a vast increase. The federal Department of Agriculture reported that, for that year, cooperatives (the term here includes all forms of cooperative endeavor) had an aggregate membership of about 500,000 and a total business of $250,000,000. In money terms, one of the leading forms of cooperation in Canada is the credit union; there are now more than 1,500 credit unions in the Dominion, with a membership of around 300,000. Farmers' cooperatives for the purchase of feed, fertilizer, and other necessaries are among the most outstanding Canadian cooperative endeavors. There has been a recent and spirited development of cooperative handling of petroleum products, especially among the farmers of the West. Although they

[10] George S. Mooney, *Co-operatives Today and Tomorrow: A Canadian Survey* (Montreal: prepared for the Survey Committee, 1938), p. 80.

occupy a relatively less significant role in cooperation as a whole than similar organizations in present-day Great Britain, cooperatives handling food and clothing still constitute an important element in the Canadian cooperative picture.

The development of cooperative societies among fishermen and miners in the Maritime Provinces has been notable. Sponsored by the Extension Department of St. Francis Xavier University, at Antigonish, Nova Scotia, a network of credit unions, cooperative stores, buying clubs, and cooperative fish processing and fish marketing enterprises has been developed.

The cooperative movement has a central organization in the Cooperative Union of Canada, with headquarters in Ottawa. The credit unions are organized principally on a provincial basis. Basic to the functioning of retail cooperative groups are the cooperative wholesale societies. The most successful venture of this sort in Canada is the Saskatchewan Cooperative Wholesale Society, organized in 1929. Although started with a modest capital of $2,900, by 1940 this C.W.S. had a share capital of $104,000. Its volume of business is reported to have reached $1,400,000 in 1939.[11]

In the volume of business done by agricultural producers' cooperatives, Canada stands well up with the leading countries of the world. Western Canadian agricultural life developed relatively late and very quickly. In order to solve the acute problems of distribution and marketing, the farmers joined together almost from the first in cooperative endeavors. By the end of 1943 there were 1,675 agricultural marketing and merchandising

[11] University of British Columbia, Department of the University Extension, *An Introduction to the Cooperative Movement,* Bulletin 4, p. 2.

cooperatives, with 585,826 members. The heavy concentration was in the prairie provinces, especially in Saskatchewan.[12]

In volume and aggregate value of products the grain growers' cooperatives constitute the largest cooperative enterprise in Canada. The wheat pools of the West are vast organizations and have great power in world markets. The University of British Columbia correspondence course in cooperation declares that more than one-half of Canada's farmers are in the ranks of cooperators. Although mere membership in the cooperative movement is not conclusive evidence that an individual has been converted to the cause of the cooperative commonwealth, it can be said that participation in the cooperative movement is one of the chief roads of conversion to CCF policy. To an extent unequaled in the labor parties of Britain, Australia, and New Zealand, the CCF has stressed the accomplishment of its social and economic objectives through cooperatives. State enterprises will have their place in the socialization of heavy industry, banking and finance, and other fields, but a vast responsibility will be placed upon cooperative enterprises by a CCF government either in Ottawa or in the provinces. Thus in Saskatchewan the CCF government, promptly after its election in 1944, created a separate Department of Cooperatives headed by a minister, and enacted legislation to assist and extend cooperative endeavor.

There is much evidence to support the claim that the cooperative movement is playing the role of opening the minds of Canadians to a social consciousness that is less often developed by one who works alone. In explaining

[12] Canada, Royal Commission on Cooperatives, *Report* (Ottawa: King's Printer, 1945), p. 15.

the heavy defeat of the Alberta CCF in the election of
1944 and comparing it with the triumph in Saskatchewan
in the same year, one writer stated that Saskatchewan had
513 cooperatives with 210,000 members whereas Alberta
had 110 cooperatives with 120,000 members. He concluded: "Cooperatives are Canada's school for socialists.
With the growth of the cooperative movement, the basis
of which is unassailable, comes an understanding of the
benefits of social ownership and control, and of cooperative production and distribution. Hand in hand with
cooperatives in Saskatchewan there has marched the
C.C.F., which is the national cooperative unit, and which
can be expected to develop no more rapidly than the
theory of cooperation, and its practical application to the
affairs of the people of Canada."[13]

In 1946, when the Dominion government proposed to
subject certain cooperative earnings to the income tax,
the CCF M.P.'s became the great champions and principal spokesmen of the opposition. Their arguments that
cooperative enterprise is different in nature from commercial enterprise were widely publicized and well reported. Because a considerable number of the party's
M.P.'s are themselves participants in the cooperative
movement, they elaborated their theme with authority
and conviction.

Such support of the cooperative movement may ultimately pay dividends to the party in terms of votes. The
top leaders and managers of the farmers' marketing
groups, however, are often politically conservative and
far distant in political theory from the rank-and-file
members.

---

[13] Morris C. Shumiatcher, "Alberta Election," *Canadian Forum*, 24
(September, 1944): 127–128.

CONSERVATIVE REBIRTH

The leaders of the Conservative Party have been extremely hostile toward the CCF since its beginnings. Within three months of the Calgary conference, Prime Minister R. B. Bennett was denouncing the new party as moving "towards a government Soviet in its character."[14]

Bennett continued: "What do they offer you for dumping you in the mud? Socialism, communism, dictatorship." Woodsworth called the statement libelous and seditious.

After the defeat of Bennett's government in the federal election of 1935, the Conservative Party entered a period of decline in electoral strength from which it had not recovered a decade later. Bennett resigned leadership of the party and moved to Great Britain, where he was elevated to the peerage. For a time it appeared that the Conservative Party would find its leader in the person of Robert J. Manion, who had been Minister of Railways and Canals in Bennett's government. Although defeated in the election of 1935, Manion was chosen leader of the Conservative Party at a national convention held in Ottawa in July, 1936, and secured a seat in the House through a by-election later in that year. He was defeated in the general election of 1940 and subsequently resigned leadership of the party. In May, 1940, leadership of the depleted Conservative forces in the House of Commons had been undertaken by R. B. Hanson, who has been described as "an undistinguished New Brunswick lawyer who is heavy both in body and in mind."[15]

---

[14] Quoted by J. S. Woodsworth in House of Commons *Debates*, Session 1932–33, 2: 1688.

[15] W. H. Chamberlin, *Canada, Today and Tomorrow* (Boston: Little, Brown, 1942), p. 179.

Hanson resigned late in 1941 because of ill health. Early in November of that year Conservative members of the House and Senate met with the national executive of the party in Ottawa. It was decided to offer the leadership of the party to Senator Arthur Meighen, who, although 67 years of age, was the most experienced and gifted Conservative leader available. He had served briefly as Prime Minister in 1920 and again in 1926. He had been appointed to the Senate in 1932. In February, 1942, he resigned his seat in the Senate in order to contest a federal by-election in the constituency of York South, in Ontario. Meighen received a stinging defeat at the hands of J. W. Noseworthy, the CCF candidate.

The search for party leadership continued. At last, at a general convention held in Winnipeg in December, 1942, the course of the party in the next era was determined by the selection of John Bracken, long the nonpartisan Premier of Manitoba, as leader of the party. At Bracken's insistence the name of the party was changed to Progressive Conservative and the program adopted was regarded as an important swing back toward the center. This metamorphosis was only the latest in a long series of attempts by the Conservative Party to find an effective role in Canadian politics. Over the years the traditional lines dividing the Conservatives and Liberals have grown so obscure that the two parties have come to appear nearly identical in principles and policies. This has been one of the important factors favoring the growth of the CCF. Bennett attempted, between 1930 and 1935, to convert the Conservative Party into a vehicle to bring the "New Deal" to the Dominion, but he found it impossible to overcome the barriers set up by the narrow interpretations put on the British North America Act by the Judicial Committee of the Privy Council in London. The success of the CCF from 1942 onward encouraged the Conservatives to swing further and further away from their traditional emphasis upon protection and the Imperial connection, and also from hostility toward social services.

In the statement of policy adopted by the Winnipeg convention in 1942, the party pledged itself to an advanced program of farm and labor legislation. It declared for full employment to be achieved through "individual enterprise,"[16] and an extensive social security program. The party's declaration for conscription for overseas service was evidence that it had abandoned all hope of winning Quebec under its own name and platform.

From the beginning of his addresses as leader of the Progressive Conservative party, Bracken attempted to win over the mass of independent voters who in the last analysis determine the results of national elections. He did not attack the CCF directly, but warned against the voters' acceptance of "any plausible alternative Utopian formula, untested and dangerous though it may be, that is offered them."[17]

While Bracken was campaigning from coast to coast in 1942 and 1943, the party organization and its spokesmen in Parliament were striking out against the rising CCF. In the newspaper *Public Opinion,* published for the party, quotations of CCF leaders and documents were given to show that the CCF was isolationist and without foresight in international affairs. Like other opponents

---

[16] *Policy of the Progressive Conservative Party,* adopted at the national convention held at Winnipeg, December 9–11, 1942 (Ottawa: Progressive Conservative Party, n.d.).

[17] "Address, December 21, 1942" (Ottawa: Progressive Conservative Party, n.d.), p. 3.

of the CCF the Conservatives concentrated their fire on Harold Winch, British Columbia CCF leader, whose proclivity for vigorous statement earned him the description "stormy radical and militant revolutionary."[18]

By 1944, Bracken himself joined in the direct assaults upon the CCF. Delivering in Hamilton, Ontario, an address rejected for broadcast by the Canadian Broadcasting Corporation, he declared: "It is a most ironical paradox that the party which I lead is trying to create a cooperative commonwealth while those who parade under the banner of the CCF are advocating state socialism." After condemning the evils of bureaucracy, he continued: "The watchwords of the future must be decentralization, not centralization; cooperation, not state dictation; expanding production, not scarcity; and widening areas of trade, not restrictions on trade."[19]

In general, the tactics of the rejuvenated Conservative Party have been to carve out a place for itself between what it calls the "piecemeal policies leaning toward reaction" on the one hand and "state socialism" on the other. This is an extremely vulnerable position and represents only the latest phase of the futile quest of the Conservatives for a role between that of wallpaper and the man on the flying trapeze. The progressive pose of the Conservative Party is undermined both by the CCF's comprehensive progressive program and the Liberal government's considerable record of social legislation. The record of the Conservatives in both federal and provincial elections shows clearly that, except in Ontario, the Conservatives have declined greatly in strength during the last ten years. They appear almost entirely doomed in

[18] *Public Opinion,* 1 (December, 1943): 1.
[19] *Ibid.,* 2 (January, 1944): 3.

the four western provinces and their strength in Ontario may wane as suddenly as it rose. The Conservatives are playing a dangerous game in Quebec through their passive support of the *Union Nationale* with its extremist leaders and policies. In the Maritimes, a sturdy backlog of Conservative support exists. As the picture appears to CCF leaders, the Conservative Party will be the weaker of the two old parties that ultimately will be forced into coalition. It will have to seek; it will not be sought.

THE LIBERAL FLANKING MOVE

Liberal leaders have denounced the CCF in less blatant terms than the Conservatives. The leader of the Liberal Party from the beginning year (1932) of the CCF until 1948 was Mackenzie King. He and his more mature colleagues remembered well that they were faced with a progressive ferment in 1921 which appeared likely either to alter the two-party system or to sweep one of the old parties out of existence. King rode out this political storm, and within half a decade the progressive movement was virtually dead or swallowed up by the Liberal Party. Senator T. A. Crerar, leader of the Progressive Party in the federal House in 1921–22 and subsequently a member of the Liberal cabinet, stands as mute evidence of the power of the Liberal Party to assimilate political reformers.

Accordingly, the Liberals' approach, at least in the House of Commons, has been rather conciliatory toward the CCF. The latchstring has been left out for a possible coalition, and King has of late years cultivated Coldwell assiduously, but the CCF has been conspicuously reluctant even to consider joint action with the Liberals. The CCF position has been that as the new party rises in power the two old parties representative of the capitalist system will be forced into coalition as they have been in British Columbia and in Manitoba.

The Liberal Party is so broad-based that it finds it more convenient to operate without a platform. Its last full statement was written in 1919 at the time King became political leader. The doctrines of the party must be drawn from its record in office over the years. In general, the Liberals have stood for Canadian nationalism as opposed to domination by Great Britain, and for internationalism in trade. While Liberal tariff policy has been less extremely protectionist than was the Conservative, it has been far from a free-trade policy. The Liberal Party has long stood nominally for a program of social legislation, but its actual achievements in this line were meager indeed until 1944.

The Liberal Party had very great national electoral strength in the period 1935–1941. At one time in 1940 it held a majority not only in the House of Commons but also in the legislature of every province except Alberta, which was Social Credit. This strong position has since been lost; the Liberals from 1944 to 1948 actually operated the governments of only the three Maritime Provinces. Quebec constitutes paradoxically a source of great Liberal strength and one of the Liberals' most acute problems. Like the Solid South in the Democratic Party, Quebec demands respect and representation and yet is an extraneous, often discordant, element.

Although King was, especially in the last days of his leadership, reasonably polite toward the CCF and almost deferential to Coldwell, some of his colleagues have attacked both with great vigor. This has been especially true of M.P.'s who, like Gardiner, the Minister of Agriculture, saw their own provinces and constituencies falling under the control of the hated socialists. The CCF M.P.'s from Saskatchewan have attacked the Liberal machine of that province relentlessly, and had the satisfaction in 1944 of gloating over the defeat of the entrenched Liberals and in 1948 of repeating their victory. Occasionally, Liberals from the Province of Quebec have attacked the doctrines of the CCF on the floor of the House of Commons; frequently in the 1930's, when the ban of Cardinal Villeneuve on socialism was still in effect. In the conscription controversy of 1942 the CCF took a point of view which led many of the French-Canadian M.P.'s to demonstrate new respect for the party. The CCF provided the French Canadians who opposed conscription for overseas service a fairly logical justification of their views. They argued that if conscription of man power was to be invoked, it must be accompanied, hand in hand, by conscription of wealth.

The Liberal organizations often have attacked the CCF vehemently in the provinces, especially in the western provinces, where the CCF has the Liberals on the run. Some of the Liberal leaders in the western provinces have made the mistake of trying to refute the CCF arguments for reform with anti-utopian expressions. Most of these counterarguments have been in terms of debunking the promises of the CCF and reviewing the history of other political ferments in Canada to show how little was actually accomplished by the U.F.A., the U.F.O., and Progressive regimes. A classic expression of anti-utopian sentiment was provided by G. V. Ferguson, former editor of the *Winnipeg Free Press*, in 1943:

... a prostrate and lovely Canada lies groaning under the yoke of two old and greedy and cynical and highly capitalistic

political parties—and behold, over the horizon, on a white
and fiery stallion comes prancing the young Prince Charm-
ing, equipped as no one has ever been equipped before with
every nostrum, salve, and unguent to drive away the evil-
doers and bind up and heal the wounds and bruises of the
beautiful maiden, who will doubtless arise promptly into a
permanent and enduring alliance with her saviour. "I took
only one bottle of your wonderful liniment. The pain left
me and I have voted CCF ever since."[20]

The better strategy for Liberal opponents of the CCF
would have been to offer a series of legislative enactments
on social matters, like the Weir health plan in British Columbia, while there was still a Liberal government in
office. Now that Liberals have been eliminated from provincial office except in the Maritimes, this effective coun-
terweapon can have only limited application.

The Liberal party at the opening of 1949 appears to be
at the crossroads. It has held national power for twenty-
one of the last twenty-seven years. Now, however, its
venerable Mackenzie King has retired from the leadership and the adequacy of his successor, Louis St. Laurent,
has yet to be proved. To judge from provincial general
elections, Liberal electoral strength is still declining. The
CCF is winning over considerable numbers of its more
progressive supporters. The Conservatives, under George
Drew, a bold and aggressive leader, are making their most
effective appeal to the country since 1930. In spite of all
these challenges, however, the Liberals still retain majority power in the House of Commons and may be able in
the parliamentary session of 1949 to enact enough social
legislation to take the wind out of CCF sails and also to
present as accomplished fact some of the bids for popular-

[20] *Canadian Journal of Economics and Political Science* (hereafter cited
as C.J.E.P.S.), 9 (August, 1943): 313.

ity made by the Conservative program. The most effective flanking attack on the CCF has been the enactment of child allowance legislation.

COMMUNIST OVERTURES

At the time the CCF was founded, its critics concentrated upon damning it as a Communist or fellow traveler organization. These criticisms have declined in recent years and even the bitterest opponents of the CCF are now inclined to confess privately that the movement is not a tool of Moscow. On the other hand, the CCF is still criticized as supporting a form of socialist totalitarianism which is compared with that of Russia.

From time to time the Communist Party of Canada made overtures to the CCF, seeking to enter the federation on a national basis as a constituent body. This request for affiliation was parallel to the repeated applications of the Communist Party in Great Britain for admission to the British Labour Party. The CCF national conventions in 1933 and 1934 adopted a policy of noncooperation with the Communist Party and with Communist-controlled organizations. In 1935 a controversy arose over the fact that the CCYM had affiliated with the League against War and Fascism, which was alleged by some to be a Communist-front organization. T. C. Douglas, as president of the CCYM, had spoken to a meeting of the League. After a discussion of the question, the National Council adopted a resolution declaring that CCF organizations can enter into alliances with no other political party or group. This apparently applies to provincial as well as national levels.[21]

---

[21] Minutes of the National Council, Winnipeg, November 30–December 1, 1935, pp. 8–10.

The Friends of the Soviet Union organization requested in 1937 that the CCF join with it in the celebration of the twentieth anniversary of the U.S.S.R. The National Council declined to participate actively in the proposed celebration, but asked that the refusal be not interpreted as criticism of the Soviet Union or opposition to the celebration. An amendment to the motion which would have added expression of sympathy with the celebration and recognition of the accomplishments in Russia was defeated.[22]

In the meantime, the Communist Party had experienced the exigencies which harassed Communist organizations in other countries. The party was organized, in Canada, in 1924. In 1931, eight of its leaders were sentenced to imprisonment after a trial in the Ontario courts. The section of the criminal code under which they were convicted was later repealed, and the party operated legally until the beginning of World War II. In 1939–40 the party was outlawed by federal action, and its leader, Tim Buck, went into hiding, presumably in the United States. During this period, however, the *Tribune,* a newspaper representing the Communist point of view, continued publication in Toronto. Buck was able to return to Canada without molestation in 1943, and together with other prominent former Communists he then joined in the formation of a new party called the Labor-Progressive Party. A considerable volume of literature was issued from the Toronto office, and headquarters were opened in Hamilton, Niagara Falls, Kitchener, Windsor, Port Arthur, Winnipeg, and other places. The party was launched formally in August, 1943. It dropped the use of the name "Communist" and adopted a plat-

[22] Minutes of the National Council, Winnipeg, July 24, 1937.

form which called for immediate invasion of the continent of Europe by the Allied forces, national unity of
workers and farmers, and a socialist Canada.[23]

The constitution adopted declared prominently, ". . .
there is no place in this party for any individual or group
seeking to undermine, subvert, or abrogate democracy."
The preamble declared, ". . . the party rejects and re-
pudiates any proposal to forcibly impose socialism upon
Canada against the will of the majority of her people."[24]

In the program adopted at the 1943 constitutional convention, the Labor-Progressive Party called upon the
CCF, which had become "a major force in the political
life of our country," to join with other democratic movements to win the war and prepare for postwar reforms.[25]

Tim Buck declared at the launching convention that
"the question of unity with the CCF is a question in
which is involved the whole future of democratic progress
in Canada."[26]

Almost immediately the Labor-Progressive Party applied for affiliation with the CCF. The application was
considered by the National Council in September, 1943.
A resolution rejecting the application was adopted, reading as follows:

That this Council reaffirms the decisions of previous national
conventions in refusing to affiliate in any way with the Communist Party in Canada; that in view of the fact that the
newly organized Labor-Progressive Party is only the Canadian Communist Party under a new name, we reject the application of the Labor-Progressive Party for affiliation to the

[23] *Manifesto of Unity, Victory and Prosperity* (Toronto: Labor-
Progressive Party, 1943).
[24] *Constitution and Bylaws of the Labor-Progressive Party*, p. 2.
[25] *Program of the Labor-Progressive Party*, p. 19.
[26] Tim Buck, *Victory through Unity* (Toronto: Labor-Progressive Party,
1943), p. 56.

CCF; that we urge and invite those truly interested in labor unity to join the CCF; and, finally, that this Council prepare and issue a statement explaining our position in this matter."[27]

The resolution was adopted by a vote of twenty-three to four.

Buck wrote again to the CCF on December 23, 1943, asking for the affiliation of the Labor-Progressive Party with the CCF and requesting the allocation of constituencies for the next federal election. The National Council considered the matter and unanimously rejected the application. The national secretary wrote to Buck on January 3, 1944, informing him of the decision of the National Council, declaring that "the CCF is the party through which the unity of labor, farmer, and other groups can unite into a democratic people's movement."[28]

There seems no possibility that the CCF will admit Communist elements into the party. The disadvantages in accepting Communists far outweigh the advantages. The Communists, if admitted, would bring to the CCF the stigma of external control. To judge by their fluctuations in policies and tactics over the past ten years, they would constitute an extremely unstable element. Public confidence in the CCF would unquestionably be undermined. On the other hand, the Communists do have great energy and devotion to their cause. They are hard workers, and do a wonderful organizing job on limited funds and resources.

The consequences of Labor-Progressive exclusion from the CCF are minor, and irritating rather than acutely dangerous. In order to achieve "unity" Mr. Buck will declare that his party will not enter a candidate in a

[27] Minutes of the National Council, Calgary, September 5-6, 1943.
[28] *Saskatchewan Commonwealth*, January 12, 1944, p. 3. This reply was approved by the National Council, January 2, 1944.

constituency when the result might be the victory of a "capitalist" candidate. Yet one of the first Labor-Progressive candidacies announced for the 1945 federal general election was in Vancouver East, which has been represented in the House of Commons since 1930 by Angus MacInnis, perhaps the most authentic spokesman for the labor movement in the House. In British Columbia, Manitoba, and Ontario there was enough concentration of Labor-Progressive voting power to throw the 1945 election from the CCF to the Liberals in seven constituencies.[29] A. A. Heaps, former CCF M.P., was defeated in Winnipeg North in 1940, largely because a Communist candidate contested the election. Labor-Progressives have two seats in the Ontario legislative assembly and one in the Manitoba legislative assembly. Formerly they had two members of the House of Commons, Mrs. Dorise W. Neilson, who represented North Battleford, a rural Saskatchewan constituency, and Fred Rose, who won a federal by-election in Cartier, a Montreal constituency, in 1943. Mrs. Neilson was defeated by a CCF candidate in the 1945 election; Rose was convicted of delivering atomic bomb secrets to Soviet agents and is now incarcerated.

During the war, and until the arrest of Rose, the Labor-Progressives often supported Liberal and Conservative governments. The two Labor-Progressive legislators in Ontario supported the Drew government (Conservative) upon many important occasions. Mrs. Neilson and Rose, former Labor-Progressive M.P.'s, were conciliatory toward the Liberal government in Ottawa, and the national leader, Tim Buck, wrote and spoke frequently in support

---

[29] Had the CCF candidates received the votes cast by Labor-Progressives, they would have won additional victories in one Manitoba, one Ontario, and five British Columbia constituencies.

of the Mackenzie King government. During the 1948 general election campaign in Saskatchewan, the Labor-Progressives embarrassed the CCF government by publicly declaring their support of CCF candidates.

Since the summer of 1943, a significant movement of business leaders opposed to the CCF has been launched. It was conceived by Gladstone Murray, former director-general of the Canadian Broadcasting Corporation. Murray projected the development of a vast anti-CCF campaign which would extend over at least three years and cost at least $100,000. He has called his project "A Brief for Free Enterprise in General." Clearly the campaign is directed against the CCF and organized labor. A favorite device of Murray's was to refer to a conspiracy among the CCF-C.C.L.-C.I.O.

The channels of publicity employed by Murray in his crusade against socialism are the usual ones. The daily press is almost exclusively in the hands of conservative-minded people, and Mr. Murray's arguments have been constantly stressed in news story and editorial. He also proposed the extensive use of the privately owned radio stations, of which there are some seventy-five of importance in Canada. A great deal of the work of this anti-CCF movement has been directed to rallying businessmen in support of their traditional institutions.

The last time that Canadian business was seriously threatened, at the close of World War I, large amounts of money were raised and spent in the campaign against free trade and the Progressive Party. S. D. Clark has reported that the Canadian Manufacturers' Association raised a million dollars in 1920 to carry on propaganda work.[30] The maximum danger to manufacturers at that time was the abandonment of protectionist policies; a thorough campaign against the broader threat of socialism should lead to even greater money raising.

The crusade against the CCF reached its height in the months preceding the 1945 general election. It was spearheaded by B. A. Trestrail of Toronto, who used the organizational names "Public Information Association" and "Society for Individual Freedom—against State Socialism." Trestrail claimed that, on the basis of test groups in Ontario, from 25 to 40 per cent of the people can be dissuaded from voting for a "state socialist" candidate if they get the "proper" information in the "proper" manner.

His campaign, obviously well financed, centered initially around a pamphlet entitled *Stand Up and Be Counted,* and later featured *Social Suicide,* a 24-page tabloid magazine. It was reported in the press that three million copies of *Social Suicide* were printed. CCF spokesmen asked how so large a quantity of paper could have been diverted for the purpose when the restrictions on the supply of paper were normally so rigid.

The general tenor of the Trestrail campaign was that the CCF advocated a thinly diguised scheme of "national socialism" and totalitarianism. Making the most of slogans like "free enterprise" and "freedom of opportunity," Trestrail painted the CCF goal of a cooperative commonwealth a striped pattern of red Communism and brown Fascism.

Most observers are of the opinion that the anti-CCF campaigns reduced somewhat the vote of the party in the

[30] S. D. Clark, "The Canadian Manufacturers' Association," *C.J.E.P.S.,* 4 (November, 1938): 505–523.

126   *The Third Force in Canada*

1945 federal election. They probably affected most seriously the Ontario provincial election, in which the change of a few thousand votes could have affected the results in dozens of constituencies, so close did the three parties run.

SOCIAL CREDIT

Since it has been the Social Credit movement that has constituted a major obstacle to the development of the CCF in Alberta and a minor one in Saskatchewan, British Columbia, Manitoba, and Quebec, a consideration of this organization and its program appears justifiable. William Aberhart and his Social Credit colleagues came into office following the 1935 Alberta provincial election, in which they won an overwhelming victory over the senile U.F.A. government. During much of the period 1935–1940 Social Credit held 56 of the 63 seats in the legislature. Although this majority was considerably reduced in the elections of 1940 and 1944, Social Credit has remained the predominant political force in Alberta, and in August, 1948, again swept the province by securing 50 out of 57 seats in the new legislature. In addition to the early interest in Social Credit demonstrated by Coote, Spencer, and Irvine in the House of Commons, the U.F.A. representatives in the provincial legislature had also evidenced curiosity over the panacea. In 1934, the agricultural committee of the Alberta legislature took testimony on the "Douglas system of Social Credit" from Major Douglas, Aberhart, and others.[31]

Interest in Social Credit continued so long as the U.F.A. government held power. Major Douglas was employed by the government to study the applicability of

[31] *The Douglas System of Social Credit: Evidence Taken by the Agricultural Committee of the Alberta Legislature, Session 1934* (Edmonton: King's Printer, 1934).

Social Credit ideas to Alberta. In a report dated May 23, 1935, which Douglas signed as "Chief Reconstruction Advisor to His Majesty's Government of Alberta," appeared the following: "Action initiating in Alberta . . . is both possible and desirable and . . . such action must have as its first objective access to the financial credit which is presently based upon the resources and the people of Alberta itself."[32]

Appended to this report were certain extracts from a radio broadcast by Aberhart and a request by the provincial attorney-general that Douglas comment upon them. Douglas replied: "As a matter of opinion, I think Mr. Aberhart has made the common tactical mistake of elaborating his detail to a general audience to too great an extent, but if this detail is to be taken seriously, I think Mr. Aberhart should as a matter of courtesy be asked whether such details are, or are not, a matter of principle with him."[33]

This marked the beginning of a schism between Douglas and Aberhart which was to endure until Aberhart's death in 1943.

It appears likely that Aberhart did not understand the economic doctrines of Major Douglas. Certainly he was less cautious than Douglas on the matter of what could be done on a provincial basis. In the 1935 campaign, Aberhart promised a minimum of $25 per month for every bona fide citizen, not from taxes, but, as one writer has said, from the "cultural heritage."[34]

---

[32] *First Interim Report on the Possibility of the Application of Social Credit Principles to the Province of Alberta* (Edmonton: King's Printer, 1935), p. 10.

[33] *Ibid.*, pp. 12–14.

[34] A. F. McGoun, "Alberta Economic and Political, I. Social Credit Legislation: A Survey," *C.J.E.P.S.*, 2 (November, 1936): 512–524, esp. p. 516.

The Hon. William Aberhart was a remarkable man. This Calgary school principal had built up a great following by his extracurricular activities, chiefly lay preaching in the Bible Institute of Calgary. He had an unusually persuasive radio voice and he kept telling the people of Alberta the things they wanted to hear. In 1935 he promised, in addition to the $25 per month dividend, to establish a new credit mechanism, to lend money without interest, to end unemployment, and to establish new industries in the province.

In office, Aberhart was somewhat sobered by his responsibilities. Before long he was asking the voters to accept honest government as a substitute for Social Credit. About 1937 it appeared that the Social Credit party would split between those who followed Aberhart and the insurgent M.L.A.'s who wanted a vigorous application of the Douglas theories. The threatened revolt did not occur, however, and the legislature during 1936 and 1937 enacted what has been called "the most drastic reform measures ever seen in Canada."[35] On April 1, 1936, Alberta became the first province in the Dominion to default on a principal maturity of its debt. This was a step of the Alberta government toward refunding of the provincial debt from its original 4.9 per cent interest rate to around 2.5 per cent[36]—no small achievement in itself.

Unable to make much progress toward introducing Social Credit because of the strictly limited powers of a province in the Canadian federal union, the Social Credit government seized upon the idea of dated stamp scrip. This scheme was not a part of the Social Credit doctrine of Major Douglas, but it provided an interesting experi-

[35] *Ibid*, p. 512.
[36] G. E. Britnell, "Alberta, Economic and Political, II. The Elliott-Walker Report, Alberta Review," *C.J.E.P.S.*, 2 (November, 1936): 524–532.

ment with an idea that has long agitated the minds of monetary reformers. The scrip was called "Prosperity Certificates." It was handsomely printed on good paper and made to look like a dollar bill. On the face of it was the declaration: "The provincial treasurer will pay to the bearer the sum of $1 on the expiration of two years from date of issue hereof upon presentation hereof provided there are then attached on the back hereof 104 1¢ certificate stamps." The stamps had to be purchased with real money. On the reverse side were squares containing dates beginning with the date of issue and continuing weekly thereafter for two years. The certificates were issued in payment as wages for work on the public roads beginning in August, 1936. A total of $175,000 in certificates was issued for July road work. The government did not accept scrip in payment of taxes; most retail stores refused to accept the certificates in payment for goods.[37]

In April, 1937, the abandonment of the scheme was announced. Just as the suspicions of human nature prevented the creation of the confidence necessary to make this scrip circulate as money, so the human proclivity for mementoes prevented the experiment from being disastrous to the Alberta treasury. A very large proportion of the scrip issued was never offered for redemption at the treasury, and even today the Prosperity Certificates are much in demand for keepsakes and curios.

Social Credit government's aspirations toward drastic reform were frustrated on August 17, 1937, when the Dominion government used its power to disallow three Alberta acts. This power of disallowance had not been used

---

[37] V. F. Coe, "Dated Stamp Scrip in Alberta," *C.J.E.P.S.*, 4 (February, 1938): 60–91. The attempts to paste these one-cent stamps on the backs of certificates which had passed through thousands of dirty hands were one of the humors of the time and place.

at all between 1924 and 1937. The effect of the disallowance was to wipe the laws off the statute books, declare them null and void, and make them inoperative. Two months later, the Lieutenant-Governor of Alberta exercised his power of reservation to keep three additional bills from having force. The power of reservation had not been used since 1920.

Prevented by insufficient provincial power and by federal opposition from achieving its program, the Alberta government next turned to less drastic but much-needed reforms. The schools were much improved. A school district consolidation law was enacted which resulted in improved services and lower costs.[38]

A minimum wage law for labor was enforced, mortgage foreclosures were curbed by a moratorium, and other progressive steps were taken. In the 1940 campaign the Social Credit party was able to point to a record of accomplishments that compared favorably with any achieved during the fourteen years of U.F.A. control, and it could show that it had attempted yet more fundamental reforms but had been defeated in its efforts by federal meddling. The 1940 election was won by Social Credit with a generous use of the slogan, "Kick Aberhart out and you invite the sheriff in," which referred to the antiforeclosure program of the government.

In the 1945 and 1948 provincial election campaigns, Social Credit forces were under the leadership of Premier E. C. Manning, Aberhart's young successor. There was a strong overtone of "We saved you from socialism" in these campaigns, especially that of 1948, and much collaboration between Social Credit and the old parties to prevent a CCF victory.

---

[38] Winston W. Crouch, "Alberta Tries Consolidation," *National Municipal Review*, 32 (January, 1943): 21–25.

The Social Credit movement is not yet declining. Although its main strength is centered in Alberta, the party polled more than 100,000 votes in other provinces in the 1945 federal election. Having successfully curbed the advance of Social Credit in Saskatchewan and Manitoba, the CCF now finds that movement making some headway among the French Canadians of Quebec. This is especially disturbing because it diverts the attention of the economically depressed people in Quebec toward "funny money" schemes and away from the fundamental social and economic reforms which the CCF maintains will be necessary.

The contributions of the Social Credit M.P.'s to the debate on national problems have been meager indeed. Possessed of no long tradition and no general philosophy, they have ridden their hobbies and given vent to their prejudices. The latter have included rabid anti-Semitism on the part of more than one Social Credit M.P., with loud and frequent denunciations of "international money-changers." If and when the Social Credit movement has run its course, some of the leaders and most of the followers may be attracted to the constructive and many-sided program of the CCF. It is the deep-seated belief of many of the CCF leaders that in due time all the wandering sheep will return.

RELATIONS WITH THE ROMAN CHURCH

The CCF has suffered a great disadvantage in Quebec, and in other provinces to a lesser degree, through the unfavorable attitude adopted by the former Roman Catholic head, the late Cardinal Villeneuve, toward the CCF and the socialism for which it stands. At one time, Cardinal Villeneuve denounced the CCF and directed Catholics to avoid affiliations with it. CCF leaders worked hard to break down the opposition in Church circles. This was done in part by getting archbishops who were not under the jurisdiction of the Quebec cardinal to issue statements that good Catholics could participate in the movement. Such a statement, for example, was obtained from the Archbishop of Regina in 1934. Evidently the objections of some Catholic churchmen to the CCF arise from fear that the individual property owner may be subjected to deprivation of his rights, from concern over the growth of a huge state bureaucracy, and from apprehension that the CCF may somehow be associated with the concurrent spread of materialism and atheism.

In 1943 all the archbishops and bishops joined in issuing a general statement regarding social welfare in the Dominion. They declared their support of cooperatives and stated that Catholics are free to support any party which is not Communist. If one may judge from the editorial comments in Catholic journals, the statement was intended to clarify the Roman Catholic attitude toward the CCF. Such a release was an important prerequisite to any successful organizational campaign by the CCF in Quebec. Its leaders do not anticipate any further wholesale opposition from the Church, although it is possible that the minor clergy may continue to oppose local attempts at organization.

Another weakness of the CCF in French Canada arises from the confused trade union situation. The Church has been hostile toward international unions generally and has fostered the development of national Catholic unions based upon the principle of craft unionism. The Catholic unions have developed almost entirely since the turn of the century. In 1940 there were more than 70,000 members of these unions, or syndicates, as they are commonly known.[39]

These unions are aggregated in the Canadian and Catholic Confederation of Labour, which was originally organized under a different name. The syndicates have never been aggressive in their relations with either government or employers. The Confederation is forbidden by its constitution to affiliate with a political party. According to the figures of the federal Department of Labour, the national Catholic unions in 1940 embraced 275 of the 675 trade union branches in Quebec.

Now that the formal barriers to organizational progress among Roman Catholics have been broken down, the CCF is free, or at all events freer than it was, to seek the ear of the large numbers of Canadians who are subject to clerical influence. The direct conversion of French Canadians to the CCF cause has so far been meager. Besides clerical controls, there is the ever-present spirit of French nationalism to be reckoned with, jealous and fearful of the Anglo-Saxon and his economic domination, which, along with his language, carries him in the direction of the American republic. It may prove advisable, in view of this separatist sentiment and the nervous individualism of Quebec, to foster there the development of a provincial party under a distinctive name and only loosely affiliated with the CCF in national politics. It would seem that both of the old-line parties may presently be compelled to work along just such lines.

[39] Canada, Department of Labour, *36th Annual Report on Labour Organization in Canada,* 1946 (Ottawa: King's Printer, 1947).

CHAPTER V

Elections and Prospects

THE ACID TEST of the effectiveness of party organization
and the attractiveness of party policy is found in election
returns. The ballot box is the pay-off for the politician.
How, then, is the CCF doing in terms of votes? Can forecasts be made from these data?

NATIONAL ELECTIONS

Four federal general elections have been held since the
CCF came into being. In 1935, 1940, 1945, and 1949,
voters across Canada have weighed the claims of the several parties and rendered their verdict. The Liberal Party
has seemingly won a great victory on each occasion. The
basic figures on these four elections are presented in
table 1.

The most striking fact revealed by these figures is the
distortion produced by the single-member-district plurality system of electing legislators. In 1935 the Liberals
enjoyed a landslide in seats won, yet failed by a large
margin to poll a popular majority. Indeed, in the four
elections, the Liberals won a majority only in the election of 1940, when they enjoyed the advantage of
governing in the early war period. The Conservatives appear to have a hard core of more than a million voters
who stuck with the party throughout the period under
review. For the CCF, the votes reveal little progress between 1935 and 1940, but it must be recalled that in 1940
the party's attitude toward the war was far from clear.

TABLE 1

NATIONAL ELECTIONS, 1935–1949: POPULAR VOTE AND SEATS WON,
BY PARTIES

Party	1935		1940	
	Popular	M.P.'s	Popular	M.P.'s
Liberal.................	1,955,727	171	2,536,514	178
Conservative...........	1,311,459	39	1,416,257	39
CCF...................	390,860	7	393,230	8
Social Credit and New Democracy...........	182,767	17	123,443	10
Communist Labor-Progressive...........	5,685	0	14,616	0
Other (and rejected ballots)	606,177	11	136,200	10
Totals.............	4,452,675	245	4,620,260	245

Party	1945		1949	
	Popular	M.P.'s	Popular	M.P.'s
Liberal.................	2,170,625	125	2,875,054	190
Conservative...........	1,455,453	67	1,735,968	42
CCF...................	822,661	28	770,207	13
Social Credit and New Democracy...........	214,998	13	135,203	10
Communist Labor-Progressive...........	111,892	1	31,820	0
Other (and rejected ballots)	470,501	11	288,767	7
Totals.............	5,246,130	245	5,837,019	262

Although the CCF vote of 1945 was more than twice that
of 1940, the election returns were regarded both in and
out of the party as a defeat of major proportions. CCF
disappointment was even keener over the 1949 losses. The
unfulfilled expectations were based on rising strength revealed in provincial elections and in the Gallup poll. In

The Third Force in Canada

percentages of total vote, the CCF got 8.9 per cent in 1935, 8.5 in 1940, 15.6 in 1945, and 13.6 in 1949. One surprising feature, especially in 1935 and 1945, is the large size of the small-party vote. In 1935 it was swelled

TABLE 2

TRENDS IN PARTY SENTIMENT, 1940–1946

	Liberal	Con-servative	CCF	Bloc Populaire	Other
Actual, March, 1940.....	55	31	8	..	6
January, 1942...........	55	30	10	..	5
September, 1942.........	39	23	21	..	17
February, 1943..........	32	27	23	7	11
September, 1943.........	28	28	29	9	6
January, 1944...........	30	29	24	9	8
September, 1944.........	36	27	24	5	8
January, 1945...........	36	28	22	6	8
April, 1945.............	36	29	20	6	9
May 16, 1945	38	29	19	6	8
May 26, 1945...........	39	28	19	6	8
June 2, 1945...........	40	27	19	5	9
June 9, 1945...........	39	29	17	5	10
Actual, June, 1945.......	41	28	16	3	12
November, 1945.........	44	26	17	4	9
January, 1946...........	45	24	16	5	10
May, 1946..............	44	26	16	5	10
September, 1946.........	41	27	17	5	10

by the Reconstruction Party, a split off the Conservative Party. In 1945 the *Bloc Populaire,* a French nationalist group, and the Labor-Progressives each polled more than 100,000 votes. More than 1,000,000 votes in 1935 and 1949, and more than 1,500,000 in 1945, went to other than the two major parties. But the CCF cannot hope to win all these voters who have left the old party groove. The party has little appeal to Quebec nationalist extremists. The Communists would certainly not vote CCF.

Winning over people who previously voted Social Credit offers more promise, for they have learned to dissent and will sooner or later become disillusioned with that panacea—apparently, in the light of the 1948 Alberta provincial election, later rather than sooner.

Thorough analysis must await presentation of figures by provinces, but it is plain to see that, while a CCF majority in the House of Commons at the next election is extremely unlikely, CCF progress comparable to that made from 1940 to 1945 might produce a House in which no party had a majority. There is an outside chance that the CCF might have the largest group in the House. If it did and were offered a chance to form a government and govern for a while, the prestige value to the party would be enormous. Such a situation might force the immediate merger of the Liberal and Conservative parties.

The CCF cannot seriously expect to win a clear majority in the federal House, except on a fluke, until it has tripled its 1949 popular vote. This will require the conversion of hundreds of thousands of voters who by family tradition and by conviction, reinforced by daily propaganda, have always voted in accordance with one of the old-party lines.

Because the polls of the Canadian Institute of Public Opinion are taken more frequently than general elections are held, they are of the utmost interest in gauging trends in party sentiment. The Institute reported[1] fluctuations in sentiment between 1940 and 1946 as shown in table 2. Assuming that the Gallup poll accurately portrayed public opinion between elections, an election in September, 1943, might have resulted in a CCF plurality in the House of Commons.

_____

[1] *Public Opinion Quarterly*, 10 (Winter, 1946–47): 633.

BRITISH COLUMBIA

Resources, People, and Industries.—British Columbia is one of the richest and most promising provinces of the Dominion. It has an abundance of natural resources—great forests, minerals, water power, fish, some rich valley land, and a mild climate. The population of the province (1941: 809,203) is a varied one, drawn from eastern Canada, Great Britain, continental Europe, and the United States, with some seasoning from the Orient. The people of British Columbia have utilized their heritage of natural resources to produce a standard of living higher than that of any other province. The per capita income for 1928–29 was $594; for 1933, $314.[2] For both years, the British Columbia income was the highest among the nine provinces.

The economic strength of British Columbia is highly developed. In mineral production, British Columbia ranks second or third in Canada, exchanging positions frequently with the Province of Quebec. In forest products, British Columbia produces approximately one-half the total of Canadian lumber, both by quantity and value. In agriculture, British Columbia is outranked in value of production by all provinces except Nova Scotia, New Brunswick, and Prince Edward Island, but her fruits and vegetables play a very important part in Canadian consumption habits. Largely because of its salmon catch, British Columbia's fisheries account for nearly one-half the total value of Canadian fish products. In manufactures, British Columbia ranks third after Ontario and Quebec in gross value of products; its production of man-

---

[2] Canada, Royal Commission on Dominion-Provincial Relations, *Report*, Bk. 1, p. 150. This contrasts, of course, a high prosperity year with a mid-depression year.

ufactured goods has increased greatly with the expansion
of shipbuilding and aircraft construction during World
War II. In hydroelectric power generation, British Columbia ranks third after Quebec and Ontario. With the
opening of the Panama Canal and the development of
trade in the Pacific area, British Columbia has come to
occupy an important role in the shipping industry of
North America. Unlike the neighboring provinces, British Columbia can ship her products to market by ocean
transportation instead of depending solely upon the long
railroad haul to the head of the Great Lakes.

Political Background.—British Columbia entered the
Confederation in July, 1871. Up to that time there were
two separate British colonies on the western coast: the
mainland was known as the colony of British Columbia;
its insular neighbor was the colony of Vancouver Island.
These colonies were united in 1866 by royal proclama-
tion and the name "British Columbia" was applied to all
their territories. Before the turn of the century, party
lines appear to have signified very little in the politics of
British Columbia. The first distinctly partisan government was that of Richard McBride, which began in 1903
and ended in 1915. McBride was a Conservative, but he
enjoyed some early Socialist-Labor support. During his
long period in the premiership he corrected the chaotic
financial situation of the province and managed to pay
off its debt. Near the end of his regime, the province again
went into debt in order to foster internal railway expansion.[3]

Soon after McBride's retirement in 1915, the Conservative government was badly defeated in a general election

[3] F. W. Howay, *British Columbia: The Making of a Province* (Toronto: Ryerson, 1928), pp. 241–248.

and a period of Liberal rule followed, from 1916 to 1928. The progressive ferment of the immediate postwar period was felt in British Columbia in the 1920 election, in which there appeared a "Provincial Party" with a reform platform. A Conservative government headed by Simon F. Tolmie held office from 1928 to 1933. In 1933 the pendulum again swung to the Liberals and T. D. Pattullo took the premiership. Following the election of 1941, in which no party succeeded in securing a majority, Pattullo resigned and a Liberal-Conservative coalition government, headed by John Hart, was formed. It continued after a victory won in the 1945 provincial election.

The Socialist movement has long exerted noticeable strength in British Columbia. As far back as the election of 1904, four Socialists won seats in the legislature. By 1916 the number declined to one, and he subsequently resigned. At the close of World War I, the Socialist Party of Canada (British Columbia) split, as did Socialist parties all over the world, between those who persisted in their belief in social democracy and those who followed the path of revolutionary socialism.

Electoral Strength.—Nine elections have been held in British Columbia since the birth of the CCF. From the first of these, the provincial election of 1933, the new party has been among the major contenders for the popular vote of the Pacific province. In the 1933 election, which was the first contested by the CCF in any province, about 115,000 CCF votes were polled and seven M.L.A.'s were elected. Since that time, the party has polled more than 100,000 votes at every federal and provincial election except one. So strong did the party become that, following the 1941 election, the Liberals and Conservatives were forced into coalition in order to form a provincial government with majority support. Excluding the 1933 election, for which complete data are not available, the election returns have been as table 3 shows (pp. 142–143).

The most remarkable thing about these figures is the evenness of the three major-party votes. In recent elections, the CCF polled the highest popular vote in two, the Liberals in three, and the Conservatives in one; in two the coalition led. Had the old parties fought the 1945 provincial election separately, with rival candidates, the CCF probably would have emerged with a majority of seats in the legislative assembly, and a plurality of the popular votes. By making in advance of the election an electoral agreement the parties to the coalition forestalled what might have been the second CCF government in Canada.

The position of the British Columbia CCF is a strong one. It has been the official opposition and the obvious alternative to the coalition government since 1941. A swing of the pendulum of sentiment from the government could easily put a majority in the legislature for the CCF, and create, possibly, a popular majority as well. Two federal by-election victories in British Columbia in 1948 both added to the CCF strength in the House of Commons and augmented third-party hopes for success in the forthcoming federal and provincial general elections.

The British Columbia CCF enjoys other assets, not revealed by election totals. The geographic distribution of party strength is unusually even throughout the province. The party wins both rural and urban constituencies, and polls a respectable vote in nearly every district. Both the party organization and the caucus personnel reflect the broad base of the B. C. section of the CCF. They

TABLE 3

British Columbia Provincial and Federal Elections, 1935–1949: Popular Vote and Seats Won, by Parties

Party	October, 1935 Federal	October, 1935 Seats won	June, 1937 Provincial	June, 1937 Seats won	March, 1940 Federal	March, 1940 Seats won	October, 1941 Provincial	October, 1941 Seats won
Liberal..................	91,729	6	151,476	31	136,065	10	148,554	21
Conservative..............	71,034	5	117,639	8	110,619	4	140,642	12
CCF.....................	97,015	3	113,761	7	103,181	1	150,422	14
Communist Labor-Progressive....	1,555	0	....	..	....	..	....	..
Other...................	11,882	2	21,568	2	13,279	1	11,389	1
Totals..............	292,423	16	404,444	48	363,144	16	451,007	48

TABLE 3 (Continued)

Party	June, 1945		October, 1945		June, 1949			
	Federal	Seats won	Provincial	Seats won	Federal	Seats won	Provincial	Seats won
Liberal	125,085	5	} 261,157[a]	37	169,115	11	} 428,779[a]	39
Conservative	128,529	5			128,686	3	245,291	7
CCF	125,068	4	175,960	10	137,406	3		
Communist Labor-Progressive	25,128	0	16,479	0	3,887	0	} 24,783	2
Other	13,864[b]	2	14,161	1	14,101	1		
Totals	417,674	16	467,757	48	453,195	18	698,853	48

[a] Liberals and Conservatives in coalition.
[b] Includes popular vote, and a seat won by H. W. Herridge, "Independent CCF."

include people of diverse backgrounds, interests, and occupations. The party is stronger as a result, for it cannot justly be charged that it is the political front for the trade unions only, or the farmers, or the depressed folk. It is a province-wide party the unity of which flows from common socialist ideology and a common program.

ALBERTA

Province of Promise.—Alberta, like Saskatchewan, became a province in the Confederation in 1905. Its population has grown steadily, rising from 374,295 in 1911 to 803,330 in 1946. Alberta's next greatest resource is its land and its resultant leading industry, agriculture. Farming in Alberta, however, follows a more diversified pattern than that in the other two prairie provinces. Although Alberta is an important producer of wheat, it has great potentialities, partly realized, in the production of livestock, dairy products, and other food and fiber. In gross values of agricultural production, Alberta, in recent years, has been exceeded only by Ontario and Quebec.

Alberta is also richly endowed with other natural resources that place her in an envied position among the prairie provinces. She has valuable deposits of coal, immense petroleum reserves, and ceramic clays. In 1943, Alberta produced more coal than any other province in Canada; the runner-up was Nova Scotia. In the same year, the province provided 99 per cent of the total petroleum produced in the nine provinces, excluding the Northwest Territories, and in 1949 it bids fair to supply within a short time the demands of all western Canada. In the production of natural gas, Alberta accounts for 80 per cent of the total Canadian production. In total value of mineral production, Alberta ranks fourth in the

Dominion, being exceeded by Ontario, Quebec, and British Columbia. In the field of manufacturing, Alberta is far behind Ontario and Quebec, the principal industrial provinces, but she does rank fifth among the provinces. The presence of resources like coal, natural gas, and petroleum may in the future bring industries to Alberta. In total value of production of all industries and gainful employment, Alberta ranks fourth in the nation, exceeded only by Ontario, Quebec, and British Columbia.

During the depression, Alberta suffered the second largest decline in per capita income among the provinces: between 1929 and 1933 her per capita income dropped 61 per cent. In the former year, Alberta enjoyed the third highest per capita income in Canada; in 1933, her income was even lower than that in Quebec.[4]

The impact of the depression on Alberta was severe; but the relief burden was not nearly so heavy as that of Saskatchewan, because flat crop failures in Alberta were few, climatic conditions being more favorable, and because irrigation was practiced in some areas, and the greater dependence upon mixed farming contributed to the same result. Although Alberta's provincial debt remains one of the highest in Canada, this is less attributable to relief cost than is true of any other western province.

Politics, Alberta Model.—From 1905 to 1921, the province of Alberta was governed by three governments, all of which were Liberal. In the election held in June, 1917, the Liberals won 34 of the 58 seats in the legislature. In July, 1921, the legislature was dissolved and a provincial election was held. The agrarian ferment of the time was

[4] Canada, Royal Commission on Dominion-Provincial Relations, *Report*, Bk. 1, p. 150.

at high tide and the United Farmers of Alberta carried 36 of the 61 seats. Amid much excitement a convention of the U.F.A. was assembled, and Herbert H. Greenfield was chosen leader of the farmers' group. By August, Premier Greenfield named his cabinet and the farmers' government was sworn in. Greenfield, who was born in England, had a career somewhat typical of agrarian Alberta. He came to Canada in 1892 and worked first as a hired man, and later homesteaded in Alberta and became a successful farmer. He was vice-president of the U.F.A. at the time he was chosen political leader.

But the outstanding man of the U.F.A. was H. W. Wood. Wood had come to Alberta some twenty years before from Missouri, where he had been active in the Populist movement. The spread of the U.F.A. through the province was due in large part to Wood's vision and organizing ability. He preferred a nonpolitical approach, but about 1920 he was persuaded that the time had come for the farmers to enter the political arena. Power was won in 1921 unexpectedly. After Wood declined the political leadership—a great surprise to many of his followers,—the U.F.A. convention turned to Greenfield.

The first two years of the Farmers' government were discouraging. Greenfield proved weak as a leader, and the government he formed did not greatly differ from the kind Alberta had known previously. In 1925, Greenfield yielded the premiership to his attorney-general, J. E. Brownlee, a Calgary lawyer.

From 1925 to 1934, Brownlee and his colleagues gave Alberta a reasonably honest and efficient government along standard lines. The policies followed were chiefly conservative. Patronage was reduced to a minimum. Neither the hopes of the farmers for fundamental reform, nor the fears of drastic change expressed by the vested interests, were justified by the record. After the coming of the depression in 1930, attacks by the Liberal opposition were renewed with fury. Since there was inadequate material for condemnation of the government on the usual grounds of spoils and patronage, certain incidents in the personal lives of cabinet members were amply publicized. First was the minister of highways, who was divorced and remarried with what was characterized as unbecoming celerity. Soon afterward, spectacular charges were brought against Premier Brownlee by a young woman who had been befriended by the Brownlee family. As the result of a verdict of guilty in the widely publicized trial that followed, Brownlee resigned the premiership and was succeeded by Richard Reid in July, 1934.

Into this mixed situation came a new political movement.[5] The attention of the people of Alberta had long been directed toward the money question. The M.P.'s elected under the U.F.A. banner particularly had shown an interest in the writings of Major C. H. Douglas, the father of the Social Credit movement. Between 1932 and 1934, Irvine, Spencer, and Coote, federal U.F.A. members, had sponsored an inquiry by a committee of the House of Commons into the whole question of financial credit and its relationship to the economic life of the state. However, before the CCF elements could formulate the attitude they desired to assume concerning the many theories of Douglas, a Calgary schoolteacher named William Aberhart lifted certain phrases from the writings of the English theorist and formed a political movement with slogans and promises so attractive that they were

[5] An excellent description of the Social Credit movement is contained in Malcolm G. Taylor, *The Social Credit Party in Alberta* (unpublished M. A. thesis, University of California, Berkeley, 1943).

destined to sweep Alberta in 1935 and, despite nonful-
fillment, to help maintain the group in power through
three more elections to the present, although pure
Douglasites are now anathema in official circles. In addition to his work as principal of the Calgary high school,
which everyone conceded was extremely well done, Aberhart engaged in high-powered evangelical preaching, and
won himself an extraordinary following by his sermons
and talks over station CFCN, Calgary. Much of the fervor
of his air audiences he was able to transfer to the political
field. He carried 57 out of 63 seats in the legislature in
the 1935 election, and write-up men came from all over
the continent to interview him.

Electoral Strength.—At the time the CCF was formed
in 1932 the situation in Alberta was looked upon as more
favorable to the CCF movement than the state of affairs
in any other province in Canada. Not only was the provincial government of Premier Brownlee apparently entrenched in office, but the U.F.A. held 9 of the 16 Alberta
seats in the federal House of Commons. The 1930 federal
general election in Alberta gave the Conservatives the
largest vote with 67,808 and 4 M.P.'s; the Liberals with
60,148 votes elected 3 M.P.'s; the U.F.A. with 60,924 took
the lion's share with 9 seats.

The next test of electoral strength came in 1935 when
the Social Credit ferment was at its height. In the provincial election of that year, the U.F.A. was swept out of
office and failed to retain a single seat in the legislature.
The federal election was equally devastating to the CCF.
Social Credit candidates polled 111,627 votes and won 15
seats. The Liberals and Conservatives, with 50,539 and
40,236 votes respectively, got one M.P. each. The CCF
popular vote was only 29,066, and the 9 U.F.A.-CCF

members, including Irvine and Spencer, were swept out
of office. The CCF inherited in Alberta the tarnished
reputation of the discredited U.F.A. political movement,
and has not yet been able to overcome this liability carried over from the pre-CCF era. The election results are
shown in table 4 (pp. 150–151).

These figures give the CCF little cause for enthusiasm.
Although the party has doubled both its provincial and
its federal vote in Alberta over the period of ten years, it
is still far from the day of victory. Its best vote in a provincial election, that of 1944, was just under 25 per cent
of the vote cast; its maximum in a federal election was
reached in 1945, with more than 18 per cent of the popular vote. On the other hand, the picture is not entirely
bleak. Even when they have joined efforts in provincial
politics, the old parties have proved much weaker than
the CCF and appear unlikely ever again to make a strong
bid for provincial power. The Social Credit movement
has in the meantime played the role of continuing Alberta along the third-party path. If and when the province
tires of Social Credit, the CCF might sweep into power
very rapidly on a flood of third-party votes.

The CCF has been handicapped in Alberta provincial
elections by the preferential voting system used there,
and particularly by the tactics of the other parties in
advising their adherents to throw their second choices
away from CCF candidates. The second choices of Liberals and Conservatives almost invariably go to Social
Credit candidates.

Should the CCF come into power in Alberta, it would
have an exceptional opportunity to make an outstanding
showing. Alberta is so dowered with resources and so
varied in products that a CCF government could engage

TABLE 4

Alberta Provincial and Federal Elections, 1935–1949: Popular Vote and Seats Won, by Parties

Party	August, 1935 Provincial	August, 1935 Seats won	October, 1935 Federal	October, 1935 Seats won	March, 1940 Provincial	March, 1940 Seats won	March, 1940 Federal	March, 1940 Seats won
Liberal	69,845	5	50,539	1	130,603[a]	19	102,060	7
Conservative	19,358	2	40,236	1			35,116	0
CCF	......	..	29,066	0	34,316	0	35,082	0
Social Credit	163,700	56	111,627	15	132,869	35	93,032	10
Communist Labor-Progressive	......	..	2,672	0	......	..	......	..
Other	48,849[b]	0	6,967	0	11,076	3	4,062	0
Totals	301,752	63	241,107	17	308,864	57	269,343	17

[a] Liberals and Conservatives in coalition.
[b] Includes 33,063 votes for U.F.A.

TABLE 4 (Continued)

Party	August, 1944		June, 1945		June, 1949	
	Provincial	Seats won	Federal	Seats won	Federal	Seats won
Liberal.................	47,236ᵃ	3	67,662	2	116,614	5
Conservative...........		2	58,077	2	56,949	2
CCF...................	70,307	0	57,077	0	28,223	0
Social Credit..........	146,367	52	113,821	13	126,395	10
Communist Labor-Progressive....	12,003	0	14,136	0	2,201	0
Other.................	6,190	0	....	..	4,598	0
Totals...........	282,106	57	310,773	17	334,980	17

ᵃ Liberals and Conservatives in coalition.

in a range of industrial enterprises that would be impossible in Saskatchewan. In an acute depression, Alberta might still be able to maintain a fair standard of living by full utilization of her own timber, mineral, and land resources.

The CCF will need a majority of Alberta's federal seats in order to achieve even a plurality in the House of Commons. CCF progress in Alberta federal elections will probably follow victory or great gains on the provincial front. Therefore, the work of the two CCF M.L.A.'s in the legislature is of the utmost importance to the party nationally. The task of the CCF in Alberta is being made easier by the obvious drift of the Social Credit party from the role of a movement of revolt to that of passive office-holding, with the support of the vested interests who were once the windmills at which the late William Aberhart tilted. However, the election of 1948 confirms the position governmentally of Social Credit till 1952—by an overwhelming majority of seats in the legislature.

SASKATCHEWAN

The rise of the CCF to a paramount position in the province of Saskatchewan is traced in chapter vii, "Saskatchewan under CCF Rule"; hence the election returns will be set forth here with a minimum of comment. In the eight elections since 1932, Saskatchewan voters have molded the patterns shown in table 5 (pp. 154–155).

The Saskatchewan CCF appears strong enough in provincial politics to face without serious consequences a coalition of Liberal and Conservative forces.[6] If such a coalition extended to federal affairs, the CCF might lose

---

[6] This judgment was fully sustained by the provincial general election of 1948.

heavily in this stronghold. The CCF vote in the landslide victory of 1944 exceeded in percentage of popular vote that received by the Liberal party in every provincial and federal election recorded. It was the only time in the period in which a party has secured a clear majority of all votes cast; but in 1948 the CCF failed, though by a narrow margin, to repeat this achievement.

In Saskatchewan the CCF has passed the pinnacle of success. Its representation in the federal House of Commons was reduced sharply in the election of 1949. Its strength in the legislative assembly since the 1948 election is certainly as high as it should be if the opposition is to have any effective voice at all. Whether this happy situation will long continue depends most upon the record of the CCF government in Regina.

MANITOBA

Economic Background.—Manitoba, gateway of the prairie provinces, is not only an agricultural producer, but has also served, through its capital Winnipeg, as a great distributing center. The population of the province in 1946 was 726,923. Although its total population is the smallest among the three prairie provinces, its urban center of Winnipeg is the leading city in the area and the fourth largest in Canada.

In net value of total production Manitoba ranks slightly behind the other western provinces. In gross value of agricultural products Manitoba ranks fifth among the nine provinces, being exceeded by Ontario, Quebec, Alberta, and Saskatchewan. Its farm products, however, are more diversified than those of the other prairie provinces. Manitoba is less dependent upon the production of wheat, and places relatively more emphasis

TABLE 5

SASKATCHEWAN PROVINCIAL AND FEDERAL ELECTIONS, 1934–1949: POPULAR VOTE AND SEATS WON, BY PARTIES

Party	June, 1934		October, 1935		June, 1938		March, 1940	
	Provincial	Seats won	Federal	Seats won	Provincial	Seats won	Federal	Seats won
Liberal	206,191	50	134,914	16	200,370	38	159,530	12
Conservative	114,873	0	71,285	1	52,366	0	52,496	2
CCF	103,582	5	73,505	2	82,568	10	106,267	5
Farm-Labor	......	..	......	..	......	..	......	..
Communist Labor-Progressive								
Social Credit		..	63,593	2	69,720	2	12,106	0
Other	9,173	0	4,239	0	35,249	2	40,134	2
Totals	433,308	55	347,536	21	449,273	52	371,134	21

TABLE 5 (Continued)

Party	June, 1944 Provincial	Seats won	June, 1945 Federal	Seats won	June, 1948 Provincial	Seats won	June, 1949 Federal	Seats won
Liberal	139,183	5	124,191	2	152,395	19	161,811	14
Conservative	44,197	0	70,830	1	37,985	0	52,884	1
CCF	211,308	47	167,233	18	236,820	31	152,380	5
Farm-Labor								
Communist Labor-Progressive		..	3,183	0	1,303	0	1,531	0
Social Credit		..	11,449	0	40,268	0	3,474	0
Other	3,026	0	....	..	29,210	2	697	0
Totals	397,714	52	376,886	21	498,081	52	372,777	20

on farm animals and on dairy and poultry products. Manitoba has an abundance of water power, exceeded only by that of Quebec, British Columbia, and Ontario. Although far behind the leaders in manufacturing, Manitoba ranks fourth in the Dominion in value of manufactured products. It is in the field of external and internal trade that Manitoba plays a premier role in the Canadian economy. The great volume of prairie wheat flows to market through Manitoba, either by rail to the Lake Superior terminals of Port Arthur or Port William, or by rail to the Manitoba port of Churchill on Hudson Bay. The latter route has been much publicized in the prairie provinces during recent years as an efficient and direct route for shipping Canadian wheat to the European market, but expert opinion is very largely opposed to it. Manitoba's role in the handling of western wheat makes her prosperity depend appreciably on the prices and volume of that crop. Manitoba plays a modest part as well in mining, forestry, and the fur trade of Canada.

During the depression of the 1930's, Manitoba had a burden of relief heavier than that of any province except Saskatchewan. The relief problem was concentrated mainly in the metropolitan area of Winnipeg, where the impact of depression and drought struck those who handled the products of the prairies and the commodities of eastern Canada that normally flowed back to the producers.[7]

Political History.—Manitoba changed its status from Red River Colony to that of province in 1870, three years after Confederation. Because it was the only prairie province admitted to the Dominion until Saskatchewan and

---

[7] Canada, Royal Commission on Dominion-Provincial Relations, *Report,* Bk. 1, p. 168.

Alberta were formed in 1905, and because it was the part of the West most accessible to the East, Manitoba's population reached noteworthy totals at an early period. In 1901 it had more than 250,000 people; in 1911 there were more than 460,000; in 1921 the figure topped 610,000. The increase in the last twenty years has been no more than modest.

In the past political history of Manitoba perhaps the outstanding event was the controversy over "separate schools" for the Roman Catholic population. The Manitoba schools question was projected on the national political scene by the legislative action which, in 1890, abolished the separate schools which from the beginning of the province had served the considerable French-speaking Roman Catholic population. A demand was made by Quebec political leaders that the action of the legislature should be disallowed or overridden by federal authority. The federal general election of 1896 was fought chiefly on this issue. Sir Wilfred Laurier maintained that the question should be settled by conciliation, not by coercion. The Liberal government won the election—but lost Manitoba.

In provincial politics Manitoba showed an early proclivity for alternating between Liberals and Conservatives. Between 1900 and 1915 the Conservatives were in power, with Sir R. P. Roblin as premier. From 1915 to 1922 the Liberals held office under Premier T. C. Norris.

In 1922 the politics of Manitoba entered a new phase, which may be called the "coalition era," when John Bracken, president of the Manitoba Agriculture College, was persuaded to accept the premiership. The election of 1922 produced a situation in the legislature in which no party had a majority and some kind of coalition was necessary in order to conduct the affairs of government. Bracken headed the government for more than twenty years, resigning only after his selection as Dominion political leader of the rejuvenated Conservative Party in December, 1942. Bracken and his coalition colleagues gave Manitoba a good, honest, mildly progressive administration. The existence of this generally satisfactory coalition probably had much to do with the lack of organizational progress made by the CCF in Manitoba during the 1930's.

The history of left-wing political movements in Manitoba is among the most interesting and spectacular afforded by any province. Many of its first leaders were single taxers, followers of Henry George. Others were Socialists. In 1910 they began a drive for labor representation in the Winnipeg city council and in the Manitoba legislative assembly. The Manitoba Labour Party was formed and the leader of the group, Fred Dixon, was put up for M.L.A. He lost in 1910 but was elected under the label "Independent Progressive" in 1914 and reëlected in the general election of 1915. In 1919 came the famous Winnipeg general strike. It was called by unions affiliated with the Trades and Labour Congress, and nearly all the organized workers of Winnipeg participated in it. In the violent struggle which followed, the federal government intervened, arrested strike leaders on general warrants, and broke down the resistance of the labor movement. Dixon, John Queen, J. S. Woodsworth, and several others were imprisoned. Dixon was acquitted after a brilliant speech as his own attorney, but Queen and others remained in jail through the 1920 provincial election campaign. Dixon was reëlected, and Queen and others who were in jail won seats in the legislative assembly.

In the meantime, the political organization of the labor element was undergoing change. The Dominion Labour Party formed under Trades and Labour Congress auspices was split by the struggle between the more conservative interests in the T. and L. C. and the "One Big Union" launched by left-wing critics in the labor movement. The Independent Labour Party was created in part to avoid the ill effects of the split. In the next general election, ten M.L.A.'s were elected under the I.L.P. banner.

The Manitoba political situation has been full of contradictions. From 1922 to 1942, Premier Bracken maintained in office a nonparty government with broad popular support. The elements in the government have in recent years included Conservatives, Liberals, Independents, and representatives of Social Credit and of the CCF. Precluded by popular enthusiasm for the Bracken government for making much headway with the electorate, the Manitoba CCF M.L.A.'s decided in 1940 to join the Bracken coalition. This action was opposed vigorously by the CCF National Council and National Executive, and in 1943 the CCF withdrew from the coalition. At the same time that the CCF was doing so poorly in provincial politics, Manitoba was sending to the House of Commons in Ottawa the prime mover of the CCF, J. S. Woodsworth. Woodsworth was first elected to the House of Commons for Winnipeg North Centre in 1921 and was reëlected at every election from that time until his death in 1942. Between 1935 and 1940, Winnipeg also sent to the federal House of Commons A. A. Heaps, a CCF leader.

For much of the interval between the wars, Winnipeg has had a municipal administration under Labor-CCF

TABLE 6

Manitoba Provincial and Federal Elections, 1935–1949: Popular Vote and Seats Won, by Parties

Party	October, 1935		July, 1936		March, 1940		April, 1941	
	Federal	Seats won	Provincial	Seats won	Federal	Seats won	Provincial	Seats won
Liberal[a]................	100,535	12	91,338	23	151,285	14	57,285	27
Conservative Progressive........	75,574	1	71,934	16	82,240	1	34,317	15
CCF..................	54,491	2	31,996	7	61,448	1	26,267	3
Social Credit..........	5,751	0	23,413	5	5,831	0	2,723	2
Communist Labor-Progressive.....	9,229	0	5,864	1	....	:	....	:
Other................	39,009	2	29,892	3	15,884	1	42,970	8
Totals........	284,589	17	253,457	55	316,883	17	163,562	55

a Principal party of government coalition in provincial elections.

TABLE 6 (*Continued*)

Party	June, 1945		October, 1945			June, 1949	
	Federal	Seats won	Provincial	Seats won		Federal	Seats won
Liberal[a].............	111,863	10	72,679	25		144,752	11
Conservative Progressive........	80,303	2	38,964	14		70,709	1
CCF................	101,892	5	73,853	10		83,256	3
Social Credit..........	10,322	0		2		....	..
Communist Labor-Progressive........	15,984	0	33,534[b]	1		6,523	0
Other...............	2,451	0		3		15,868	1
Totals...........	322,815	17	219,030	55		321,108	16

[a] Principal party of government coalition in provincial elections.
[b] 1945 provincial election figures on popular votes of minor parties not available separately.

control. The late John Queen, one of the leaders in the
1919 strike, served as mayor of Winnipeg from 1919 to
1937 and from 1938 to 1943. The Winnipeg council has
regularly had from four to twelve representatives of the
CCF-I.L.P. group.

Electoral Strength.—In part because of the long persistence of a spirit of collaboration that led to coalition
governments, headed first by Bracken and later by Gar-
son, the CCF has not made the headway it should have
achieved in Manitoba. During a portion of the recent
war period, the CCF itself participated in the coalition.
Until recently, the CCF organization and leadership in
Manitoba have been considerably weaker than in some of
the other provinces. On the other hand, Winnipeg has
a tradition for progressivism, born of the 1919 strike and
the racial medley of its people. The province has a large
urban population and a considerable number of industries; trade unionism is fairly strong, especially among
the numerous railway workers. The farmers have shown
much interest in prairie progressivism of the past; their
economic life rests on a broad base of mixed farming,
rather than leaning wholly on the vulnerable thin reed
of a wheat crop. The election returns for Manitoba are
shown in table 6 (pp. 160–161).

Rising steadily in showings made in federal elections
and very sharply with respect to provincial elections, the
CCF may be able to capture the lion's share of both in the
next elections.

ONTARIO

Economic and Historical Background.—For the CCF,
Ontario is both the greatest electoral prize and one of the
most elusive of the provinces. It is the largest province in
population in Canada, and occupies the position of great-

est influence in national affairs. In politics it has a reputation for conservatism. The average standard of living is relatively high. The farmers, being close to their markets and engaged in diversified agriculture, have enjoyed a measure of prosperity and security denied to western farmers. Until the last decade, organized labor had not been able to make much headway despite the industrialization of the province.

The few times that the spirit of revolt has entered Ontario politics, it has been largely an agrarian ferment. In 1894, the Patrons of Industry managed to secure the election of 14 members to the provincial legislature. The influence of the Patrons soon waned in Ontario as it did in the rest of Canada. The years from 1905 to 1919 were a continuous period of conservative rule in Ontario. During this time, and especially during World War I, the spirit of revolt spread through the countryside. In the provincial election of 1919 the United Farmers of Ontario won a spectacular victory, raising their representation in the legislature from none before the election to 44 seats after the election. Joined by 11 legislators who campaigned under the "labour" label, a government was formed under the leadership of Ernest C. Drury. As pointed out in an earlier chapter, the farmer-labor government was not able to accomplish drastic reforms. The political movement of the U.F.O. gradually spent itself. After the election of 1929 only one U.F.O. member was left in the provincial parliament. Labor members of the legislature lost ground proportionately.

At the convention at which the CCF was founded in Calgary in 1932 there was no real representation from Ontario. A. R. Mosher, president of the Canadian Brotherhood of Railway Employees, came from Ontario, but if

TABLE 7

ONTARIO PROVINCIAL AND FEDERAL ELECTIONS, 1934–1949: POPULAR VOTE AND SEATS WON, BY PARTIES

Party	June, 1934 Provincial	Seats won	October, 1935 Federal	Seats won	October, 1937 Provincial	Seats won	March, 1940 Federal	Seats won	August, 1943 Provincial	Seats won
Liberal............	754,243	66	675,803	56	793,716	64	834,166	55	499,307	15
Conservative........	621,562	17	562,513	25	627,740	23	687,816	25	469,672	38
CCF............	108,961	1	129,457	0	77,744	0	61,166	0	418,520	34
Communist Labor-Progressive......	9,775	0	8,945	0	404	0	....	..	14,843	2
Other.............	67,285	6	231,526	1	71,827	3	26,266	2	1,596	1
Totals.........	1,561,826	90	1,608,244	82	1,571,431	90	1,609,414	82	1,313,938	90

TABLE 7 (*Continued*)

Party	June, 1945				June, 1948		June, 1949	
	Provincial	Seats won	Federal	Seats won	Provincial	Seats won	Federal	Seats won
Liberal..................	474,817	11	745,571	34	515,846	13	910,783	54
Conservative............	774,982	66	757,057	48	727,412	53	758,832	26
CCF....................	390,910	8	260,502	0	465,834	21	306,617	1
Communist Labor-Progressive......	44,252	2	36,333	0	17,654	2	12,810	0
Other...................	55,183	3	15,504	0	32,515	1	32,678	2
Totals...........	1,740,144	90	1,814,967	82	1,759,261	90	2,021,720	83

he represented any group it was the national union of which he was head. He was present at Calgary undoubtedly as a shrewd observer in the interests of the Railway Employees.

Electoral Strength.—With its 82 federal M.P.'s, its large population, and its central location, Ontario holds the key to much of the prestige and influence needed by the CCF, if that party is to rise to power throughout the Dominion. Election returns in the province have been as table 7 shows (pp. 164–165).

It will be noted that the CCF vote in Ontario is subject to violent fluctuation. After a good beginning in 1934 and 1935, the depths were reached in 1937 and 1940. Then came the striking upturn in the 1943 election, followed by a decline recorded in 1945 and a resurgence in 1948. While there are several rationalized explanations for the reduced CCF vote in Ontario in 1945, they should not be allowed to obscure the fact that the Conservatives have greatly improved their positon over that of 1943, presumably, in part at least, through the record of their government in office from 1943 to 1945.

The explanations of the CCF decline are numerous. First, the vicious attacks that were made on the party by Trestrail and others were concentrated most heavily on Ontario. Second, the CCF provincial leader, Jolliffe, made some very spectacular charges about "Gestapo tactics" allegedly used by government secret police. Since he lacked newspaper support to publicize these charges effectively, they backfired. Third, the labor movement was split wide open by Communist forces determined to block further CCF advance. Finally, the provincial and federal elections were called so close together that the CCF, relying on volunteer help and a minimum of money, was unable to make full preparations for either. The 1948 election probably represented a fair plebiscite of party strength in a normal election.

A constituency-by-constituency analysis of the Ontario federal and provincial election returns of 1945, and those of the provincial election of 1948, reveals that the greater share of CCF strength in the province is found in the urban and industrial centers. Relatively little progress has been made with the Ontario farmer, who was once in the vanguard of political and social reform.

QUEBEC

People and Resources.—The Royal Commission on Dominion-Provincial Relations identified three distinct economies within Quebec. One is the trade and processing economy of the Montreal metropolitan area, which is dependent upon the east-west commercial intercourse of the Dominion. A second is based upon the mining and pulpwood resources of the north country and is highly dependent upon export markets. The third type of economy, subsistence agriculture, is concentrated along the valley of the St. Lawrence.[8]

Quebec is second in population and in production among the provinces of the Dominion. The 1941 census gave its population as 3,331,882, just under 29 per cent of the nation's total. Quebec's people are more urban than rural; for every resident of the province who lives in the country, nearly two live in cities and towns. This degree of urbanization is considerably higher than that of the country as a whole. Quebec contains the largest metropolitan area of Canada; Greater Montreal in the census of 1941 had 1,139,921 inhabitants, and the city proper

---

[8] *Report,* Bk. 1, pp. 190–191.

showed slightly more than 900,000. In religion, an all-important factor in Quebec, the province is overwhelmingly Roman Catholic. The birth rate in Quebec is the highest in Canada. In 1942 it was estimated at 28 births per 1,000 population; the death rate among infants in 1942 was second highest, being exceeded only by that of New Brunswick, which also has a very large French-Canadian population.

In agriculture, Quebec ranks second after Ontario in gross value of production. Dairy products constitute a particularly large element of the province's farm output. In recent years, mining has been much developed; mineral production in Quebec has exceeded that of all the other provinces except Ontario, although British Columbia in some years displaces Quebec for second place. Quebec's principal metals are gold, aluminum, and copper; it also produces most of the world's visible supply of asbestos. Nature endowed Quebec with the greatest water power resources of any province, and so greatly has this been developed for electric power generation that Quebec has nearly one-half the developed horsepower capacity in Canada. The forests of Quebec produce most in value among the provinces of Canada; provincial production is approximately one-third that of the nation. Quebec's forest products are mostly pulpwood, of which the province contributes about one-half the total value of Canadian production. Next to Ontario, it is Canada's most industrialized province; in net value of manufactured products it supplies about 30 per cent of the Dominion's total.

Political Background.—Ever since the conquest of Quebec in 1759, the French problem has been a dominating one in attempts to govern British North America. The great majority of the French population of Quebec is distinct, and is resolved to remain distinct, from English-speaking Canada in language, religion, and culture. Although Britain and France in recent times have been drawn close together politically, French Canada has had few contacts with France in the century and a half since the French Revolution. The French Canadian is a devout Roman Catholic. His family and religious life is considered by some to be more like that of the pre-1789 French villager or peasant than of the modern Jean Baptiste. The plain fact is that on the two sides of the St. Lawrence, spilling over into New Brunswick and Ontario and the United States, there is an island of unassimilated French population clinging to the past and defying all North American traditions of assimilation.

The political consequences of this situation are very great. Politically, the declaration that "As goes Quebec, so does the Dominion" has more basis of fact than the expression, "As Maine goes, so goes the nation." In the early days of Confederation, a majority in Quebec voted Conservative. Between 1867 and 1891, in only one election did the Liberals win more Quebec seats in the House of Commons than the Conservatives. This has been attributed to the skill of Sir John A. Macdonald, the Dominion's first Prime Minister, and of his lieutenant, Sir Georges E. Cartier. From 1891 to the present, the Liberals have had the great majority of Quebec M.P.'s; on one occasion they won every one of the 65 seats allocated to the province. This in turn has been attributed to the great qualifications of leadership of Sir Wilfred Laurier, the first Prime Minister of Canada drawn from the French population, and the only one prior to the elevation of Louis St. Laurent in 1948.

The pivotal role of Quebec in Canadian politics results in part from the fact that Quebec has 73 seats in the House of Commons out of a total of 262, as arranged for in a recent amendment of the British North America Act. While it is mathematically possible for a national party to win power in Canada without Quebec's support, it is far more likely that Quebec will hold the balance of power, depending upon the party alignment of the time.

The Liberals encountered great difficulty over the conscription issue during the period of World War II. Quebec was overwhelmingly opposed to conscription and overseas service. The imposition of conscription in World War I by the government of Sir Robert Borden put the Conservatives in the doghouse so far as Quebec was concerned and there they have remained. In World War II, a Liberal prime minister found it necessary to walk the tightrope to retain Quebec's support and yet provide the man power necessary for effective prosecution of the war. In the conscription debates of 1942 it appeared at times that the Liberal hold upon Quebec had been shaken loose, but Mackenzie King demonstrated remarkable political agility in securing discretionary conscription powers from Parliament. When these powers were at last invoked in 1944, it appeared for a time that the reaction in French Canada might bring down the King government, but the wounds healed rapidly. Unable to make progress in Quebec under its own name, the Conservative Party has stood aside while its former leaders in Quebec have participated in provincial politics under the name *Union Nationale*. This party was and is led by Maurice Duplessis, former provincial leader of the Conservative Party. The *Union* was formed in 1935; at first it appeared as a coalition of forces of the new *Action Libérale*

Nationale headed by Paul Gouin, a sort of ginger group seeking to win control of the Liberal Party, and of the Conservative forces headed by Duplessis. In the course of the campaign for the provincial election of 1935, Duplessis squeezed Gouin out. The *Union* won a great electoral victory, polling 60 per cent of the popular vote. Duplessis was appointed premier. During its four years in office this *Union* government sponsored some modest social legislation, but its most conspicuous actions were attacks on international unions, censorship of films and literature, and restrictions on radical political activities.

Duplessis's forces were overwhelmingly defeated in the general election of 1939, and the Liberals came into power with Adelard Godbout as premier. This Liberal government gave Quebec its most progressive administration in years. The government took over ownership and control of the Montreal Heat, Light, and Power Company, the largest privately owned utility in the Dominion. Its record in social legislation was notable. Godbout was criticized primarily for his cordial relations with the Liberal government in Ottawa and his support of the war effort. In the election of August, 1944, his government was displaced and the *Union Nationale,* still headed by Duplessis, won 46 of the 91 seats in the legislative assembly. In this campaign a new party, the *Bloc Populaire,* made its appearance. The *Bloc* took an even more extreme view than the *Union* in opposition to the war effort and to what it called imperialism. The Duplessis government won a renewed mandate in 1948, with an electoral majority more overwhelming than ever.

Electoral Strength.—The lack of any foothold by the CCF in Quebec is shown most clearly by the election returns. In the federal elections held since the CCF was organized, a very poor showing has been made. In 1935 the CCF entered four candidates and lost its deposits on all of them, except in Verdun, where George Mooney made a spirited contest. In 1940 there were three candidates for M.P., but no one of them came near election. All three constituencies contested were in Montreal. The Canadian press tabulation of election returns showed 7,610 Quebec votes for CCF candidates.[9] In both the 1936 and the 1939 provincial elections one CCF candidate was nominated, and defeated.

Until the election of August, 1944, the Quebec CCF made no serious bid for seats in the provincial legislature. At that time, however, the CCF entered 24 candidates for the 91 seats. A total of nearly 33,000 votes was polled, largely in English-speaking industrial areas. The total vote appears to indicate that the Canadian Institute of Public Opinion polls taken in 1944 are substantially correct in their indication that between 6 and 7 per cent of the Quebec voters prefer the CCF. The campaign produced more dividends for the CCF than the single CCF M.L.A. who was elected. It gave the CCF access to free time on the radio and provided an occasion for the distribution of educational literature in areas which had been untouched by previous organizing efforts.[10]

THE MARITIMES

The Maritime Economy.—The Maritime Provinces of Nova Scotia, New Brunswick, and Prince Edward Island constitute a distinct region. The Maritime area was set-

---

[9] The figures given in *Canadian Parliamentary Guide*, 1942, show a total of 10,585 for the three CCF candidates.

[10] F. R. Scott, "Quebec Election Improved CCF Position," *CCF News* (B. C.), August 17, 1944. David Cote, who was elected as CCF member of the Quebec Assembly, subsequently left the party.

tled early because of its accessibility to Europe by ship, and it developed an economy based upon the obvious resources of the area. Fishing is one of the major activities of the Maritime Provinces. Although the value of fish products of the Maritimes amounts to much less than that of British Columbia, it does constitute nearly one-third the total of all Canada. The Maritime economy rests in part upon agriculture, but not in so large measure as on the prairies. Prince Edward Island, Nova Scotia, and New Brunswick together account for a total agricultural production less than that of Manitoba alone. Nova Scotia plays an important part in Canada's mining. In value of production it is exceeded each year by Ontario, Quebec, and British Columbia and ranks nearly equal with Alberta. Nova Scotia's greatest contribution is in coal mining. Nova Scotia is also the leading producer of gypsum. The Maritimes, and particularly Nova Scotia, have long been noted for shipbuilding, and this industry was greatly revived along the Nova Scotia coast during World War II. In manufacturing, none of the Maritime Provinces is a leader, but Sydney, Nova Scotia, has one of the four great steel mills of Canada. It utilizes the iron ore deposits of Newfoundland. New Brunswick is an important producer of timber. In recent years its wood products have ranked fourth among the Dominion's. A large proportion of this is pulpwood.

The Royal Commission on Dominion-Provincial Relations described the Maritime economy as "the most mature, and the most chronically depressed, regional economy in Canada."[11]

In many ways the Maritimes are more firmly tied to the New England States by their economy than to the

---

[11] *Report*, Bk. 1, p. 187.

other regions of Canada. The United States constitutes the best market for fish products, and probably for wood pulp as well. The Maritime Provinces have suffered from the depletion of their natural resources, including their ablest young people, and from an inability to adapt themselves to changed conditions.

In population, the Maritime Provinces have about one-tenth of the people of the Dominion. In 1941 the population of Nova Scotia was 577,962; of New Brunswick, 457,401; and of Prince Edward Island, 95,047. Population in this area has increased very slowly through the years. Prince Edward Island has about 10,000 less than in 1881. The chronically depressed economy of the Maritimes has caused the young people to seek their fortunes in other areas. The withdrawal of the Cunards, of Beaverbrook, and of hundreds of other potential leaders to other parts of Canada, to the United States, and to Great Britain, from their native Maritime Provinces, has left the region without its rightful share of able local leadership. Moreover, the movement of population away from the Maritimès has produced a difficult social and financial problem. As the proportion of the older population has increased, it has become necessary to provide for the care of those who can no longer produce. This has placed a burden on government finance. In normal years the marriage rate in Nova Scotia and Prince Edward Island is the lowest in Canada.

Political History.—Nova Scotia, New Brunswick, and Prince Edward Island were important participants in the beginning of the move for confederation. In 1864, leaders of the three Maritime colonies met at Charlottetown to discuss union. Later in the same year, they participated in the conference at Quebec City which laid the basis for the confederation subsequently enacted in the British North America Act. When the British North America Act came into effect in 1867, both Nova Scotia and New Brunswick entered the Confederation. In Prince Edward Island, as in Newfoundland, the proposal for union was defeated. P. E. I., however, entered the Confederation in 1873; Newfoundland has waited till 1949.

The politics of reform has not affected the Maritime Provinces so much as it has affected the provinces of the west or even Ontario. The regular pattern of politics in Nova Scotia, New Brunswick, and Prince Edward Island has been to alternate between Liberal and Conservative rule. In the period of ferment after World War I, Nova Scotia elected eleven insurgent M.L.A.'s, of whom four were labor and seven were farmers. For a brief period they replaced the Conservatives as the official opposition. In the New Brunswick provincial election of 1921, seven United Farmers' candidates secured election as M.L.A.'s. The United Farmers' movement enjoyed no political success in Prince Edward Island. Between wars the Maritime Provinces resumed their habit of alternating between the two old parties. After the launching of the CCF in 1932, there were sporadic attempts to set up a CCF organization in the Maritimes. In the 1933 Nova Scotia provincial election two CCF candidates were nominated for Cape Breton constituencies; together they polled only 2,336 votes.

Electoral Strength.—Among the four provinces east of Ontario, only Nova Scotia has enough CCF strength to justify detailed analysis of its elections returns. In that province, as we have seen, the votes have come mainly from the Cape Breton Island area. From the toehold secured there, the CCF hopes to spread its influence

TABLE 8

Nova Scotia Provincial and Federal Elections, 1935–1949: Popular Vote and Seats Won, by Parties

Party	October, 1935		June, 1937		March, 1940		October, 1941	
	Federal	Seats won	Provincial	Seats won	Federal	Seats won	Provincial	Seats won
Liberal........................	142,334	12	165,397	22	151,731	10	138,915	23
Conservative..................	87,893	0	143,670	8	112,206	1	106,133	4
CCF...........................	....	..	....	..	17,715	1	18,583	3
Other.........................	45,296	0	3,396	0	....	..	....	..
Totals.................	275,523	12	312,463	30	281,652	12	253,631	30

TABLE 8 (Continued)

Party	June, 1945		October, 1945		June, 1949			
	Federal	Seats won	Provincial[a]	Seats won	Federal	Seats won	Provincial	Seats won
Liberal.........	141,911	8	124,473	28	177,534	10	134,597	26
Conservative....	114,214	3	74,295	0	126,375	2	30,846	7
CCF...........	51,892	1	35,808	2	33,263	1	7,912	2
Other..........	2,650	0	634	0	....	..	....	..
Totals........	310,667	12	270,210	30	337,172	13	173,355	35

[a] For double-member constituencies, in which the voter has two votes, only the party's highest candidate is included in the popular-vote figures.

throughout the Maritimes. That it is a slow job, even in Nova Scotia, is shown in table 8 (pp. 176–177).

The trend is mildly encouraging from a CCF point of view, but unless it is accelerated greatly the party will wait a long time indeed before there is a CCF government in Halifax and the province sends a majority of CCF M.P.'s to Ottawa. The Liberal vote is surprisingly stable in both provincial and federal elections, and it is obvious that the CCF has not seriously challenged it. In provincial elections the Conservatives have shown a steady decrease in popular votes, culminating in the ridiculous result of 1945 when with nearly 75,000 votes the Conservatives received no seats at all. This gave the CCF an unexpected opportunity to become the official opposition with a meager contingent of two M.L.A.'s.

Until the provincial general election of August, 1944, CCF candidates were rare in New Brunswick. One CCF candidate appeared in the 1939 provincial election and managed to poll 712 votes in Saint John City. In 1940, 761 votes were polled in the federal general election. In the 1944 provincial election, there were 41 CCF candidates for the 48 constituencies. The results gave the CCF candidates approximately 15 per cent of the total vote, but none was elected. The CCF candidates ran strongest in the urban centers, especially in Saint John City.

The CCF entered a Prince Edward Island election for the first time in the provincial general election of September, 1943. Its nine candidates were defeated.

ELECTORAL PROSPECTS

From the statistics presented in this chapter it may be seen that the CCF, despite a substantial beginning, is still far from winning power nationally or in a majority of the provinces. Many elections were held in 1944–45, and therefore few in 1946–47, either federal or provincial. The first returns from a new series of elections beginning with 1948 indicate that CCF strength is fluctuating widely. The writer believes that economic conditions prevailing in Canada, or in any of its provinces just at election time, will determine whether the CCF can challenge successfully the old-party supremacy.

The new party is in an electoral position not unlike that of the Labour Party in Great Britain around 1920. It has a socialist program that appeals to the voters. It is recovering from the impact of the war and from an election called to coincide with celebrations over victory in Europe. It is charged with being not "fit to govern." From a somewhat similar situation, the Labour Party rose to form the first Labour government in January, 1924. Of course there are many differences. The Liberal Party of Canada still has a formidable machine, unencumbered by the rust and corrosion that coalition politics brings to an organization. The trade union movement of Canada is disunited and far from closely tied to the CCF.

In the next federal election, if the CCF were able to double its popular vote of the 1949 election, it would probably secure a minimum of 65 seats. This estimate is based on the assumption that the parties would compete freely, without electoral agreement among them. Further, it is predicated on the old apportionment and the old number of seats (245), rather than the new apportionment and number of seats (262). There are so many uncertainties that the estimate of 65 M.P.'s perhaps ought to be considered only a guess. The CCF did more than double its popular vote in the period between the 1940 election and that of 1945. If this can be repeated, and the vote is distributed among the constituencies as it was in 1949, 65 or more seats may be expected. Should the CCF vote be doubled in every constituency contested in 1949, however, the party would still be largely western in its parliamentary representation, 53 of the 65 coming from west of Ontario.

Unless there is a landslide to the Conservatives, or the country turns decisively back to the Liberal standard—both of which events are unlikely in view of the diverse complexions of provincial governments today,—a situation with no party in the majority in the House of Commons appears possible. If this led to a coalition of Liberals and Conservatives, the CCF would gain much new importance as the official opposition and the alternative government. If the CCF should win a plurality in the House, it might form a minority government and govern for several months before meeting Parliament. By introducing bold socialist legislation at the first parliamentary session, the CCF government could choose the ground on which it would be challenged in a vote of nonconfidence. Careful management of its relations with the Governor-General might enable the government to secure a dissolution of the House and then ask the country for a mandate to carry out its program.

CHAPTER VI

The CCF in Parliament

BECAUSE the number of CCF members in the House of Commons has not yet been large, the operation of the party caucus has not constituted a complex problem. A major party with numerous M.P.'s and diverse elements is confronted with difficulties in organizing and disciplining its members. This has been shown in the history of the British Labour Party and other major parties in various countries.

The CCF caucus has never yet included many more than thirty M.P.'s. While they have come from provinces as remote from one another geographically as British Columbia and Nova Scotia, in ideology they have been closely akin. It is fortunate also for the CCF that it has had in the national parliament few members who were temperamentally unsuited to teamwork. On the whole, the CCF caucus in the House of Commons has operated on an extremely democratic and cooperative basis.

BEGINNING OF THE PARLIAMENTARY CAUCUS

After a federal general election, the M.P.'s elected under the official CCF label join the party caucus in the House of Commons. At the time the CCF was organized in 1932, several M.P.'s—including J. S. Woodsworth, Angus MacInnis, William Irvine, E. J. Garland, and A. A. Heaps—decided to adhere to the new party and constituted themselves the CCF caucus. The group was so small and so well experienced in parliamentary life that no elaborate or formal caucus rules were necessary. Whenever the opportunity presented itself, members of the group directed the attention of the House of Commons to the emerging program of the new party.

The election of 1935 brought changes in the composition of the CCF group. Irvine and Garland were defeated in the Alberta Social Credit landslide. The three reelected M.P.'s were joined by M. J. Coldwell and T. C. Douglas of Saskatchewan and Grant MacNeil and J. S. Taylor of British Columbia. Taylor became involved in a B. C. factional fight not long after his election. He followed the Rev. Robert Connell, deposed British Columbia CCF leader, and backed Connell's "Social Constructive" ticket in the 1937 provincial election. For this he was expelled by the constituency and provincial CCF. The National Council called upon Taylor to withdraw from the "Constructive group," but he refused, so it recognized his expulsion from the party. He automatically ceased to be a member of the caucus.

The small-team tradition continued after the 1940 election. MacNeil and Heaps were defeated, but there was a considerable group of newcomers, including G. H. Castleden, A. M. Nicholson, and P. E. Wright of Saskatchewan, and Clarence Gillis of Nova Scotia. In the course of the term, they were joined by by-election victors J. W. Noseworthy of Ontario, J. W. Burton of Saskatchewan, and William Bryce and Stanley Knowles of Manitoba. Knowles rewon for the CCF the seat vacated by the death of J. S. Woodsworth. In the years 1940–1945 the caucus was still small enough to meet often and to discuss virtually every important subject that came up in the House. During parliamentary sessions the group met in the office of the leader once a week or oftener. It was presided over by Woodsworth at first, and later by Coldwell as his deputy and successor. Until her election as M.L.A. in British Columbia in 1941, Mrs. Grace MacInnis, daughter of Woodsworth, served as caucus secretary. She was followed by G. H. Castleden, whose functions as secretary were modified somewhat after a full-time parliamentary secretary was appointed in December, 1943. The national secretary, David Lewis, attended caucus sessions and participated actively in the work of the parliamentary group as legal adviser and researcher. His presence also insured attention to the problem of keeping the parliamentary group's actions in harmony with party policy declarations.

In this important formative period, 1940–1945, the members of the caucus fell naturally into specialization in particular fields. The lines were not hard and fast, but it was apparent from their interests and speeches in the House that M. J. Coldwell concentrated upon foreign affairs and finance, Angus MacInnis and Clarie Gillis were primarily interested in labor, J. Noseworthy and G. H. Castleden specialized in educational matters, A. M. Nicholson was preoccupied with housing, and P. E. Wright, J. W. Burton, and William Bryce made their chief contributions in the field of agriculture. T. C. Douglas (1935–1944) and Stanley Knowles (from 1943) were men of well-rounded experience, able to help in several fields.

In arguing the case for more adequate staffing of the national office, A. M. Nicholson, the national treasurer, once declared concerning these specialties:

It is not a case of selecting Cabinet Ministers before our eggs are hatched, but when a trade union writes to us regarding a labor problem it is referred to our two labor members. When farm organizations enlist our help, the subject is referred to the C.C.F. member who is our agricultural expert. Since each of our M.P.'s is responsible for at least two departments, he should have at least two assistants doing research work, helping him to formulate C.C.F. policies for the many departments of modern government. It is obvious that the member receiving $4,000 a year, out of which he must pay at least $1,000 income tax, make contributions to his constituency, provincial, and national organizations, meet his telephone and telegraph and Hansard reprint bills, cannot engage a private secretary to handle each of his two or three departments.[1]

Although the parliamentary group is now significantly larger, the load on CCF M.P.'s is still very heavy and the assistance available remains meager.

THE PARLIAMENTARY GROUP, 1945 MODEL

The 1945 election produced a number of CCF M.P.'s nearly three times the highest previously obtained. Of the eighteen new M.P.'s only one (William Irvine) had served in the House of Commons before; indeed, few had served previously in any public office. The larger group necessitated a considerable alteration in the methods of doing business. The caucus moved to a larger room, but continued to meet weekly. David Heaps presently returned from military duty overseas and joined the group as parliamentary secretary. The task of keeping all hands informed was multiplied, there were so many new members to coach in parliamentary procedure and to indoctrinate with the self-sacrificing and Spartan tradition of a CCF legislator. On the eve of the opening of the new Parliament, M. J. Coldwell, at a banquet given by the Ottawa CCF, told his new colleagues: "The influence of

---

[1] A. M. Nicholson, "C.C.F. National Office Has Vital Role," *Saskatchewan Commonwealth*, October 28, 1942.

the C.C.F. group in the House of Commons has always been many times as great as the actual number of members. The C.C.F. is in Parliament to fight for every good measure and fight against every bad one. You are entering a group in Parliament which has always prided itself upon its reputation for hard work, accuracy and careful attention to the duties that are placed upon a member of the House of Commons."[2]

As the new M.P.'s one by one made their maiden speeches, Coldwell was at his front-row desk, speaking words of encouragement, injecting verbal thrusts at would-be hecklers, explaining to Mr. Speaker, "with great respect," why the freshman member was not out of order. To an interested spectator in the gallery of the House, the leader appeared like the schoolmaster he is, proudly launching his promising trainees in the field of politics. The party has been fortunate that successive elections have produced a very able and devoted group of M.P.'s.

The new parliamentary group met in Regina the week end of July 8, 1945, and proceeded to plan and organize for the opening of Parliament. As national president and leader, M. J. Coldwell is House leader and caucus chairman. The caucus selected Angus MacInnis as deputy leader and vice-chairman. G. H. Castleden was reëlected secretary. Stanley Knowles was chosen chief whip, and E. L. Bowerman deputy whip.

After Parliament convened, CCF M.P.'s were assigned to caucus committees, nineteen in number plus nine subcommittees. With the announcement of the allocations went an explanation that work in the fields in which committees were set up was not restricted to those mem-

---

[2] *Saskatchewan Commonwealth,* September 12, 1945.

bers who were appointed committeemen. Each member is free to dig and delve where he likes. The allocation simply assures that each department and field will be covered. The CCF caucus committees for the twentieth Parliament (beginning in September, 1945) and their chairmen were as follows:

1. Agriculture .... Wright
    a. Marketing Service..................... McCuaig
    b. Prairie Farm Acts........................ Argue
2. External Affairs............................. Coldwell
3. Finance .... Knowles
    a. Housing .... Nicholson
4. Fisheries .... Bryce
5. Justice .... Jaenicke
6. Solicitor-General .... McKay
7. Labor .... MacInnis
8. Mines and Resources.................. Townley-Smith
    a. Immigration .... Zaplitny
    b. Indian Affairs........................ Matthews
9. National Defence (Army)...................... Probe
    a. Defence (Navy) .... Moore
10. National Defence (Air)..................... Castleden
11. National Health and Welfare.................. Strum
    a. National Health .... McCullough
12. National Revenue .... Thatcher
13. Post Office .... Campbell
14. Public Works .... Irvine
15. Reconstruction and Supply.................... Gillis
16. Secretary of State .... Bowerman
17. Trade, Commerce, and Cooperative Movement.. Burton
18. Transport............................... Archibald
    a. Civil Aviation .... Knight
    b. Radio .... Stewart
19. Veterans' Affairs .... Bentley

Those who know the backgrounds of these M.P.'s will recognize how appropriate many of the appointments were. Percy Wright was a veteran of World War I who settled on prairie land and made a success of it. Coldwell was a Canadian delegate to the San Francisco U. N. Conference. MacInnis knows the labor movement from many years of experience as a workman, a unionist, and a champion of labor in the House of Commons since 1930. Zaplitny is son of an immigrant. Probe served overseas as a captain in the army in World War II. Moore was elected at the close of a tour of duty as a stoker in the navy. Castleden flew in the R.A.F. in World War I. Gillis fought in that war, and returned to the struggle for existence of a Cape Breton miner. Burton is a farmer who pioneered in the development of the cooperative movement.

Through the use of committees and subcommittees every CCF M.P. was made a chairman of some field of caucus interest. Each member also received one or more appointments to standing and special committees of the House of Commons, and, in keeping with CCF traditions, takes the responsibility very seriously.

CAUCUS RELATIONS TO THE NATIONAL PARTY

The problem of caucus relationships with external party agencies is often a difficult one. So far in the CCF there have been few occasions of friction. This relative smoothness is due to the simplicity of the situation, the carefully conceived machinery of liaison, and the democratic spirit of the leaders. Never having come even close to national office, the party group in Parliament has been limited to the less responsible tasks of opposition. The stakes are much less when a party is in opposition than when it is running a government, and the pressures are not nearly so great.

The national CCF is well organized to promote harmony between parliamentary group and national organization. The same person holds the offices of leader of the group and national president of the party. The national secretary and parliamentary secretary, both of whom provide services to the caucus, are employees of the party organization. As many as one-third of the National Council and an even larger proportion of the National Executive are usually chosen from among the M.P.'s.

Idyllic as it may seem, there is still a close connection between the leaders of the CCF, both in and out of Parliament, and the rank and file of party members over the country. Coldwell and other top leaders are constantly on the move when the House is not in session. A leader covering a vast country like Canada, talking with its people, renewing old acquaintances and making new ones, would be callous indeed if he were insensitive to what goes on at the "grass roots" level. The leadership of the CCF came from the ranks, most of it within the last ten years, and a good deal of it risked jobs in entering politics. When one remembers the life of Ramsay MacDonald and the flaw in his career, it is difficult to see how CCF leaders could lose touch with their people for long without themselves losing their leadership.

At the time of the conscription plebiscite in 1942, the parliamentary group decided to vote affirmatively on the proposal to free the government from its obligation not to impose conscription for overseas service. Some rank-and-file members of the CCF in the country took exception to the stand of the caucus. Because it was impossible to assemble the National Council in time to consider the question, a telegraphic poll of provincial officers was taken.

As the number of CCF M.P.'s increases, it will be necessary to work out more elaborate machinery for management of the parliamentary caucus. Under no circumstances should the regular caucus meetings be dropped, for they are an essential part of the democratic political process. If the party gains power, there may be a temptation for the government to avoid the caucus. Unquestionably a caucus might overreach itself, but the dangers are greater still that a cabinet will insulate itself too thoroughly from the opinions of the backbench M.P.'s. When the parliamentary group exceeds fifty or one hundred, it may prove necessary, in order to assure prompt action, to establish some kind of executive or steering committee, with jurisdiction over day-to-day tactics. The present scheme of full participation and open collaboration should be retained as long as possible.

Finally, the ties between M.P.'s and the national office are made more binding by the quaint custom of asking M.P.'s to donate a portion of their salaries to the party. Some people have assumed that such receipts, a major source of revenue since the early days, are no longer important. That is far from the fact, for even in 1945–46 around one-fourth of the party's national revenues came from this source. Money is where you find it.

LEADERSHIP

Under the British parliamentary system, the leader of the party with a majority in the popular house of Parliament is invited by the Crown to become Prime Minister. The leader of the next largest party becomes Leader of His Majesty's Opposition. This places great importance upon the method of selection of the party leader. Two methods of selecting party leaders are in vogue in various parts of the British Commonwealth. The most common is that employed in the United Kingdom, under which the party leader is elected by the caucus of party M.P.'s. The second method, usually employed by the parties of Canada, is the selection of party leader by national convention. Influenced by practice in the United States, the Canadian parties have come to recognize a need for rank-and-file party participation in the selection of a leader. This is obtained through the national convention, which is deemed sufficiently representative of the various sections of the country and factions of the party to serve in this role. The choice of Mackenzie King as leader of the Liberal Party was made by the Liberal convention of 1919. The choice of Conservative leaders of the last twenty-five years, including that of George Drew (1948), has been made largely through conventions. St. Laurent was chosen to succeed Mackenzie King by the Liberal convention of August, 1948, at Ottawa.

Confronted with the two divergent lines of precedent, the CCF has groped for a solution. It has not yet reached a final one. Technically, the leader of the party is chosen by the CCF caucus in the House of Commons. This choice is, however, subject to a sort of review by the party organization in its biennial conventions. Each two years, the national convention elects the national officers for the forthcoming biennium. It has an opportunity at that time to pass judgment on the leader who has been chosen by the group in Parliament.

The first leader of the national party was J. S. Woodsworth. He assumed this role quite naturally, for he was widely regarded as the founder of the CCF and was certainly its most venerated member. Not only did the caucus choose Woodsworth as its leader, but the various national conventions of the 1930's elected him also president of the national party. When he became too ill to continue in an active role, he wrote to the national party asking to be relieved of the presidency. After negotiations during the 1940 convention, the office of president was abolished and the office of honorary president was created. Woodsworth was elected to the new office and continued in that role until his death. At the 1940 convention, M. J. Coldwell was elected to the post of national chairman.

In his letter to the party, asking to be relieved of the presidency, Woodsworth wrote:

> Ever since the formation of the C.C.F. I have held two positions—first, that of House Leader and, second, that of President. To the first position there was no formal appointment. In 1921, when the former Labour Party was set up in the House, Mr. William Irvine made the announcement, "Mr. Woodsworth is the Leader and I am the Group."
>
> Since then I have simply carried on. Personally I am inclined to think it would be well for the C.C.F. members of the House to choose their own House Leader. However, that can be decided later. At this time under the circumstances it seems wise for me to resign.
>
> As to the Presidency, I have always been opposed to positions being held by those unable to give active service. Further, on the important question of War Policy, my personal position differs from that of the majority of the Executive and, I take it, from that of the majority of our members. It is not fair either to the organization or to myself, that I should occupy an executive position under these circumstances. Hence, from this position also, I resign.[3]

Following Woodsworth's death, the caucus selected Coldwell as its leader. The 1942 convention restored a

---

[3] Report of the sixth national convention, Winnipeg, October 28–29, 1940, pp. 3–4.

combined role by electing Coldwell to the presidency. The chairmanship was filled by the election of F. R. Scott to the post. It now appears established that the leader of the party in the House of Commons is also president of the national party. Should the leadership again fall vacant, the method of filling these positions would have to be improvised. Presumably the initial selection would be made by the parliamentary caucus, for it is relatively easy to assemble. The national convention, meeting only biennially, is likely to be in the position of ratifying or rejecting the decision already made by the caucus. Should the convention dislike the caucus choice, its failure to elect the leader to the office of president might be taken as a vote of nonconfidence. Since no leader could long remain without the confidence of the rank and file of the party, one repudiated by a convention would feel constrained to resign. This would make possible consultation in the party in order to secure the selection of a leader acceptable both to the parliamentary group and to the party as a whole.

If the CCF should obtain in a federal general election a majority or a plurality of the 262 seats in the House of Commons, the Governor-General, as representative of the Crown, would be obligated to ask the CCF leader to form a government. Acting as Prime Minister, the leader-president would be responsible for the selection of his ministers. It is the view of M. J. Coldwell that that Prime Minister-designate should consult the National Council of the party, but that the final responsibility must rest upon the leader. In the selection of his cabinet the CCF Prime Minister would doubtless seek to represent the various geographic sections of the Dominion and the various factions of the party.

PARLIAMENTARY COMMITTEES

Under the rules of the House of Commons, its standing committees are selected by a committee elected for that purpose. This committee on committees is set up by a motion of the Prime Minister in which he names its proposed personnel. The committee on committees balances with care the representation of the various parties and groups. In the Parliament since 1940, nearly every committee of importance has included one or more CCF representatives. Special committees of the House of Commons have often performed functions as important as those of standing committees. The CCF has been given proportionate representation in their personnel.

CCF members of standing on special committees in the House of Commons devote much time and energy to committee work. During the Parliament of 1942, for example, M. J. Coldwell played a vigorous part in the investigation of radio broadcasting; T. C. Douglas brought an extraordinary background to a special committee on war expenditures; and Angus MacInnis attacked with rare devotion and conviction the problems posed by the Defence of Canada Regulations.

Standing committees are playing an increasingly important role in Canadian parliamentary procedure. When the CCF wishes to attach an amendment to a bill pending before the House, it attempts to do so in the committee stage of consideration. Amendments are usually drawn up in caucus, or at least reviewed by the parliamentary group before submission. When amendments are included only for an opportunity to express disagreement with a pending bill, they are submitted on second reading on the floor of the House.

PROCEDURE ON THE FLOOR

As representatives of a party of the opposition, the CCF M.P.'s utilize fully their opportunity to question members of the government on special matters of policy and administration. The M.P.'s submit questions which are of particular interest to their constituents or to them as specialists for the CCF in particular functions of government. The question period is one of the most valuable in a British-modeled legislative assembly. It provides an opportunity to reveal to the public certain details of the operations of ministers and administrative agencies which otherwise might easily be neglected, or, as in the United States, made subjects of extravagant charges and allegations.

On second reading of bills before the House of Commons there occurs the primary debate, dealing with the general principles of the proposed act. On each bill of importance the CCF produces at least one full-dress speech. On matters of greater importance often two or more take part. The main CCF speaker in opposition to a leading bill usually offers an amendment (at its second-reading stage). Typical of a motion to amend was that made by Angus MacInnis in the debate on conscription for overseas service, at the 1942 session:

That all the words after "that" in the said motion be struck out and the following substituted therefor: "this bill be not now read a second time but that it be resolved that the principle of the bill before the house is inadequate and inequitable, permits the governor general in council to conscript men for overseas service without reference to parliament, and is, therefore, contrary to the peace, order and good government of Canada."[4]

[4] House of Commons *Debates*, Official Report, daily edition, vol. 80 (June 15, 1942), p. 3638.

In their major speeches on important bills in the House of Commons, CCF spokesmen deliver addresses that are ably prepared and studded with facts. Into each one goes careful marshaling of data, often with the assistance of the parlimentary secretary and the research secretary of the national office, and thorough discussion of the issue with colleagues, both informally and in caucus. The CCF M.P.'s are unusually diligent about attendance in House sessions. They do a disproportionate amount of heckling of their opponents whenever any alleged misrepresentation concerning the CCF is uttered. Skilled parliamentarians like M. J. Coldwell and Stanley Knowles enjoy thoroughly the give and take that marks a controversial debate.

In recent sessions of the Parliament, Coldwell has been one of the most active participants in debate on the floor of the House. Since 1940 he has emerged as the center of greatest interest to the spectators in the galleries of the House of Commons. Analysis of the House of Commons *Debates* since 1941 shows that Coldwell is one of the most frequent contributors to the proceedings of the House. In the first session of the Twentieth Parliament (September–December, 1945), for example, the index reveals that participation by the CCF leader exceeded in quantity that of all other M.P.'s except C. D. Howe, Minister of Reconstruction, J. L. Ilsley, Minister of Finance, and John Bracken, Conservative leader.

Prospective Prime Minister

If the CCF secures a majority in the House of Commons in the next few years, the Prime Minister of Canada will most likely by M. J. Coldwell. He was born in England of English parentage in 1888. He was educated at Univer-

sity College, Exeter. At the age of twenty-two he emi-
grated to Canada and took up schoolteaching, first in
Alberta and later in Saskatchewan. Two years after his
transfer to Canada, he married Nora Gertrude Dunsford
of Somerset, England. They have two children. Through
the decades of the 1910's and 1920's, Coldwell was a successful teacher and school principal. From 1922 onward,
he engaged in local politics in the city of Regina. He
served as alderman on the city council on two occasions.
He achieved national recognition as secretary-treasurer
and as president of the Canadian Teachers' Federation.

In politics, Coldwell was from the beginning connected
with the labor and progressive forces of Saskatchewan.
He first ran for M.P. in the Regina constituency in 1925.
In 1934 he was a CCF candidate for M.L.A. in the provincial general election of that year. Both times he was
defeated. Contesting the rural constituency of Rosetown-
Biggar in 1935, he won a seat in the federal House of
Commons. His pluralities in this constituency have been
comfortable ones, but the combined vote of his Conservative and Liberal opponents in 1940 left him with
only a small majority.

It is widely conceded, even by his opponents, that this
former Saskatchewan schoolteacher has the qualities of
a first-class political leader. He combines character of the
highest order with rare charm and real political skill. In
ideology, Coldwell may be classed as a moderate socialist
on domestic issues and as an internationalist in foreign
affairs. When the leadership of the CCF was left vacant
owing to the ill health of J. S. Woodsworth, Coldwell was
admirably suited both in ability and in his views to face
the public questions of the day as leader. His vigorous
support of the war effort did much to overcome the

pacifist reputation the CCF had gained under Woodsworth's leadership. Coldwell was a member of the national executive of the League of Nations Society of Canada; his only son went overseas with the R.C.A.F.

His entry into politics and his role as leader of the party have required of Coldwell very great sacrifices. There was a storm in Regina when he began to run for office as a partisan candidate. Trouble with his school board (he was principal of Thomson School, Regina) began in earnest in 1934 when he ran for M.L.A. He was unable to obtain a leave of absence in order to make a proper campaign. When the federal election of 1935 came round, his application for extended leave was denied again; when he did not return to his post on time, the school board dismissed him. At the next school board election in Regina, a new slate of board members, headed by Dr. Hugh MacLean, was elected largely on the issue of "Reinstate Coldwell." The new board restored Coldwell to his post. He never resumed it, but instead offered his resignation in order to take up his duties as an M.P.

As leader of the CCF, Coldwell's strength and resources have been taxed to the maximum in recent years. His modest salary as M.P. is soon exhausted in supporting his family and making contributions to the national party. Furthermore, he has imposed upon himself a very heavy burden by meetings and speaking engagements in various parts of the country. Like other M.P.'s, he is able to travel upon the railways on pass, but berth and meals must be paid for. Through the courtesy of the House of Commons, Coldwell receives the services of a full-time secretary; since late in 1943 he has had the assistance of a CCF parliamentary secretary, initially Alex J. Macdonald, later David Heaps, and at the present time Allan O'Brien, who keeps informed of the business of the House and performs the many services required by the leader, including the compiling of necessary information on current issues.

That M. J. Coldwell is an extraordinarily attractive political leader is agreed to by friend and foe alike. From the day he gave his maiden speech, on February 13, 1936, in the debate on the Address in Reply to the Speech from the Throne, he was marked as a promising House of Commons man. In that speech he focused attention on the problems of the prairie provinces; in a parliamentary wrangle with Minister of Agriculture James Gardiner, Coldwell handled himself so ably that he succeeded in getting a damaging quotation into the record without final denial by the minister. After he had finished, a political opponent declared of his speech: "I have been in public life for many years, in the provincial house and in this house, and I have never listened to the maiden speech of a member of Parliament with greater interest than I did to the speech of the honorable member who has just taken his seat. I predict that this young man will go far in the public life of this country."[5]

Bruce Hutchison, one of Canada's top journalists, calls Coldwell "a man of superb political talent, who has taken like a duck to the water of Canadian politics."[6]

CCF PARLIAMENTARY PERSONNEL, 1945–1949

Although it is not possible to describe a composite or typical CCF M.P., one can tabulate facts about essential characteristics. On the basis of such data it is possible to speculate and generalize a good deal.

---

[5] House of Commons *Debates*, session 1936, I: 177. The compliments were from T. A. Thompson (Lanark). For Coldwell's maiden speech see *ibid.*, pp. 171–177.

[6] *Fortune*, August, 1945, p. 201.

The most obvious attribute for initial comment is age. At the time of their election in 1945, the CCF M.P.'s averaged 47.6 years; the average for the whole House was 51.8 years. The CCF average is higher than might be expected in so young a movement, but Canada has always been slow, even in her radicalism, in recognizing talented youth. If we take the CCF M.P.'s in ten-year age groups, there were two in their twenties, five in the thirties, five in the forties, twelve in the fifties, and four in the sixties. While the median age of the group is around that in other national legislative bodies, it is too high for a party that may not have an opportunity to form a government for several years.

In place of birth the group is like a cross section of the Canadian adult population. Eighteen of the twenty-eight were born in Canada, seven in the United Kingdom (three in Scotland, three in England, one in Northern Ireland), two in the United States, and one in Germany. Half of the Canada-born members list a prairie province as their birthplace.

Canadians of many walks of life, while proud of being Canadians, also take pride in their ancestry. CCF people are less inclined to allege "purity" of the family stock than are some of their opponents, but one's origin often stands out in a name or a biographical fact. Ten of the twenty-eight M.P.'s listed themselves as of Canadian ancestry; nine claimed Scottish forebears; four were of English origin; and one each was of American, Irish, German, Yugoslav, and Ukrainian family background.

The educational level is relatively high among CCF parliamentarians, reflecting a democratic educational system for which Canada deserves much credit. Fifteen of the M.P.'s attended a university or other higher institution of learning; six had high school education; two had elementary training only; the remainder did not report.

When Parliament turned its attention to military or veterans' affairs, the CCF had in its group a number who could speak authoritatively. Four of the 1945 M.P.'s served in World War I, and four in World War II.

Like most people in political life, the CCF M.P.'s have participated in the life of other organizations. In the biographical sketches of the twenty-eight, eleven mentioned connections with cooperative societies; nine, agricultural groups; seven, veterans' bodies; eight, fraternal orders; five, professional (mostly teacher) associations; three, trade unions; two, learned societies.

The group was most unusual in occupations. There was only one lawyer, whereas most legislative bodies have more attorneys than anything else. The largest element, occupationally, consisted of farmers, of whom there were eight. The next in size was made up of teachers. There were four former clergymen, three laborers, and a businessman or two.

Especially in the occupational field, the CCF has brought into the House of Commons some unique elements. The most surprising is its reliance for leadership on teachers and preachers and workers. To a noteworthy degree the teachers and clergy represent the intelligentsia, especially in the western provinces. They have shown much courage and self-sacrifice in risking their security by participating in political activities.

PARLIAMENTARY OPPOSITION

The role of an opposition party in a parliamentary system, with rigid party discipline, when the government has a clear majority, is not a happy one. If the task of the

CCF group in Parliament were to defeat the government's bills, then it has been a failure indeed. In modern Canadian history no government possessing a majority in the House of Commons has ever been brought down by an adverse vote. Party lines are so rigid, and discipline through the whips is so thorough, that individual M.P.'s on the government side almost invariably support the government. Therefore, the CCF uses its opposition role for more fruitful purposes.

First, the parliamentary party is preparing itself to take office. Members of the group are receiving training both in handling themselves on the floor of the House and in acquainting themselves with the functions and problems of the several departments. Both in the debates on specific bills and in the general speeches that discuss the government's policy in the debate on the Speech from the Throne, the M.P. is learning to be a "House of Commons man," able in exposition and quick in repartee. Through work on caucus committees and committees of the House, members become acquainted with the details of departmental operation and have opportunities to think about future public policy in the various fields.

Second, the CCF, like other parties, uses the House of Commons as a platform from which it proclaims its party program to the country. The long job of persuading voters to abandon traditional party allegiances and follow a new party is carried out in part by the conduct of CCF representatives in Parliament. Of course, the stand taken by the CCF on a given matter may offend more people than it pleases, for the party does not shift its position with every gust of public opinion. Reliance must be placed on the ultimate acceptability of the CCF program to the Canadian electorate.

To carry out with maximum effectiveness this use of the House of Commons as a sounding board, full and fair reporting of parliamentary debates is needed, but it is not available. The radio, largely owned and operated as a public corporation, handles news from Parliament rather objectively, but the brevity of treatment in news broadcasts limits greatly the impression made on the listener. Most of the daily and weekly newspapers of Canada are actively opposed to the CCF and its program. Even though some sections of the press protect the integrity of their news columns through straight reporting, they often nullify through editorial attacks any favorable impressions of the CCF thus obtained. Facing a preponderantly hostile press, the CCF has developed its own newspapers across the country, and has supplied them with a press service which is thoroughly biased in favor of the party point of view and always full of the news of the party's own M.P.'s.

Third, the M.P.'s play a highly important role in the party's organizational picture. Liberated by their parliamentary salaries from most of the normal occupational concerns, CCF M.P.'s are expected to devote full time to party and parliamentary work. Over the last dozen years, Parliament has been in session on an average of hardly less than six months in each year. When the House meets, the CCF members are on hand; their attendance record is remarkably high. When a House session is adjourned, the M.P. is expected to take on organizational tasks for the party. A few examples will illustrate the heavy burden this work entails. After J. W. Noseworthy was elected to the House in 1942, he was in constant demand by party organizations everywhere. In the last five months of 1942 he addressed 145 meetings in more than 70 cities and

towns. A. M. Nicholson covered the country from end to
end in the performance of his "honorary" duties as national treasurer.

Clarie Gillis and Angus MacInnis are sent from province to province to meet with labor leaders and to speak
at trade union affairs. The week end is a time of rest for
some in Ottawa, but the CCF M.P. may be found in his
office or on a train headed for a party rally in Quebec or
Ontario. The newly elected M.P. is asked to do many
things in the new party that might not be expected of
him some years from now, because he has for the time
being a special prestige, and his presence at a party occasion is living evidence that constituencies can be won.
Also not to be neglected is the financial side; the M.P.
has a pass on the railways, and so he can reach a distant
place with a cash outlay limited to payments for sleeping-
car space, meals, and incidentals. The tasks of opposition,
then, are exacting, and the satisfactions rarely are complete. The larger CCF group elected in 1945 demonstrated the proclivity for hard work and the tenacity
characteristic of previous groups, and its record was a
good omen for the groups yet to come.

TECHNIQUES OF OPPOSITION

The ideas of the emerging Cooperative Commonwealth
Federation were first brought to the attention of the
House of Commons through a series of resolutions introduced in each session of Parliament. Woodsworth introduced the first of these in the 1932 session; it declared
that "the government should immediately take measures
looking to the setting up of a cooperative commonwealth
in which all natural resources and the socially necessary
machinery of production will be used in the interests of

the people and not for the benefit of the few.'" A similar resolution in the next session was supported in speeches by Macphail, Coote, Heaps, Garland, MacInnis, and Irvine.

By 1934 a few Conservative and Liberal members of the House took the trouble to attack the new party. Woodsworth reviewed the Regina Manifesto and read the list of affiliated organizations. Regularly, speakers in opposition to the resolution conceded the sincerity of Woodsworth but made bitter attacks on the movement. One member declared that the mild-mannered leader would be replaced later "by a Robespierre" as "was Kerensky by bolshevik dictators."[8] In 1935, before the federal election, Woodsworth was able to tell of electoral gains in British Columbia and Saskatchewan, where the CCF had become the official opposition. Opponents displayed unusual interest in finding out which M.P.'s adhered to the CCF standard, a question to which the party itself might have liked answers. Neither Agnes Macphail nor Humphrey Mitchell would state whether they were or were not members of the party.[9]

The purpose of these "cooperative commonwealth" resolutions, and of the many others on insurance, banking, pensions, unemployment, and other matters, was to get the speeches in the record and to force M.P.'s to declare themselves on vital subjects.

In more recent years, CCF M.P.'s have made full use of the device of moving an amendment to the Address in Reply to the Speech from the Throne. Not only do these amendments include declarations of nonconfidence in

[7] House of Commons *Debates*, session 1932, I: 726.
[8] *Debates*, session 1934, I: 275–276.
[9] *Debates*, session 1935, I: 721.

the government of the day, but they also include a list of shortcomings in the conduct of national affairs which could be remedied by the use of CCF policy.

CCF leadership in the House of Commons has so thoroughly mastered parliamentary procedure that the group misses few opportunities to point up and expound CCF doctrine. Nevertheless, Coldwell has proved himself the most consistent exponent in the House of the rights and privileges of the backbench M.P., whether he be political friend or foe.

The value of the CCF constructive opposition is well illustrated by the party's role during House of Commons consideration of constitutional legislation in the autumn of 1949. The St. Laurent government proposed, in an "address to the King," to alter the British North America Act by providing that Canada might amend her own Constitution, except with regard to provincial matters and minority school and language rights. The CCF supported the Liberal government's motion, which was opposed by both Conservative and Social Credit M.P.'s. On the second day of the debate, Stanley Knowles offered an amendment which specified that a session of Parliament must be held each year and that a Parliament's maximum life be five years. The Prime Minister accepted this amendment, with the modification that the House of Commons might, in time of war or insurrection, prolong its life by a two-thirds vote.

CHAPTER VII

Saskatchewan under CCF Rule

IN SASKATCHEWAN, heart of the Canadian prairies, the CCF developed early its greatest organizational and electoral strength in the Dominion. Saskatchewan has, for the most part, been settled since the turn of the century, and became a province in the federation only in 1905. Its population increased rapidly, stimulated by a land boom which ended after World War I. The maximum population of the province was recorded in the census of 1936 as 931,547. The census of 1941 showed a decrease to 887,747, and that of 1946 to 832,688.

ECONOMIC AND POLITICAL BACKGROUND

Saskatchewan is primarily an agricultural province. It includes only three cities of any considerable size—Regina, Saskatoon, and Moose Jaw. Although some of the farming land is of good quality, many of the farmers of Saskatchewan live on marginal land and stake nearly everything on a wheat crop, which in turn depends upon the exigencies of the weather—hail, rain, snow, sleet, drought.

In 1926–1928, wheat accounted for 81 per cent of total cash receipts from sale of farm products in Saskatchewan. The very great dependence of the province on the wheat crop is emphasized further by the fact that in the same period 62 per cent of Saskatchewan income was derived from agriculture.[1]

---

[1] Canada, Royal Commission on Dominion-Provincial Relations, *Report*, Bk. 1, pp. 121 and 122.

In the 1930's Saskatchewan wheatgrowing was stricken by both world depression and drought. The Royal Commission on Dominion-Provincial Relations reported: "If the repercussions upon other sections of the Dominion were widespread and severe, the conditions in Saskatchewan were nothing short of disastrous. Economically, this area was the most vulnerable in Canada. No other province was so completely dependent upon the fluctuations in the export market. Nowhere was production so dependent upon the vagaries of the climate."[2]

Between 1930 and 1937, the burden of relief in Saskatchewan was unbearably oppressive. In 1937, when about two-thirds of the farm population suffered crop losses from drought, the expenditures for direct and agricultural relief reached 163 per cent of total provincial and municipal revenues.

There is ample evidence that Saskatchewan is the poorest province west of Quebec both in money income and in potentialities. It is distant from the principal markets for its products; it has few mineral or forest resources which can become the basis for major industrial development. If Saskatchewan is to prosper, it will require favorable world economic conditions and the province will have to utilize effectively what resources it has. Of course, there is always the chance of big-scale oil.

In the 1920's, Saskatchewan was fourth among the nine provinces in average money income per capita. In 1928–29 this figure was $478; in 1933, it had declined to $135, a decrease of 72 per cent in four years. This made Saskatchewan the lowest in per capita income of all the Canadian provinces for 1933.

The geographic and economic background of Sas-

---

[2] *Ibid.*, p. 169.

katchewan should have predisposed her in favor of politics of radical reform; yet between 1905 and 1944 Saskatchewan showed a decided preference for the mildly progressive Liberal Party, and once, between 1929 and 1934, the province turned to the Conservatives. In the thirty-nine years from its admission to the Confederation to the CCF landslide of 1944, Saskatchewan had thirty-four years of Liberal government. In their years of power, the Liberals, under the redoubtable "Jimmy" Gardiner, built up a political machine of astonishing strength. Enjoying both provincial and federal patronage over the greater part of those years, the Liberals, at least up to 1929, managed the whole provincial organization from the top down. Patronage was distributed liberally in the form of jobs, road improvements, and relief.[3]

The Grain Growers' movement was particularly strong in the Saskatchewan area. Projecting a progressive platform, the Grain Growers' Association concentrated upon economic problems, focusing its main attack on the high interest rates charged on farm debts. Later it went into trading activities, encouraging the farmers to buy seed, twine, lumber, and other commodities collectively. After a period of diffusion in organization in which the more radical farmers joined the Farmers' Union, the Association and the Union amalgamated in the formation of the United Farmers of Canada (Saskatchewan Section). The U. F. of C. fostered cooperative enterprises, but later turned also to educational work and pressure politics. Its research and educational activities led to the establishment of several successful cooperatives, including the Saskatchewan Cooperative Wheat Producers, Ltd., which

[3] Escott Reid, "The Saskatchewan Liberal Machine before 1929," *C.J.E.P.S.*, 2 (February, 1936): 27–40.

now markets more than one-half the wheat of the province, the Saskatchewan Cooperative Livestock Producers, Ltd., and other endeavors of varied fortunes.

In pressure politics, the U. F. of C. strove initially for marketing legislation and for mortgage moratoriums. Later it turned to direct political action. Under the leadership of George H. Williams, the U. F. of C. joined hands in 1932 with the urban Independent Labour Party and began contesting elections under the label of "the farmer-labour movement."

Provincial Elections, 1934–1944.—In 1932, at the time the CCF came into being at Calgary, the government of Saskatchewan was a coalition which included Conservatives and Independents. The coalition, however, interrupted only briefly (1929–1934) the long Liberal control over the province dating from 1905 when Saskatchewan entered the Confederation. In the provincial general election of 1934 the CCF managed to become the official opposition by capturing 5 of the then existing 55 legislative seats. A Liberal government headed by James G. Gardiner took office. Between 1934 and 1938 the Liberal governments (Gardiner to 1935, with Patterson succeeding him) had 50 supporters among the 55 members of the House.

In the meantime the federal election of 1935 was held. As was expected, the Liberals polled the largest vote in a rather heterogeneous field, with the CCF second, Conservatives third, and Social Credit fourth. The popular vote of the Liberals was approximately 135,000, which won 16 seats in the House of Commons; the CCF's 73,500 votes won 2 seats (M. J. Coldwell and T. C. Douglas); the Conservatives' 71,000 votes secured only 1 seat; Social Credit with 63,500 votes won 2 seats.

In 1938 the provincial general election, held in June, attracted very great interest. One of the outstanding features of the campaign was the popular following developed in Saskatchewan by Premier Aberhart of Alberta, who drew thousands to Social Credit meetings. The CCF put on a vigorous campaign, but the results were disappointing to the young movement. The Liberals, proceeding in their traditional fashion in the province, placed particular stress upon securing the vote in rural areas that were stricken by drought and poverty. Liberal strength in the legislature was reduced to 36. The CCF won 10 seats, Social Credit got 2, and the Independents 2. In popular vote the Liberals polled a plurality but not a majority. The Liberals had 200,000 out of 440,000 votes cast, CCF was second with 82,000, Social Credit third with 69,000, and the Conservatives fourth with 52,000. No Conservative candidate won a seat. It was plain after the election that the Social Credit invasion had actually aided the Liberal government to maintain control. Social Crediters competed with CCF candidates for reform votes, and in several places the votes of the two parties, if combined, could have defeated the victorious Liberal candidate. The power of the Liberal machine was illustrated in the election returns from the relief and drought-stricken areas, which voted mainly for Liberal candidates. As in the 1935 federal election, the CCF ran strongest in the more well-to-do farming areas.

The 1940 federal election gave the Saskatchewan CCF confidence in its ability to gain in popular support despite some losses in other parts of the country. As in 1935, again the Liberals led; for nearly 160,000 votes they won 12 seats. The CCF, with a popular vote of 106,000, elected 5 M.P.'s; the Conservatives, now down to 52,500, elected 2.

Between 1940 and 1944 the CCF engaged in an aggressive and persistent campaign to break down the Liberal supremacy in the province and to prepare the people for CCF government. In the legislature, the 10 M.L.A.'s, later made 11 through a by-election victory, opposed vigorously the major legislative enactments of the Patterson government and tirelessly covered the province, explaining to farmers and townspeople the shortcomings of the provincial administration. Premier Patterson was in a difficult position. Realizing the government's relative insecurity so far as the electorate was concerned, he sought to retain as long as possible his preponderant Liberal majority in the legislature. A provincial election was due in 1943, but rather than face the electorate at that time the Liberal government enacted "Bill 13," which extended the life of the legislature another year, to July 10, 1944. All over the country the CCF voiced protests over the prolonging of the legislature's life. Earlier pronouncements by Mackenzie King and Sir Wilfred Laurier were quoted to show that postponement of elections was contrary to public policy and to Liberal practice. When the 1944 session ended in April without the passage of another bill to extend the life of the legislature, it was obvious that the CCF was to face the election for which it had waited so long. At last the election was announced for Thursday, June 15, 1944. The Saskatchewan section of the party entered the campaign with the most thorough organization ever developed by the CCF in a Canadian province.

The Election of 1944.—The CCF nominated candidates in all the provincial constituencies. Only 51 seats were filled in the June 15 election; the election for the remaining one, a far northern seat, was deferred. The 51 CCF candidates were challenged by 49 Liberals and 38 Conservatives. There were in addition 3 Labor-Progressives, 3 Independents, and 1 Social Credit nominee. The disappearance of Social Credit was noteworthy.

From the beginning of the campaign the CCF took the initiative. Both Premier Patterson and former Premier J. G. Gardiner, now federal Minister of Agriculture, concentrated greatest attention upon criticizing CCF plans. As in the Ontario election campaign, both Liberals and Conservatives attempted to pin the label of "national socialism" and dictatorship on the CCF. The Liberals also defended their own record in office with some vigor. They pointed to progress in the field of agriculture, in which, through collaboration with the federal government, markets had been assured to Saskatchewan producers. They told of achievements in soil conservation and reclamation. They claimed credit for halting farm foreclosures during the years of drought and depression.

The CCF drove home the principal planks of its platform for "security and progress." After reaffirming its faith in freedom of speech, elections, and religion, the CCF program declared in favor of a reorganization of the economic life of the province in order to assure to producers their rightful share of the products of their labor. It promised to survey the natural resources of Saskatchewan and to develop these resources under public ownership. It projected a vast program of rehousing rural and urban families and the extension of adequate health and other social services to all the people of the province. In answer to the question, "Where is the money coming from?" the CCF presented a list of possible sources of revenue which included federal aid, savings through elimination of patronage, reduction of interest from the public debt, and returns from new provincially owned enterprises, including petroleum and electric power developments, food processing, and farm machinery distribution. It is likely, however, that the CCF's general aspirations were less convincing to rural Saskatchewan than its stratified appeal to farmers. The CCF's "four-point land policy" was: (1) protection of the farmer against foreclosure and eviction; (2) protection of the farmer's crop against seizure; (3) a moratorium to compel reduction of debts; and (4) crop failure clauses in mortgages. In urban areas like Regina, Moose Jaw, and Saskatoon the power of organized labor was marshaled to put over CCF candidates in constituencies which had never before been won.

The Conservative campaign attracted little attention, for that party had neither deep roots in the province nor a program which could command the attention of the electorate. The Communists, calling themselves the Labor-Progressive Party, spent a good deal of money for advertising but were unable to secure many votes for their three candidates. In the initial stages of the campaign, the Labor-Progressives announced their support of certain CCF candidates, including those in Regina, but later this action was repudiated, ostensibly on the grounds that the CCF did not support with sufficient vigor Canada's war effort! During the last week of the campaign, Tim Buck, Labor-Progressive leader, made his astonishing offer for a Liberal-Labor coalition in the coming federal election.

One feature of the CCF campaign in Saskatchewan was the array of leaders, both national and provincial, drawn from other parts of the Dominion. M. J. Coldwell and G. H. Castleden, both of whom were Saskatchewan

M.P.'s, naturally participated in the campaign throughout. Provincial leaders Harold E. Winch of British Columbia and E. B. Jolliffe of Ontario made extensive speaking tours through the province.

After the campaign entered upon its last week, with the CCF unquestionably leading, the Liberals made violent attacks upon their principal opponent. It was charged that the CCF would take away the farmer's land, confiscate savings and insurance, discharge summarily all the civil servants, and lead eventually to dictatorship. The CCF prepared its replies and delivered them forcefully through its able leadership and competent organization. Despite the solemn warnings issued by Premier Patterson and others, the people of Saskatchewan were willing to take a chance on this new party, which had originated in the soil of the prairies.

From the earliest returns there was evidence of a landslide victory for the CCF. When the votes were finally tabulated, the CCF had won 47 of the 52 seats. Only the premier and one cabinet minister survived the avalanche. The opposition in the new legislature consisted of five Liberals. Three Service M.L.A.'s were elected later by the armed forces; all three called themselves "independent," but one was a member of the CCF and participated in its caucus.

Men and women in the armed forces serving in Canada were permitted to vote in the provincial election in their home constituencies. Tabulation of this service vote was completed near the end of June and showed the following distribution: CCF, 60 per cent; Liberals, 28 per cent; Conservatives, 10 per cent; others, 2 per cent. These returns gave the CCF renewed confidence in its prospects in the postwar period.

As required by the Saskatchewan CCF Constitution, Premier-Elect T. C. Douglas consulted with a legislative advisory committee, composed of three members of the provincial council and two M.L.A.'s, concerning the personnel of the cabinet to be formed. The committee acts in an advisory capacity only, since the Constitution stresses that final responsibility for ministerial appointments rests with the premier. On July 5th, announcement of the personnel of the cabinet was made. It was as follows:

Premier and minister of health—T. C. Douglas
Provincial treasurer—C. M. Fines
Attorney-general—J. W. Corman, K.C.
Minister of agriculture—Major G. H. Williams
Minister of municipal affairs—J. H. Brockelbank
Provincial secretary and minister of social welfare—O. W. Valleau
Minister of natural resources—J. L. Phelps
Minister of highways and public works—J. T. Douglas
Minister of education—Woodrow S. Lloyd
Minister of rehabilitation and reconstruction—J. H. Sturdy
Minister of cooperatives—L. F. McIntosh
Minister of labour—C. C. Williams

The posts of minister of labour and minister of cooperatives were new to Saskatchewan. In order to avoid additional expense to the province through increasing the number of cabinet ministers from ten to twelve, salary reductions were instituted which maintained the total expenditure for cabinet salaries at the same level as that of the Liberal government.

Classified by occupation, five of the new cabinet members were farmers, three were teachers, and one each a lawyer, a railroad worker, a cooperative field agent, and a preacher. Each of the ministers had special qualifications for the post he was to assume, although only four had served previously in the Saskatchewan legislature. Premier T. C. Douglas had nine years of experience in the federal House of Commons. The minister of education, Woodrow Lloyd, was president of the Saskatchewan Teachers' Federation. The minister of labour, C. C. Williams, was mayor of Regina, and the attorney-general, J. W. Corman, was mayor of Moose Jaw. The provincial treasurer, C. M. Fines, in addition to long experience as a school principal, had played a prominent part in the formation of the CCF in 1932, and had held various party offices since that time.

The new government was sworn in by the lieutenant-governor, A. P. McNabb, on Monday, July 10, 1944.

Election of 1948.—The 1948 provincial election was held on June 24. As in 1944, the CCF entered candidates for every seat, 52 in all. The Liberals nominated 37 candidates who contested the election under the Liberal label. Social Credit entered 35 aspirants. The Conservatives entered only 7 candidates, who sought election in full competition with the other parties. The Liberals and Conservatives joined forces in supporting joint coalition candidates for 12 seats. One Labor-Progressive and several independents completed the roster of candidates for whom ballots were cast.

The CCF campaign was based primarily on the record of its government over the past four years. The election program issued two weeks before the polling consisted of a review of achievements since 1944 and a general promise of more of the same in the next term of office. The CCF reviewed with pride the province's agricultural progress, industrial development, social services expansion, labor advance, and educational achievement. Its second term, the party promised, would be marked by further extension along similar lines.

The opposition campaigns took various tacks, but all directed vigorous attacks on the government. Liberals and Conservatives sought to arouse fears and suspicion by inferring that the ultimate goal of CCF socialism was totalitarianism in both economics and politics. They stressed the point that Labor-Progressive support of the CCF candidates (in all constituencies except one) proved the similarity of aims of the socialists and Communists. Social Credit candidates drew word pictures of the success of the Manning government in adjoining Alberta.

Polling more than 235,000 votes, the greatest number ever gained by a party in Saskatchewan history, the CCF won 31 of the 52 seats. Although this was a substantial victory, it was no landslide and represented a decrease both in percentage of popular vote and in proportion of seats won. The popular vote declined from 53 per cent in 1944 to 47 per cent in 1948. The number of M.L.A.'s elected, which was 47 in 1944, was reduced to 31 in 1948. Although the Liberals also received a reduced proportion of the popular vote, their legislative representation rose to 19 in place of the meager 5 won in 1944. Social Credit, which polled 40,000 votes, elected no M.L.A.'s. Independents and others received nearly 30,000 votes and won 2 seats. The Conservatives secured just under 38,000 votes, most of them in coalition with the Liberals, but were again left utterly without representation in the provincial legislature.

The several parties interpreted the results of the election differently. The greatest controversy centered around the role of Social Credit candidates in the field. CCF leaders were inclined to think that Social Crediters entered the campaign to draw votes away from the CCF and aid the Liberals. The Liberal leader, Walter Tucker, declared after the election that the intervention of Social Credit candidates had cost the Liberals many seats. The CCF view of this matter is that the Social Credit vote is primarily an anti-old-party expression; the Liberal contention is that it is in the main antisocialist.

For the CCF the 1948 election results offered much food for thought. Its 31 seats were won by margins varying from a few votes to a huge majority; 14 victories were secured by a plurality (less than half) vote; 17 seats were won by clear majorities over all opposition. Since the Liberals and Conservatives had few candidates in active competition with one another, further coalition efforts against the CCF will necessarily include Social Credit and independent candidates. Unless the CCF percentage of the popular vote falls below the 1948 level, the chances of a coalition victory in the next provincial election do not appear bright.

The CCF may well be concerned, however, with the trend of popular voting in various parts of the province. The 1948 returns show that the CCF has greatly strengthened its support in the cities but that some relative loss has been suffered in the rural areas. Although losses among the farmers have been exaggerated by opponents of the CCF, the shift is unmistakable, and its reversal may well constitute a primary objective of party organizational efforts in coming years.

Among the casualties of the 1948 election were two cabinet ministers, O. W. Valleau and J. L. Phelps. In August, Premier Douglas reorganized the cabinet, reducing the number of ministers from twelve to eleven and reallocating portfolios.

The portfolios and personnel of the reorganized government were as follows:

Premier, president of the council, and minister of public health—T. C. Douglas
   Provincial treasurer—C. M. Fines
   Attorney-general—J. W. Corman
   Minister of natural resources and industrial development—J. H. Brockelbank
   Minister of highways—J. T. Douglas
   Minister of education—W. S. Lloyd
   Minister of social welfare and rehabilitation—J. H. Sturdy
   Minister of cooperation and minister of municipal affairs—L. F. McIntosh
   Minister of labour and provincial secretary—C. C. Williams
   Minister of agriculture—I. C. Nollet
   Minister of public works and telephones—J. A. Darling

In perspective, the Saskatchewan CCF victory of 1948 was more remarkable than that of 1944. Federal Minister of Agriculture James Gardiner, a former premier of the province, stumped for the Liberal ticket and stimulated hopes that a Liberal victory would result in close federal-provincial relations and generous grants to Saskatchewan from the federal treasury. He also hoped to spring from the post of victorious campaigner to that of Dominion Liberal leader. The Liberal Party spent very large sums in the campaign. Under the circumstances, the Liberal defeat must rank as one of the most significant electoral accomplishments in CCF history.

Leadership of the Saskatchewan CCF.—At the beginning of the CCF in Saskatchewan there were two leaders who stood out as advocates of the new cause. From the urban community of Regina, M. J. Coldwell applied to the problems of the new party an unusual brilliance, attractive personality, and great devotion and vision. The other leader, George H. Williams, contributed to the movement his understanding of rural problems, organizing ability, and tireless effort. From the time the farm and labor elements were united in 1932, there developed a rivalry between the two leaders which over the years threatened upon several occasions to divide the party into two hostile groups.

The minutes of the first convention of the Saskatchewan Farmer-Labor Group, held in July, 1932, show how the early pattern of leadership was woven. The farm delegates were from the United Farmers of Canada and the labor delegates from the I.L.P. George H. Williams declared the convention open. M. J. Coldwell served as joint chairman. When the time came to choose a political leader, Williams nominated Coldwell. When the name of Williams was placed before the convention, he rose to speak and was greeted by "enthusiastic applause and was visibly affected" by the response. Williams then withdrew his name from consideration, to the "visible disappointment of the convention."[4]

Coldwell, who had stated earlier that the Saskatchewan leader should be a farmer, was declared elected by acclamation. He was greeted, according to the minutes, by "round after round of applause and cheers."

Within a short time, Coldwell, as leader of the group, and Williams, as president of the group, were covering the province with their propaganda work. By July, 1934, when the Farmer-Labor Group had changed its name to the CCF, Saskatchewan Section, the feud between Williams and Coldwell was already under way, aggravated by

[4] Minutes of the first annual convention of the Saskatchewan Farmer-Labor Group, held in Saskatoon, July 27, 1932, pp. 12–13 (original manuscript on file in CCF provincial office, Regina; 13 pages).

the selection of Williams by the CCF M.L.A.'s as their floor leader. The convention responded to this action by creating a "Coldwell Leadership Fund" to enable Coldwell to leave his school duties in Regina and devote full time to the work of the party.

In the 1934 provincial election, Williams and four other CCF candidates had been elected, but Coldwell, who had been chosen as provincial leader, was defeated. When the suggestion was made that one of the CCF M.L.A.'s might resign in order that Coldwell could take his seat, Williams was hostile to this proposal. A year later, in the federal general election of 1935, Coldwell was elected to the House of Commons from the Rosetown-Biggar constituency. Coldwell thereupon resigned as leader of the Saskatchewan CCF, and from that time on his primary attention was concentrated on the federal field. Williams continued as a CCF M.L.A. from 1934 on, and was both leader of the CCF group in the legislature and leader of the opposition.

A serious situation developed in 1937 when Williams refused to appear on the platform with King Gordon, a brilliant CCF orator from eastern Canada, at a public meeting organized under the auspices of the Regina CCF. His refusal was based upon the possibility of a difference in opinion over the question of neutrality. The National Executive wrote to Williams telling him that he had interpreted wrongly the CCF policy on involvement in foreign wars. The Executive declared that CCF policy was not pacifistic, and charged that Williams hindered unity by publicizing differences in the CCF.

Through these years, Williams held two offices; he was president of the provincial party and political leader of the Saskatchewan CCF. In 1935 and 1936, proposals had been made that either the CCF M.L.A.'s alone should select the political leader or that the CCF M.L.A.'s and the members of the provincial council should make the selection. The 1936 convention rejected all such proposals and continued the practice of having the leader and the president one and the same person. The convention then proceeded to elect Williams to these two offices. He continued in the dual role until early in 1941. In August, 1940, Williams was reëlected president, and Clarence M. Fines was chosen vice-president. About the same time, Williams was rejected by army medical officers as unfit for active service because of a wound received in World War I. In the fall, however, both Williams and T. C. Douglas were in the same infantry officers' training school. In February, 1941, it was announced that Williams was taking up active military duties, and his resignation was submitted. J. H. Brockelbank was chosen by the caucus as CCF leader in the legislature, and automatically became leader of the opposition. Fines, who had been elected vice-president of the provincial party, was appointed chairman by the provincial council.

As soon as Williams had withdrawn from the political scene, energetic steps were taken to reorganize the provincial party leadership. The first step was the appointment by the Executive of J. T. Douglas as provincial organizer. J. T. Douglas had been manager for the federal constituency of Rosetown-Biggar since 1934 and was otherwise closely associated with Coldwell. The appointment of Douglas was opposed by the Williams faction because it was feared that Douglas would undermine Williams' leadership. Apparently the CCF M.L.A.'s had agreed to supply $50 each in support of a provincial organizer. After J. T. Douglas was appointed, however,

Williams wrote a bitter letter refusing to make his contribution. At least one party official resigned over the appointment of J. T. Douglas.

In the provincial convention of 1941, T. C. Douglas, M.P., was elected president over George Williams by a vote of approximately three to one. Fines was elected vice-president over Brockelbank. The next morning, the secretary-treasurer of the provincial party resigned. The year 1941–42 was a period of uncertainty over the leadership of the Saskatchewan CCF. On the surface, it appeared that the controversy was one of principle: (1) Should the offices of president and leader be separated, or should they be combined? (2) How should these two officers be selected? Actually, the conflict was a factional struggle for control between the supporters of Williams, whose greatest strength was in the legislature, and the Coldwell group, which was in effective control of the provincial party organization. As early as 1940, the federal M.P.'s had submitted a brief to the Saskatchewan party, recommending that the two positions be separated. The provincial council referred this question to a constitutional committee for study. In the end, an amendment was adopted which would separate the political leadership from the post of president if the CCF should be called upon to form a government. In December, 1941, a crisis was precipitated over remarks made by Fines at a Regina meeting featuring an address by M. J. Coldwell; Fines referred to T. C. Douglas as "the future premier of Saskatchewan." In the controversy which followed, Fines defended his statement on the grounds that the president of the Saskatchewan CCF had been *ex officio* leader since 1936. The provincial council considered the question of leadership and decided to refer it to the 1942 convention.

That convention finally decided to separate the offices of president and political leader. Four names were presented to the convention for the latter office: T. C. Douglas, George H. Williams, J. H. Brockelbank, and O. W. Valleau. Douglas was elected leader; Fines was elected president; and Brockelbank, vice-president. The fact that Williams was overseas on active service with the army greatly strengthened the case of those who supported Douglas.

Just on the eve of the 1944 election, Williams, then a major, was returned from overseas service and given a medical discharge from the army. During the 1944 campaign he participated loyally. In addition to winning his own seat at Wadena, he strengthened the CCF by rallying rural support in other constituencies. Premier-Elect Douglas appointed him minister of agriculture in the new cabinet, in which he served until February, 1945, when illness caused him to resign. I. C. Nollet was appointed his successor. Williams' death in Vancouver in September, 1945, was mourned throughout the CCF movement as the loss, as Premier Douglas said, of "one of its earliest and ablest champions."

Thomas C. Douglas, the first CCF provincial premier, was born in Scotland in 1904, and was brought to Canada by his parents in 1910. He received most of his education in Manitoba, except for three years passed in Scotland at the time of World War I. After the war, he worked for five years as a printer. He left this trade to return to his studies, on which he concentrated from 1924 to 1930. In this period he received the degree of Bachelor in Theology from Brandon College, Manitoba, and his Master of Arts degree, which was granted by MacMaster University, Ontario, after he had completed some advanced study at the University of Chicago. He spent five years, from 1930 to 1935, as minister of the Baptist church at Weyburn, Saskatchewan. In 1931 he became interested in the farmer-labor political movement and wrote to J. S. Woodsworth about his interest. He was referred by Woodsworth to a Regina school man, M. J. Coldwell. Douglas then formed a branch of the Independent Labour Party in Weyburn. In 1934 he ran unsuccessfully for M.L.A. In 1935 the Weyburn constituency CCF chose him as its candidate for the federal election that year. He was elected, and served in the federal House of Commons until his resignation on the eve of the Saskatchewan election of 1944.

Douglas had no difficulty with his church over his entry into politics; his experience in this regard is unlike that of most of his colleagues who came from school and church work. In the House of Commons, Douglas demonstrated unusual ability in debate. He took on the most experienced parliamentarians in the House and drove them to cover by the vigor of his exposition and repartee. Being young and energetic, a former light-weight boxing champion, Douglas is able to cover the far corners of Canada in party organizational work. Although in Saskatchewan the CCF was stronger proportionately than in any other province, much of its ablest political leadership had been diverted into the federal field. The calling of G. H. Williams to army duty cleared the way for the selection of Douglas as provincial leader in 1942. After the landslide victory of the CCF in the 1944 provincial election, he became premier of the first socialist government in North America.

The Party and the Legislative Group.—The provincial organization of the Saskatchewan CCF has already been described in comparative terms. It may be advisable, however, to stress here the organizational excellence that made possible the CCF provincial victory in 1944 and the capture of eighteen of Saskatchewan's twenty-one House of Commons seats in the federal election of 1945. A description of the provincial organization requires superlatives from the vocabulary of Hollywood. The Saskatchewan CCF has the largest membership, raises the greatest amount of money, enjoys the most active youth movement, maintains the largest CCF newspaper circulation, and supports the best-manned provincial office.

Statistics alone are inadequate to explain what a large part CCF party activities play in the life of the people of Saskatchewan. That story has to be told in terms of individuals like, for example, the farm hand who contributes two months' wages because he believes in the party, or the pastor of a far north country church who risks his little job when he campaigns for CCF candidates, or the railroad worker who spends his off hours pushing doorbells in the essential work of canvassing. At the peak of its membership, achieved in 1944 before the provincial election victory, approximately one in every seven families of the province held paid memberships in the party. Proportionately to total population, the CCF of Saskatchewan then had a higher paid-up individual membership than the British Labour Party, and probably had the highest of any democratic party in existence.

One of the things that has been particularly well done is the reporting of legislative affairs. Beginning with the 1939 session, the Saskatchewan CCF had issued a summary of the record of the legislative assembly. At first called "Notes for Speakers," this report, after 1941, bore the title, "The C.C.F. in the Legislature." Through these mimeographed reports, and through the *Saskatchewan Commonwealth,* supporters of the party were kept informed of what went on in the legislature. Major pieces of legislation were discussed and explained, and each important roll call was recorded. During its years in opposition, the CCF attacked the Liberal governments and put forward its own program through the media of the question hour, private members' bills, addresses in the debates on the Reply to a Speech from the Throne, and criticism of government bills.

After the formation of the CCF government in July, 1944, the role of the CCF group in the legislature was greatly changed. The task of opposition in the parliamentary system allows much latitude for the individual member. Criticism is inherently easier than constructive support, for it requires less discipline and is freed from direct responsibility for public policy. These considerations are especially telling in a democratic political party. The question of what use to make of the rank-and-file "backbenchers" when the party has attained power, plagued acutely both the first and second Labour governments in Great Britain. The present British Labour government has sought to utilize the talents and energies of "private" M.P.'s (those not holding ministerial office) by organizing a series of caucus committees, corresponding roughly to the jurisdiction of the major ministries.

In the Saskatchewan CCF, as in the British Labour Party, there are three principal elements to be considered in the formulation of the public policy. First, the premier and his ministerial colleagues have effective control over both executive and legislative machinery and are primarily responsible for carrying out the party program. Second, the caucus, composed mainly of nonministerial members of the legislative body, while possessing the ultimate power to overthrow the government by an adverse vote, is restrained by party discipline and by the power of dissolution, which is practically in the premier's hands. Third, the party organization considers itself the custodian of party policy, as determined in convention, and bends its efforts toward the sometimes contradictory tasks of supporting actions of the government and of pressing the government to careful stewardship of platform declarations.

Following a year of CCF government, a need was felt for closer contact between the cabinet and the rank and file of the party. Although expressed chiefly in terms of gauging public response to the CCF program, the machinery of consultation chosen was the provincial party organization and the CCF caucus in the legislature. As outlined in September, 1945, the plan called for more frequent consultation between: (1) cabinet members and other CCF M.L.A.'s; (2) the premier and the provincial president of the CCF; (3) CCF M.L.A.'s and the CCF provincial council; and (4) government and the CCF legislative advisory committee.[5]

The legislative advisory committee, previously mentioned as advising Premier Douglas on ministerial appointments, is composed of three members appointed by and from the provincial council, and two members elected by and from the CCF M.L.A.'s. Its general responsibility is to aid the legislative group in preparing legislation in conformity with CCF policies. In 1945, Dr. Carlyle King and P. G. Makaroff were appointed by the provincial council to revise the party constitution. Among the changes proposed by them to the 1945 con-

[5] *Saskatchewan Commonwealth*, September 4, 1945.

vention was one altering the duty of the legislative advisory committee from "preparing legislation" to "advising the CCF Legislative Group concerning the implementation of the CCF program."⁰ This amendment was urged as necessary, now that the CCF government was in power and itself prepared and introduced all major pieces of legislation. Although favored overwhelmingly in preliminary votes taken in provincial constituencies, the proposed changes were not adopted, and hence the legislative advisory committee continued with the impossible assignment of preparing legislation for a legislative group in power.

The Saskatchewan CCF has gone to unusual lengths to insure appropriate discipline on the part of public officers elected under its banner. No person may be nominated by the CCF for the offices of M.L.A. and M.P. without having been a member of the party for one year. Moreover, the candidate for M.L.A. is required to sign a "recall agreement." The recall procedure involves (1) a petition signed by at least 100 members, (2) a hearing at a special constituency convention, and (3) a two-thirds vote for recall. Of course the party has no power except through the display of the signed recall agreement to compel an M.L.A. to resign his seat, and so this procedure, if carried out, would amount to expulsion from the party only.

THE CCF IN POWER

It is now nearly six years since the CCF first won control of the government of Saskatchewan. Although this period has been far from normal, covering as it did the final months of the war and the initial period of readjustment,

⁰ *Delegates' Handbook, Tenth Annual C.C.F. Provincial Convention ... Saskatoon, November 5, 6, 7, 1945, Resolutions and Proposed Amendments to the Constitution*, p. 83.

it may be used for a provisional judgment of what the CCF does in power on the provincial level. The reader should bear in mind several qualifying factors. First, the war brought a period of comparative prosperity to Saskatchewan, but the war's end confronted the province with acute problems of reconstruction. Second, a Canadian province is constitutionally limited in powers and is subject to federal controls and interference to an even greater degree than an American state. Third, Saskatchewan carried into the 1940's a burden of debt and obligations incurred in the disastrous 1930's.

Dominion-Provincial Relations.—The *Report* of the Royal Commission on Dominion-Provincial Relations in 1940 represents the most thorough study ever made of a federal system in operation.[7] Issued in wartime, the report never received the attention it deserved. The federal government made two separate attempts to get action on the Rowell-Sirois report, one in 1941 and one in 1945–46, but both ended in failure. Because Premier Douglas played a leading role in the second conference, a review of its work seems appropriate here. It must be borne in mind that Douglas spoke as premier of a prairie province perhaps more than as a CCF premier. Had E. B. Jolliffe been there as premier of Ontario, it is possible that he would have approached the federal proposals somewhat differently, but he would have been in substantial agreement with Douglas, and in any event certainly not as obstructive as the then premier of Ontario, Mr. Drew.

The original Rowell-Sirois recommendations were placed before the provincial premiers by the federal government in 1941. They provided both for a reallocation of functions between federal and provincial governments

---

[7] Canada, Royal Commission on Dominion-Provincial Relations, *Report* (3 vols.; Ottawa: King's Printer, 1940).

and for a reassignment of revenue sources. For provinces with insufficient resources to provide a minimum standard of welfare services, federal aid would be provided. The 1941 conference failed to reach an agreement.

Prime Minister W. L. Mackenzie King proposed a modified version of the Rowell-Sirois report to the conference that opened in August, 1945. It provided for the reallocation of functions by agreement rather than constitutional change. The provinces must agree to withdraw the imposition of taxes on personal incomes, corporations, and estates. In exchange, the Dominion offered to increase per capita subsidies to the provinces, pay the cost of old-age pensions for persons of 70 and over, pay one-half of pensions for persons 65 to 70, pay unemployment assistance to out-of-work employable persons, and make grants for some provincial and local public works projects.

Although stating his preference for the original Sirois recommendations, Douglas gave general and strong support to the federal proposals.[8] Throughout the conference, he stressed the need for Dominion-wide minimum standards in social welfare—a floor below which no person need go, irrespective of the relative poverty of the province in which he lives. The Saskatchewan premier also used the conference as a platform from which to advocate many other items of national and provincial CCF policy. In May, 1946, the conference adjourned in deadlock. Premiers George Drew of Ontario and Maurice Duplessis of Quebec refused to agree to the reallocation of revenue

---

[8] The premier's suggestions may be found in *Saskatchewan and Reconstruction* (Regina: Bureau of Publications, 1945) and *The Dominion-Provincial Conference on Reconstruction, 1945–46: The Reply of the Saskatchewan Government to the Proposals Submitted to the Conference by the Dominion on August 6, 1945* (Regina: Bureau of Publications, 1946).

sources, which was fundamental to the whole scheme.[9] Among the general principles laid down by Premier Douglas before the Dominion-Provincial Conference was one item of pressing immediacy: "We believe that no province should be discriminated against because of the political philosophy of the government which the people have seen fit to elect."[10] From the day it took office, the the CCF government was harassed in both petty and important matters by actions of the King government in Ottawa. Some federal-provincial disagreements are inevitable in a federal system, because it is not possible to distribute authority satisfactorily. In Saskatchewan, however, the fierce Liberal versus CCF rivalry intensified the normal squabbles into major rows.

The Lieutenant-Governorship.—Under the Canadian constitutional system, the lieutenant-governor of each province is the formal representative of the Crown and performs functions such as the designation of the premier, the granting of dissolution, and the reading of the Speech from the Throne. By custom the lieutenant-governor exercises most of his powers on the advice of the government of the province, just as the Governor-General in Ottawa acts on the advice of the Dominion government. On the other hand, the lieutenant-governor is, as Hugh McD. Clokie has pointed out, "appointed, instructed, and paid by the Dominion government."[11] The lieuten-

---

[9] Drew was reported in the press as declaring that the wealth of Ontario was created by the brains and virility of its people. Duplessis wrote into the Speech from the Throne: "The Government considers that it belongs neither to a majority of the provinces nor the Ottawa Government to bring about changes to the Canadian Constitution. I firmly believe that the BNA Act is a pact of honour between the two great races; it intends to respect it, it exacts that respect."—*Montreal Star*, February 8, 1945.

[10] *Saskatchewan and Reconstruction*, p. 20.

[11] Hugh McD. Clokie, *Canadian Government and Politics* (Toronto: Longmans, Green, 1944), p. 208.

ant-governor controls the royal assent to provincial bills; he still possesses the power to reserve legislation for the Governor-General's approval. In addition, the Governor-General has power to disallow a provincial bill within one year of its enactment; this power is exercised on the advice of the Dominion prime minister.

Shortly after the CCF came to power in Saskatchewan, the Hon. A. P. McNabb, who had been lieutenant-governor for eight years, resigned. The Douglas government indicated plainly its preference for leaving the post vacant, and considered the duties so few that they could be performed by the chief justice of the province in addition to his judicial duties. Chief Justice W. M. Martin read the Speech from the Throne and performed other services, between the resignation of McNabb in 1944 and the appointment of his successor in March, 1945. From March until his death in June, 1945, the Hon. Thomas Miller held the titular executive post. A veteran Moose Jaw journalist, he had been for nine years president of the Saskatchewan Liberal Party, a post from which he resigned only a month before his appointment. He was succeeded later in 1945 by the Hon. R. J. M. Parker, who had long been in Liberal politics and was a member of the Patterson cabinet swept out of office in the 1944 CCF landslide. Parker died in March, 1948, and the post was filled by the appointment of Dr. J. M. Uhrich, former minister of public health, who had served twenty-three years as a Liberal member of the provincial legislature.

In the meantime, the Saskatchewan government closed Government House, the residence of the lieutenant-governor, and offered its use to the federal government for a convalescent and rehabilitation center for returned servicemen. Part of the furnishings were sold in 1945.

Ultimately the building will be a provincial museum. CCF hostility toward the lieutenant-governorship appears based on (1) concern lest the power of reservation or some other form of federal intervention will be used, and (2) a desire to use the money previously spent on pomp for matters of social significance.

The Disallowance Controversy of 1945.—The power of disallowance is a veto exercised over provincial legislation by the Dominion government acting through the Governor-General. Unused between 1924 and 1937, it was exercised to void three acts of the Social Credit government in Alberta in the latter year.[12] In 1945, petitions asking for disallowance of three Saskatchewan acts were filed in Ottawa with the federal Department of Justice. The three acts were the Farm Security Act, the Mineral Taxation Act, and amendments to the Local Government Board Act. The requests for disallowance were made by the Canadian Pacific Railway and the Dominion Loan and Mortgage Association. The Farm Security Act provided that farmers might not be evicted, through mortgage foreclosure, from their farm homes, including up to 160 acres of land; it also relieved farmers of repayment on the principal of loans in years of crop failure. The Mineral Taxation Act was an attempt to secure either tax revenue or forfeiture to the province by levying a tax of three cents per acre on holders of mineral rights and by a mineral holding tax based on the assessed value of minerals. The Local Government Board amendments provided for final and binding debt adjustments by the board, whether or not bondholders should agree.

---

[12] *Ibid.*, p. 209. See also Eugene Forsey, "Disallowance of Provincial Acts, Reservation of Provincial Bills and Refusal of Assent of Lieutenant-Governors since 1867," *C.J.E.P.S.*, 4 (February, 1938): 47–59.

The case for Saskatchewan was handled by Attorney-General J. W. Corman. He argued that the power of disallowance was as outmoded when used on the provincial level by Ottawa as it was on the Dominion level by London. Mass meetings were held and resolutions were passed by farm, labor, and other groups. Premier Douglas went on the air and declared for no retreat from the province's position. In late November, 1945, the decision of the Dominion government not to disallow was announced. The crop failure clause of the Farm Security Act was declared void in November, 1948, by the judicial committee of the Privy Council in London.

The Seed Grain Debt.—The great drought of 1937 was the climax of nearly a decade of depression for Saskatchewan farmers. The crop failures of that year were widespread. The meager wheat crop was shipped and sold at the low prices then prevailing. In order to get seed for the 1938 planting, farmers appealed to their rural municipalities for assistance. Their credit rating was so low that it was necessary to obtain both provincial and federal governmental guarantees for the loans. The total loan was about $16,500,000, at 4 per cent interest. Prices paid by farmers for various goods were high as compared with market prices for farm products. Repeatedly, farm groups and municipalities offered to pay half the debt, the other half to be paid by the guaranteeing governments.

During the 1944 provincial campaign, the CCF repeatedly declared for a settlement of the seed grain debt that would be "fair" to the farmers. Meanwhile, the federal government paid off the bankers who held the loan, and itself took the role of lender. As soon as the CCF government was installed in office, the federal government demanded payment. The provincial government offered its treasury bills (I.O.U.'s) for the full amount at 3 per cent interest; but although treasury bills of other provinces and of Saskatchewan previously had been accepted by the federal treasury, they were flatly rejected for the seed grain debt.

In February, 1945, the federal government took the drastic step of withholding the subsidy due to Saskatchewan under the wartime federal-provincial tax agreement. For six months the controversy raged in Ottawa and throughout the province. The rural municipalities, in conference, backed the Saskatchewan government position. An arbitral tribunal, composed of one appointee of each government and a third appointed by the other two, was empaneled and assigned the task of adjudicating the validity of the federal withholding of the subsidy on account of the seed grain debt. In September the tribunal decided the case in favor of the federal government, Professor Frank R. Scott (Saskatchewan appointee) dissenting.

The seed grain debt was settled within a month. On October 1, 1945, an agreement was reached under which the province promised to pay the federal government more than $7,500,000 over a period of eleven years. The balance was to be collected from farmers by rural municipalities and transmitted to the Dominion treasury by mid-1948.

Provincial Radio License Denied.—In 1946 the province sought to purchase a Moose Jaw radio station, CHAB, and transfer its broadcast license to a "crown company." Permission to make this transfer was denied by the federal government, allegedly on the grounds that the Canadian Broadcasting Corporation (CBC) could not permit private companies to establish networks and that the CBC could itself render better service. Saskatchewan officials were quick to point out that they contemplated no network and that provincial ownership was scarcely private. Since station CHAB was privately owned, the choice was between private operation and provincial operation, for the Dominion had made no known move toward acquiring the station for CBC. Manitoba has two provincially owned stations, the licenses of which might be lost if the federal government imposed a general ban on provincial stations. In response to a question in the House of Commons, C. D. Howe, federal Minister of Reconstruction, declared: "I can say the government has decided that, since broadcasting is the sole responsibility of the dominion government, broadcasting licenses shall not be issued to other governments or corporations owned by other governments. In regard to the two stations in Manitoba discussions are taking place with the government of that province which we hope will lead to the purchase of these two stations by the dominion government."[13]

SOCIALIZED ENTERPRISES

The most striking difference between the CCF and the old parties in policy matters is found on the economic front: the CCF stands for the socialization of the principal means of production, distribution, and exchange; the Liberals and Conservatives support the private enterprise system. The limited powers and geographic area of a Canadian province make it impossible for a CCF provincial government to carry the socialization process to the party's ultimate goal. This would appear especially true in Saskatchewan, which depends so much upon wheat for

---

[13] House of Commons, *Debates*, Official Report, daily edition, 85 (May 3, 1946): 1209.

its economic well-being. On the other hand, the number and influence of vested interests actually rooted in Saskatchewan is rather small and fairly easy to identify. Most of the great corporations with stakes in the province are owned and managed from central Canada or abroad. Since manufacturing was little developed in Saskatchewan, the question of appropriating existing concerns arose to a less degree than it would in an industrialized region.

In the review of the socialized enterprises that follows, it should be borne in mind that the CCF is committed to approach socialization not only through nationalization and provincialization, but also through municipal and cooperative endeavor. The reader should give particular attention to the fields chosen for socialization. On the one hand, the province has sought to take over or provide competition for corporations that are alleged to exploit the people; in this category may be classified those handling electric power, those manufacturing farm implements, and those selling insurance. On the other hand, the CCF government has entered various light industries closely related to the processing of the province's raw materials; these include its brick plant, wool mill, tannery, shoe factory, fish filleting plants, and others. Through these years under CCF rule, there has been a preoccupation with broadening the economic base of the province. The great depression came early and stayed late in Saskatchewan, and recollections of it are deeply etched in the minds of the people. If another economic collapse occurs, the government hopes to have an industrial plant sufficient to process the raw materials of the province and to provide from within itself housing, clothing, and food for its people.

Most of the provincialization of economic enterprises in Saskatchewan has been accomplished through the legal mechanism of the "crown company." Under the Crown Corporations Act, broad powers were given to the government to create provincially owned companies to operate industrial and commercial enterprises. The appropriate minister, with the approval of the cabinet, may lease, purchase, or appropriate properties needed. The crown company is not under direct departmental control, but a majority of the directors (usually two out of three) are ministers or deputy ministers.

Insurance.—After studying statistics on the cost of insurance premiums and the amount of benefits paid in Saskatchewan, the CCF government concluded that the costs were excessive.[14] The Saskatchewan Government Insurance Office was opened in June, 1945, and offered policies to protect against fire, automobile, liability, and other losses. Financial stability was assured by providing for advances from the provincial treasury. At the end of the first year of operation, the office was reported to have written fire insurance policies with an aggregate coverage of more than $30,000,000; the central office staff had been increased to fifty, and some five hundred agents had been appointed.

Although government entry into the insurance field was opposed by existing companies and agents doing business in the province, the sharpest opposition came to the surface in 1946 when compulsory automobile insurance was introduced. Advertising even in the CCF paper,

---

[14] O. W. Valleau, Minister of Social Welfare, 1944–1948, quoted figures for the ten-year period 1935–1944, indicating that for fire insurance Saskatchewan people paid out about $28,000,000 in premiums and received about $7,000,000 in loss payments. See *Saskatchewan Commonwealth*, November 28, 1945.

the *Saskatchewan Commonwealth,* insurance interests attempted to head off the compulsory plan. Government spokesmen argued that compulsory insurance was necessary to protect society against the irresponsible driver, and that its plan provided greater coverage at less cost than policies with commercial concerns. The plan required that for each vehicle and driver a premium be paid at the time of licensing, ranging from $4.50 to $6 for a private car and $1 for a private operator.

The volume of the government insurance business was also increased greatly in 1946 by enactment of a law requiring schools, hospitals, and all other institutions receiving grants to place their insurance with the government office.

Electric Power.—By far the most extensive of the going concerns taken over by the Saskatchewan government is Dominion Electric Power, Ltd. Controlling interest was acquired by the purchase of common stock early in 1945. By autumn the province had acquired 90 per cent of the common stock, and the concern was thereby no longer liable to taxation by the federal government.[15] Provincial Treasurer C. M. Fines estimates that the government can pay off preferred stock and bondholders out of earnings and own the enterprise clear of debt in twelve to fifteen years.

Acquisition of the Dominion Electric Power concern not only added 6,500 customers to the Saskatchewan Power Commission, but was of great importance in building a province-wide public power system. Dominion's power plant at Estevan, burning cheap lignite coal, could be connected with the whole southeastern power system by building some thirty miles of line. Some of the savings

---

[15] *Saskatchewan Commonwealth,* August 8, 1945.

made possible by coordination were passed along to customers in the form of rate reductions in 1945. The commission also added customers and facilities through the purchase of the Prairie Power Co., Ltd., and the Saskatchewan properties of Canadian Utilities, Ltd.

Farm Implements.—The CCF government does not claim credit for originating the agricultural implement cooperative, but it has participated modestly in financing the venture. Canadian Cooperative Implements, Ltd., may prove to be an effective answer to the high prices and protective tariffs that have long characterized the farm implement industry in North America. In the fall of 1944 the governments of the three prairie provinces pledged a loan of $750,000 to help this cooperative endeavor. Saskatchewan's third of the initial $250,000 was paid in January, 1945. Other financial aid will come from other cooperatives and by the sale of shares to individuals. Operating a factory at Winnipeg, the cooperative will manufacture many types of farm equipment. The farmers of western Canada hope that it will provide effective competition for the giant Massey-Harris firm and for the several American concerns that sell their products in Canada.

Fur Marketing.—One of the first economic enterprises established by the CCF government was the Saskatchewan Fur Marketing Service. It is an agency designed to protect the trappers and fur farmers of the province by securing for them the highest possible return for their product. Operating in Regina, the service receives pelts from trappers, grades these, and assigns them to standard lots. The furs are sold at auction, the buyers coming from the major fur centers of Canada and the United States. If bids are below fair valuation, the furs are bought back by the service and offered for sale again later. The cost of operating the service is met mainly through a small selling commission. In the first year of operation, 1945, sales through the Service amounted to nearly $500,000, at four auctions. The 1946 sales were considerably greater.

Wood Products.—Saskatchewan's timber resources are much less than those of most of the provinces, but it does have forests that can be utilized. Like the furs and the fish, the province's timber is mainly in the north, where much of the population ekes out a meager living on marginal farmlands. The men of the north traditionally have gone to the woods in the long winter season to fell trees and haul out logs. In order to stimulate this activity and to assure maximum returns to those who engage in it, the Saskatchewan Timber Board was created. Its job is to buy, sell, and distribute forest products. Operating from a headquarters in Prince Albert, the board has exclusive control over all timber cut on crown lands, and markets it as pulpwood, railroad ties, telephone poles, and in other forms. The province also established at Prince Albert a box factory that employs one hundred workers. It was expropriated from former owners after a labor dispute in 1945.

The Saskatchewan timber enterprise has been vigorously attacked by C. D. Howe, federal Minister of Reconstruction, and enthusiastically supported by farmers in the province and by CCF spokesmen in the House of Commons. The elimination of the private middleman is necessitated, from the CCF point of view, by the marginal nature of timber operations in the province. The utility of a well-developed wood products industry in the event of a depression is obvious; it might enable the province to continue a home-building program in spite of generally adverse economic conditions. Since 1946, timber operations have been merged with the handling of fish products in a single corporation called Saskatchewan Lake and Forest Products, the operations of which are supervised by the Minister of Natural Resources and Industrial Development.

Fish Filleting.—Saskatchewan is not as important in fisheries as are several other provinces. An inland province, its fish catch is limited to the rivers and lakes, largely in its northern region. On the other hand, the northern lakes are well stocked and the development of the fish industry has been retarded only by the lack of processing and distributive facilities. Recognizing the potential value of these resources, and anxious to provide further employment opportunities for people in the north, the government acquired three filleting plants and created a fish marketing agency, Saskatchewan Fish Products, now merged into Saskatchewan Lake and Forest Products, as just stated.

This enterprise involves the purchase of fish from lake fishermen, inspection, and filleting. The prepared fish is then quick-frozen, wrapped, packed, and shipped to market. A modest concern, this crown company will never employ large numbers of people or make a major dent in the economic life of the province. It can, however, provide jobs in an area of low earnings, and helps to bring a valuable foodstuff to the market. There have been reports of increased prices to fishermen since the government agency has been operating this field.

Wool Mill.—In June, 1945, the government announced the formation of the Saskatchewan Wool Products Corporation, which became a unit of Saskatchewan Government Industries in July, 1946. Machinery was purchased and installed in a three-story building in Moose Jaw, and production commenced in the autumn. The mill is operated by about fifty employees. The corporation purchases Saskatchewan wool, stores it in the warehouse of the Canadian Cooperative Wool Growers' Association, and processes it into blankets and other products. This enterprise does not compete with any commercial concern already in the province.

The government decided to enter the wool business in order to assure stabilized prices and maximum returns to Saskatchewan wool growers, to supply wool products to consumers at fair prices, and to provide modest employment opportunities. The wool blankets produced are of high quality, and the volume of unfilled orders indicates a lively buyer interest in the product. With appropriate provincial pride, the department stores of Regina, Moose Jaw, and Saskatoon feature the government-manufactured blankets.

Leather Products.—Saskatchewan Leather Products, a government-owned corporation, was established in 1945. The first enterprise started by the corporation was a shoe factory in Regina. Machinery was purchased and installed in the fall of 1945. Approximately 100 employees will be required for maintenance of full operation. Beginning with the manufacture of work shoes, the plant may turn to dress shoes and other leather products as the operators acquire the necessary skills.

The same corporation in 1946 commenced operation of a tannery. Equipment was purchased from a Calgary plant and transferred to Regina. About fifty persons will be employed. Beef hides are obtained from slaughterhouses of the province; horsehides are bought from the Swift Current plant of the Saskatchewan Horse Marketing Cooperative Association, a cooperative financially backed by the government. The purpose of provincial entry into the tannery and shoe manufacturing businesses is to protect Saskatchewan producers and consumers, to diversify the economy of the province, and to provide employment.

Under the crown company consolidation effected in July, 1946, the tannery, shoe factory, and wool mill were combined in a single corporation known as Saskatchewan Government Industries. The minister of municipal affairs was made the responsible minister in charge. Some critics asserted that the merger was carried out in order to hide losses in particular enterprises, especially in the wool mill. The consolidation precipitated the resignation of the managing director of the leather products concern and terminated a questionable contract which named as sole wholesale distributor the private company he headed.

Mineral Products.—In order to utilize the clay and coal deposits of the Estevan region, and to provide both employment and a useful building material, the government purchased early in 1945 the brick-manufacturing plant of a private concern. The government concern was first known as the Saskatchewan Clay Products Corporation, but in 1946 was merged into the Saskatchewan Minerals Corporation. Its facilities are capable of producing about 10,000,000 bricks a year, and it may employ as many as 100 men during the working season. Special attention is being given by the University of Saskatchewan to the possibility of developing other ceramic products.

In mid-1946 another enterprise, a sodium sulfate plant, was launched at the small town of Chaplin, which lies between Moose Jaw and Swift Current. Production of this substance, used in processing rough pulp products, may sometime become an important industry in the province.

Horse Products.—The coexistence of an oversupply of horses in southern Saskatchewan and an acute demand for horse meat in liberated countries of western Europe led to the establishment of a horse processing plant in Swift Current. It is operated by the Saskatchewan Horse Marketing Cooperative Association, which received a $50,000 loan from the provincial government. The basic product is meat, which is sold to the Belgian government under contract. The initial agreement called for delivery of 10,000 tons of meat for an estimated $2,000,000. An important by-product is horsehide, which is sold to the government tannery in Regina. At the time the plant was established, there were an estimated 250,000 surplus horses. The farmers reportedly are now able to secure several times the previous prevailing low price for their horses.

Bus Lines.—One of the most recent proprietary enterprises entered by the Saskatchewan government is in the field of transportation. In a jurisdiction so large in area and so hemmed in by severe winters, the arteries of travel and trade assume special importance. The early pattern of settlement in the prairies was determined primarily by the routes of the railroads. By wagon and sled and boat, settlers were able to fan out over the plains. At a later period, the automobile and improved roads made possible rapid movement to most of the settled areas at most times of the year. The airplane has become of vital importance in recent development of the north country, for it has made possible the penetration of remote sections without roads but with lake surfaces for landing.

In December, 1945, the government announced that the Saskatchewan Transportation Company, a crown concern, would operate, 3,300 miles of bus lines when equipment should become available. Modern buses were purchased at a Fort William, Ontario, factory, and the first deliveries were made in May, 1946. At least one small coach line was bought out by the crown concern. The transcontinental service of the Greyhound Lines will, however, continue to pass through Saskatchewan. The principal advantage of government ownership of bus transportation services would appear to be that it makes possible a coordinated development of common carrier and highway development and perhaps a more rapid extension of good service to remote sections.

Economic Planning.—One of the basic planks in CCF platforms, both provincial and national, is the demand for economic planning. An early step by Premier Douglas was the creation of an Economic Advisory Committee, composed of members of the faculty at the University of Saskatchewan. The committee consisted of G. E. Britnell, chairman, F. C. Cronkite, and Vernon Fowke; Thomas McLeod served as its secretary. The purpose of the committee was to advise the cabinet and individual ministers concerning various aspects of problems referred to the committee.

Another agency was added early in 1946, following the arrival in Regina of George W. Cadbury, a British industrialist. Cadbury was made chairman of the Economic Advisory and Planning Board, which is composed of both ministers and others. He is also chief industrial executive and coordinator. A member of the boards of all the crown companies, Cadbury has become the directing genius of government enterprises.

A member of the well-known family of chocolate manufacturers, Cadbury has had a varied career as managing director of food processing concerns and as a member of the British aircraft mission to Washington at the time of World War II. Born in 1907, he was educated at Cambridge University and the University of Pennsylvania. The combination of business experience and of extended interest in social and economic planning as evidenced by his Labour Party membership makes his counsel of unusual value and great importance to the CCF government.

An idea for a new enterprise is referred to the Economic Advisory and Planning Board. It makes a recommendation to the cabinet. If it is favorable, the project is then sent for study to a committee consisting of Cadbury, the appropriate minister, and others. On receiving this report, the cabinet decides whether or not to create a crown company by a lieutenant-governor-in-council order as is authorized by law. New public enterprises are launched with treasury funds allocated according to Planning Board recommendations. In 1946 the cabinet decided not to charge interest on capital advanced to crown companies, thus giving them a chance to get on their feet as a private company does—by means of equity capital.

Every company has a minister who is chairman of the corporation and its spokesman. After some experimentation, it was decided that managers of the concerns should not be members of the boards. The manager is classed as a technician, whose political views are not concerned, but the boards are deliberately composed of persons who are consciously socialist.

HEALTH AND WELFARE SERVICES

Socialist parties everywhere devote much attention to social welfare services; indeed, some are so much preoccupied with labor and social legislation of a remedial type that they fail materially to alter the economic system. The CCF in Saskatchewan has achieved a nice balance in this regard. Although the record in socialization is outstanding, considering the limited powers of a provincial government and the nature of the Saskatchewan economy, the record on the welfare front, especially in health services, promises to be one of the major achievements under CCF rule.

Before describing and evaluating welfare services, one should set down some introductory words of caution. As we have seen already, Saskatchewan is economically a poor province, and it was just emerging from the finanacial wringer of the 1930's when the war started. Therefore, welfare standards are likely to look low to American and central Canadian critics. On the asset side of the ledger, however, medical care was already socialized to a considerable degree in rural areas through the device of the "municipal doctor," a physician employed on salary by rural municipalities. Approximately one-third of the rural municipalities had municipal doctors and free medical services at the time the CCF came to power. The province also pioneered in providing free treatment for cancer and tuberculosis, and early gave subsidies to hospitals throughout the province. In health services, therefore, the task of the CCF government was to go forward from the plateau which had been reached by previous municipal and provincial endeavor.

Health Planning.—At the time the CCF government was formed, T. C. Douglas assumed the portfolio of minister of health in addition to his tasks as premier. This was a fortunate solution for the problem posed. No physician was elected to the legislative assembly in the election of 1944, yet the CCF planned some of its most significant work in the health field. The fact that Premier Douglas was serving as minister of health insured high priority for health matters on the agenda of the government. He brought to the position qualities of leadership and a degree of social consciousness rarely found among medical practitioners.

Soon after the government took office, Dr. Henry E. Sigerist of Johns Hopkins University was appointed to head a survey of Saskatchewan health needs. After the Sigerist commission filed its report, revealing the deficiencies of the province in medical care, a permanent agency was created to plan the future development of health services. This continuing body is the Saskatchewan Health Services Planning Commission, established under legislation enacted in 1944. To this body Douglas originally appointed T. H. McLeod, C. C. Gibson, and Dr. M. C. Sheps. As had been expected, these survey groups found health services "spotty," ranging from relatively adequate in urban areas to nonexistent in remote rural areas.

Instead of seeking improvement through the conventional method of contributory health insurance, plans were made for free medical services to reach in the end every resident of the province. So large a proportion of Saskatchewan people is self-employed on farms that the usual sickness insurance scheme financed by pay-roll deductions would provide inadequate coverage. Studies showed also a lack of medical and nursing personnel, shortages in hospital beds, and many other deficiencies.

Health Regions.—Although greatest stress has been placed on the building of strong local health centers, Saskatchewan health planners recognized that a system based solely on local units would be spotty. In order to build larger hospitals, provide services of specialists, and buy expensive equipment, pooling of resources was necessary. Therefore the government sponsored the plan of dividing the province into fourteen health regions, each large enough to provide the essential services and facilities. As finally demarcated, these regions range in population from 12,569 to 109,619 and in hospital and nursing-home beds from 1.5 per 1,000 to 6.7 per 1,000.

The government has been very cautious about inaugurating health regions without full local approval. After local authorities request aid, provincial officials confer with them and help plan health services for the region. After the plan evolved has been discussed thoroughly, the matter is placed before the electorate in the form of a plebiscite. The first two such proposals were placed before the people in the municipal elections of November, 1945. The result was a strong affirmative vote of 71 per cent in Region 1 (Swift Current area in southwest corner of province), and 76 per cent in Region 3 (Weyburn-Estevan area in southeast corner of province). Five other regions had been organized and put into operation as of mid-1948.

Under the regional scheme, health services are rendered on three levels. At the regional center is a regional hospital, at which a central staff of doctors and nurses do their work, and from which the regional health officer directs the services of the whole area. Each region has several district hospitals, which are well-equipped smaller units, but may call specialists from the regional center. Local health centers provide the basic services to people in their home communities. Only in the Swift Current region has a comprehensive health program been established. It includes virtually all services and is paid for through taxation.

Health Progress.—One of the first problems tackled by the CCF government on the health front was a deficiency in physicians, nurses, and dentists. The legislative assembly appropriated money for a medical school at the University of Saskatchewan, and that school has been launched. In order to keep in the province the doctors trained there, consideration has been given to a possible contract between any medical student receiving a scholarship and the province, under which the student agrees to practice in Saskatchewan a definite number of years. It might be added that the financing of the medical school has embarrassed the University administration greatly, but the province has now built a $7,000,000 hospital.

In January, 1945, free medical care was extended to a group of 25,000 recipients of public assistance, including aged persons, the blind, and dependent children and mothers. To this group will soon be added some 7,000 incapacitated persons. Free diagnosis and treatment have been provided for persons suffering from cancer. All health services are now provided free for those who are mentally ill.

In order to strengthen hospital services in rural areas, the government has greatly increased its loans and grants to small community and union hospitals. This assistance is given on the basis of need for hospital facilities in the area and on the relative incapacity of the community to pay. One of the more spectacular services instituted by the province is an air ambulance, which transports persons stricken with illness in isolated communities to places where hospital and medical care are available.

The 1946 legislature enacted the Hospitalization Act, which provides free hospitalization for all residents of the province. A levy of $5 per person, up to a maximum of $30 per family, was authorized to pay the costs of the plan. A hospital construction program between 1944 and 1948 nearly doubled the hospital-bed ratio in the province.

Social Welfare.—During the election campaign of 1944, the CCF declared its intention of raising old-age pensions by $5 a month (to a new total of $30) and to make other forms of public assistance more nearly adequate. Unlike many social-democratic regimes, however, the CCF government, during its first two years in office, gave more emphasis to fundamental economic reforms, and added to the social services, excluding health, in a very modest way. The minister of social welfare concentrated initially on internal improvements in his department in the way of simplifying procedures. Then, in January, 1945, free medical services were extended to aged and blind pensioners and to mothers and children.

The first budget of the CCF government provided funds for increased public assistance. Old-age pensions were raised by $3 a month, to a new maximum of $28; and mothers' allowances were increased by $10 a month, to a new maximum of $25. Although the administration of assistance was left in the hands of local governments, as was the responsibility for supplying half the funds, standards of payments were raised throughout the province to higher levels, more comparable to those in urban centers. In 1949 the old-age pension was raised to $42.50 monthly.

The first CCF budget provided an increase of $1,400,000 for social welfare services. While most of this went for increased direct aid, some was used for additional training of social workers, grants to private welfare agencies, and provision of homes for the needy, aged, and blind.

Labor Legislation.—Because the CCF is a farmer-labor party, it was to be expected that a government formed by it would give attention to the problems of both farmer and workman. Considering how little industrialized the province of Saskatchewan is, however, the record of the Douglas government in the field of labor legislation is indeed remarkable. There is abundant evidence that organized labor throughout Canada has been impressed by this record, made by a legislative assembly composed largely of representatives of rural areas.

The first and most basic piece of legislation is the Trade Union Act of 1944. It established the Saskatchewan Labor Relations Board, which is now composed of two representatives of labor, two of employers, two of the general public, and a chairman from the government. The act guarantees the right of collective bargaining and outlaws a number of "unfair labor practices." After the board has recognized a union as a bargaining agent, collective bargaining with that union by the employer is mandatory. The board is empowered to conduct elections in order to determine the wishes of employees with respect to bargaining agents. Like other labor acts adopted during the war, the Trade Union Act could be applied only incompletely to begin with, because of wartime regulations made by the federal government to be applied in war industries. The provincial acts were, however, fully enforced after July 1, 1946. Although one section of the law was held *ultra vires* by the Saskatchewan Court of

Appeal in 1947, it was later upheld in a decision of the judicial committee of the Privy Council in London in 1948.

Another law enacted in 1944 was the Annual Holidays Act, which allows to employed persons two weeks' holiday with pay. Farm laborers are not included in this legislation. The CCF government also amended the provincial minimum wage law to provide the highest minimum permissible under federal wage controls. The provincial workmen's conpensation scheme has been amended to provide injured workers with 75 per cent of their normal wages, and a minimum of $15 per week was established.

Often the acid test of a government in the field of labor relations is found in its treatment of its own employees. Within a few months after taking office, the CCF government left little room for doubt on this front. In April, 1945, the government signed with two union locals an agreement believed to be the first ever entered into by either a federal or a provincial government in Canada. The union was the United Civil Servants of Canada (C.C.L.); it represented 600 employees of provincial mental hospitals in Weyburn and North Battleford. The agreement provided for collective bargaining, maintenance of membership, wage increases, overtime pay, equal status for women, and a number of other features.[16] A second agreement, signed soon afterward, was drawn up between the government and the employees of its provincial telephone system, represented by the United Telephone Workers of Canada (C.C.L.). It provides for a minimum basic wage, sick leave, double time for work done on holidays, and several other gains for the employees. A number of other agreements between the government and unions of employees have been signed.

---

[16] *Saskatchewan Commonwealth*, April 11, 1945.

There have, however, been difficulties with the inside civil service at Regina which have proved very vexatious in solution.

Education.—Education is a particularly challenging field for the Saskatchewan CCF. First, the schools suffered greatly during the period of economic distress in the 1930's. Even in 1942 the Regina *Leader-Post* had columns of advertisements under "Teachers Wanted," the salaries offered being as low as $700 a year. At the time the CCF government took office in 1944, teaching positions were advertised with salaries as low as $900. Second, the CCF has always regarded education as one of the major roads to a better society. Equality of educational opportunity is obviously prerequisite to the social mobility necessary if each individual is to achieve the place in society appropriate to his ability and industry. Third, the leadership of the CCF has always included a strong element of teachers, many of whom have pioneered in rural schools in remote sections.

For minister of education, Premier Douglas chose the young and able Woodrow S. Lloyd. Under his direction an aggressive program of school improvement was undertaken at once.

In order to attract people to the profession of teaching, in which there was an alarming decrease, immediate steps were taken to increase teachers' salaries. For holders of permanent certificates, salaries were increased from a minimum of $700 to $1,200 per year; those with less training and experience were assured at least $1,000. At the time this minimum was adopted, in 1944, it was reported to be the highest in Canada. Experiments were made in teacher training, especially in the direction of making practice teaching realistic by confronting the student teacher during his training with the multiple-grade class of the average country school.

Tackling one of the knottiest problems of school improvement, the government encouraged larger units of school administration. Small one-room schools are rarely efficient and seldom successful in providing the essential educational services. The miniature school district often lacks the taxable property to provide adequately for its school. The smaller the school, the less the chances are of good equipment and good teaching personnel. The minister of education has urged consolidation of districts as "the basic step which must be taken."[17] The goal set, under a law enacted in 1944, was to consolidate 5,000 rural districts into 60. Under legislation enacted at the 1945 session of the legislature, a vote on the formation of a larger unit is held if 20 per cent of the ratepayers petition to that effect. By November 30, 1945, 29 larger units had been organized,[18] and by January, 1949, 46 larger units had been set up.

In order to induce the acceptance of improved standards and to shift the cost of schools more fully on the province, increased grants were made by the province to school districts. For 1947–48, provincial grants were nearly double those of the 1943–44 level. Free textbooks were supplied to elementary school pupils beginning in the autumn of 1945. Special grants were made for the schools in the north in order to improve educational services on the rugged frontier. Curricular changes have been made in the high schools to give greater freedom of choice and place more emphasis on social studies.

---

[17] Radio address, printed in full in *Saskatchewan Commonwealth*, May 2, 1945.
[18] Saskatchewan, Department of Education, *Annual Report*, 1944–45 (Regina: King's Printer, 1945), p. 10.

Great emphasis has been attached to the program of adult education. "Study-action" leaders were recruited and placed permanently in the rural areas in which they worked. At first directed by Watson Thomson, who had had much experience in the W.E.A. in Britain, the adult program sought to assist people, particularly rural folk, to study their community and its needs, and then to encourage them to take appropriate action. This phase of educational reform has been singled out for attack by the daily press. Until his resignation, Thomson was lambasted as an extreme leftist. Later, the attack centered on a study-action outline, *Atomic Future,* by Dyson Carter, who was accused of Communist affiliations.

The University of Saskatchewan has received considerable attention from the new government. In addition to the projected setting up of a medical school, mentioned previously, the general provincial appropriation to the University was increased, and a number of special grants were made. In 1946 the organic act of the University was amended and the number of members of its board of governors was raised from 10 to 14, of whom the government appoints seven.

OTHER PROBLEMS

Farm Security.—Saskatchewan farmers, now comparatively prosperous, have vivid recollections of the great depression of the 1930's. Many a farm family, hardworking and on good land, lost everything through mortgage foreclosure following crop-failure years. Tillers of the soil appeared to take all the risks and to suffer all the losses. Interest and principal payments on mortgages had to be made, and constituted the first claim on every crop, ranking above food for the farm family and seed for the next year's crop.

The CCF government sought through legislation to require the lenders of money to share some of the risks and losses of the farm debtor. The Farm Security Act declared immune from foreclosure that land, up to 160 acres, upon which the farm home stands, so long as it remains a farm homestead. Under an exemptions act, the real and personal property made free from seizure for debts was listed. For farmers this included food to meet the needs of the family until the next harvest, implements, seed grain, and livestock up to 6 horses, 6 sheep, 4 pigs, and 50 fowls.

In years of crop failure when value of produce is less than $6 per acre, the obligation of the farmers to make repayments on principal is postponed by one year. The purpose of this legislation is to assure the farmer resources enough to permit him to live and to put in his next crop. A mortgage association and the Dominion government challenged the constitutionality of the Farm Security Act before the Supreme Court of Canada, which in May, 1947, declared the legislation *ultra vires*. Saskatchewan's appeal to the judicial committee of the Privy Council in London was rejected in November, 1948.

Led by J. H. Brockelbank, minister of municipal affairs, the CCF government has worked closely with local authorities in the province. Not long after the CCF came to power, an intensive study of municipal units was launched. The demand for large units of administration is especially keen with respect to the rural municipalities. The original definition of boundaries was done in 1908 before much was known about resources and before the development of modern communications. Rural municipalities today vary greatly in population (from 465 to 5,200) and in financial capacity. Like the demand for

larger school units, the pressure for larger rural municipalities is justified on the grounds of better services and
greater efficiency. It is argued that savings can be made
by reducing the amount of overhead and by larger-scale
public works operations.

After reassuring leaders of the rural municipalities that
they would not be forced into the larger unit mold,
Brockelbank created a committee in April, 1945, to in-
quire into the question of rural municipality boundaries.
Composed of two University of Saskatchewan professors,
one official of the rural municipalities association, one of
the rural municipalities secretary-treasurers' organizations, and one of the United Farmers, the committee
would appear to be thoroughly representative of the interested parties. As this is written, no substantial changes
have been made in local government boundaries.

Financing Saskatchewan Socialism.—Coming to power
at a time of comparative prosperity, the CCF government
found it possible to expand public services considerably
without adding materially to the tax burden. Provincial
Treasurer C. M. Fines presented balanced budgets to the
legislature in 1945, 1946, and 1947. Both revenues and
expenditures were up, and the provincial debt was reduced materially both by repayment and adjustment. In
1945 the gasoline tax was increased by one cent a gallon,
in order to provide funds for road improvement. Additional revenue has accrued from mining operations
through the Mining Royalties Tax, which was amended
by order-in-council in 1945. Enacted for social purpose,
yet productive of some revenue, is the Mineral Taxation
Act. This tax, unsuccessfully challenged in the disallowance row of 1945, places levies both on holders of mineral
rights and on mineral valuations.

In its second budget, that of 1946, the CCF government removed the sales tax (called the "educational" tax) from foodstuffs, thus reducing revenues an estimated $2,000,000 a year.

If or when the honeymoon period of good times ends, it may be expected that the CCF regime will increase taxes to whatever level is necessary to assure continued expansion of the social services.

Improving the Public Service.—In order to secure supplies of the best quality at the lowest prices, a Purchasing Agency was established in 1944 by the Douglas government. It has been estimated officially that this agency effects savings of $200,000 a year.

During the 1946 session of the assembly, legislative radio broadcasts were used to keep the people informed on issues before that body. Thirty-six hours of radio time were taken for the purpose. Time was divided between government supporters and opposition on the basis of about 3 to 1. The popularity of these broadcasts was so great that they will be continued at future legislative sessions.

One of the early steps of the CCF government was to enfranchise for provincial voting young people of eighteen years of age. It was appropriate that this action should have been taken in the spring of 1945 when boys in their late teens were playing so large a part in the victories of World War II. Subsequent legislation extended the right to vote at eighteen in municipal elections as well.

In June, 1945, the government purchased a Regina printing plant for $85,000 and commenced operations as the Saskatchewan Government Printing Company, a crown corporation. Doing approximately one-half the total printing work of the provincial government, the company was expected to repay through earnings its initial purchase price in less than three years.

Cooperatives.—Even the name of the CCF proclaims its interest in the cooperatives. Saskatchewan, with 1,100 cooperatives having an aggregate of 300,000 members and assets of $71,000,000, has more cooperative enterprise than any comparable unit in North America.[19] Large sectors of its economic life are substantially under cooperative management. The creation of a department of cooperatives and the appointment of L. F. McIntosh as minister of cooperatives were evidence of the importance which the government assigns to this field. The financial assistance given by the Saskatchewan government to Canadian Cooperative Implements, Ltd., and to the Saskatchewan Horse Marketing Cooperative Association, has already been mentioned.

With a view to international cooperative collaboration, both Douglas and McIntosh have negotiated with Scottish and English cooperative officials. It is proposed that Saskatchewan provide farm products in exchange for manufactured goods produced by the British cooperative movement. A Saskatchewan trade and information office has been established in the United Kingdom.

Great attention has been given to the development of cooperative farms. Cooperative farming is thought to offer considerable utility in Saskatchewan. First, grain farming, now so greatly mechanized, requires much expensive equipment which can best be owned on a communal basis. Second, cooperative villages offer the possibility of more comfort and cultural and social life, abating the rigors and loneliness of the prairie winters.

---

[19] Figures from the *Saskatchewan News*, August 12, 1946, p. 2.

The number of cooperative farms is not large. By 1948, thirty-six were in operation. Of these, only five were cooperative farms proper, with full pooling of land and labor; others were for cooperative operation of farm machinery, grazing of stock, and other broad purposes.[20] Most attention has been given to the Matador Cooperative Farm, which is being launched in southwestern Saskatchewan by twenty veterans of World War II on sixteen sections of provincially owned land. It is a full cooperative, pooling labor, land, equipment, and livestock. Other crown lands will eventually provide farms for approximately 1,250 returned service men.

Rehabilitation.—The task of assisting war veterans to adjust themselves to peacetime pursuits was assigned to a new Department of Reconstruction and Rehabilitation, headed by J. H. Sturdy. The department provides a number of services for veterans. It offers them the long-term use of provincial lands in order to establish farming enterprises. It sponsors formation of local committees to counsel them. It conducts surveys to locate employment opportunities.

An interesting project of the rehabilitation minister is a portable spray-painting outfit manned by veterans. The idea grew out of a dual concern—to provide business opportunities and useful employment for veterans, and to improve the appearance of some 80,000 sets of farm buildings in the province, a large proportion of which had become terribly drab in the long depression years. Only small crews are needed, and hence the amount of employment created will be negligible, but the results of the project may literally change the face of Saskatche-

---

[20] Saskatchewan, Bureau of Publications, *Report of Your Government* (Regina: King's Printer, 1948), pp. 46–47.

wan. Guides to modernizing farm homes have been issued, and a survey of rural electrification has been instituted.

The ministry also has jurisdiction over two crown companies, the Saskatchewan Reconstruction Corporation and the Saskatchewan Reconstruction Housing Corporation. The former was created for the purpose of buying war assets, buildings, and equipment from the federal government, and of operating repair shops. The housing agency provides emergency living accommodations by moving and reconditioning war-surplus buildings. One of the principal locations of housing activity is Saskatoon, where temporary homes have been provided for veterans who are students at the University of Saskatchewan.

CHAPTER VIII

Party Policy

DIRECTLY after the Calgary conference, at which the CCF was born, the provisional National Council appointed a committee to frame a policy declaration for the new movement.[1] The committee was composed of N. F. Priestley and W. N. Smith. Alderman M. J. Coldwell of Regina was requested to submit a draft of a manifesto to the committee. The research committee of the League for Social Reconstruction was invited to assist in the formulation of policy. Starting with the eight points laid down by the August, 1932, conference, the committee developed in the early months of 1933 the program contained in the manifesto adopted at the first national conference held at Regina in July of that same year.[2]

THE REGINA MANIFESTO

The program of the CCF adopted at Regina in July, 1933, has remained the basic statement of party policy. Subsequent policy statements have been formulated for special situations, but the general principles of the original program have remained the same.

The Regina Manifesto presents a socialist program. The CCF aims to replace the capitalist system with a social order from which basic injustice and inhumanity will be eliminated. The general outline of the new order

---

[1] Minutes of the meeting of the provisional National Council held at the close of the Calgary conference, August 1, 1932, p. 2.

[2] Minutes of the provisional National Council, Calgary, January 24-25, 1933, p. 4.

is then presented. Economic planning will replace un-regulated private enterprise. The new social order will be achieved through democratic political action; violence is rejected as a method of achieving power. Coldwell's declaration of a year before, that the new party did not wish to take office until a majority of the people under-stood and supported its program, became at Regina the established policy of the CCF. Beyond the official policy statements of the party and the resolutions adopted at national conventions and national council meetings, the most authoritative statements concerning the CCF pro-gram are found in *Social Planning for Canada*,[3] written by the research committee of the League for Social Re-construction, and *Make This Your Canada*,[4] by David Lewis and F. R. Scott. A series of resolutions adopted at the 1948 convention constitute the "First Term Pro-gram," the latest policy statement on record.

CCF policy of today includes not only the principles adopted in the Regina Manifesto, but also the many resolutions concerning policy which have been carried at the successive national conventions. The Regina Mani-festo remains the base from which more detailed and timely statements issue. The various aspects of the CCF program will here be considered in the order in which they were presented in the Regina Manifesto, but subse-quent additions and alterations will be included under each topic.

A PLANNED ECONOMY

Planning.—The first plank in the CCF platform relates to planning. In the words of the Regina Manifesto, it is a demand for "the establishment of a planned, socialized

---

[3] (Toronto: Nelson, 1935).
[4] (Toronto, Central Canada Publishing Co., 1943).

economic order, in order to make possible the most efficient development of the national resources and the most equitable distribution of the national income.''[5]

Economic plans will be under the direction of a National Planning Commission. The task of this commission is of heroic proportions; it would plan for the production, distribution, and exchange of all goods and services, and would direct the economic life of the Dominion generally. Although the Commission would enjoy a considerable measure of independence in its technical work, it would be ultimately responsible to the Cabinet and hence to Parliament and the people. The authoritative *Social Planning for Canada* anticipates a commission of some three to five members.[6]

It is anticipated that the planning policies would be determined by the Commission after consultation with the appropriate heads of socialized industries. The master plan would be formulated by the Commission in such a way as to provide for the efficient utilization of the resources of Canada. The goal would be to achieve for all the people the goods and services they desire and need.

At the time the Regina Manifesto was adopted, the idea of national planning was being discussed vigorously in many of the capitalist countries. The journals of the United States were filled with articles describing planning in the Soviet Union and proposing various schemes for combining the idea of ordered planning with the capitalist economic system. Since the original policy declaration of the CCF, World War II has taught Canada

[5] First plank of the CCF program adopted at the first national convention, Regina, Saskatchewan, July, 1933. The document will hereafter be cited as the Regina Manifesto. It has been most widely circulated in leaflet form. The planks in the platform will be cited by number.

[6] *Social Planning for Canada*, p. 234.

and the other belligerents a great deal about national planning. The necessities of wartime caused nations to marshal their resources with maximum efficiency. Although the CCF was critical of much of the war record of the Liberal government, it has not hesitated to point out how, by reviving wartime controls, a CCF government in Ottawa might produce plenty for all.

In spite of much propaganda for "free enterprise" throughout North America, it appears unlikely that an economic system that existed before World War II can be fully restored in either Canada or the United States. Any government in Ottawa, even a Conservative government, would have been called upon to ration or allocate for specified uses raw materials and goods which remained scarce after the war was over. There is wide public acceptance of the necessity for some kind of planning.

Although national CCF policy naturally stresses national planning, appropriate emphasis will be given to planning bodies on regional, provincial, and municipal levels. In *Make This Your Canada* the provincial field includes education, hydroelectric power, rural electrification, and the distribution of bread, milk, and coal. In the same work, municipal problems mentioned are housing, slum clearance, and town planning.

Banking and Finance.—The Regina Manifesto calls for "the socialization of all financial machinery—banking, currency, credit, and insurance—to make possible the effective control of currency, credit and prices, and the supplying of new productive equipment for socially desirable purposes."[7]

It was not difficult to persuade the western farmers, who have constituted an important element in the CCF

---

[7] Regina Manifesto, plank 2.

since its beginning, that public control over banking and finance is a necessary prerequisite in the new social order. The western farmers are largely debtors and have had firsthand experience with banks and mortgage concerns. The League for Social Reconstruction (L.S.R.) stressed the extreme importance of full socialization of finance, including capital investment. The manifesto of the I.L.P. of Manitoba adopted in 1926, and the proposal for a national policy formulated by the U.F.A. in 1932, contained planks of this sort.

The socialization process would begin with the acquisition of control over chartered banks and the construction of a national banking system. At its head would be a central bank in charge of all credit and price policy. Although sentiment in 1933 was rather strong for inflation and hostile toward the gold standard, declarations concerning these matters were fortunately left out of that part of the Manifesto which related to finance. L.S.R. studies demonstrate the danger that reformers concentrating on the panacea of inflation or by following the will-o'-the-wisp of social credit, may overlook real weaknesses in the financial system. There is a vague gesture toward the Social Crediters in the plank on taxation and public finance, in which it is proposed that public works be financed by the issuance of credit based on the national wealth of Canada.

Insurance companies are to be included in the socialization of finances because of their importance as a channel for the investment of individual savings. The Manifesto charges that needlessly high premiums are exacted from policyholders.

A sharp fight took place in the 1948 convention over the timing that should govern the socialization of financial institutions. The convention rejected a compromise resolution backed by the National Council, and adopted by a vote of 94 to 56 a resolution to include chartered banks in first term nationalization plans.

Socialization of Industry.—At the very heart of socialist doctrine lies the demand for social ownership and control of the major means of production and distribution. The CCF anticipates the socialization not only of public utilities but of all major manufacturing and wholesale enterprises. The line is not clearly drawn between the concerns that will be taken over by the national government, by provincial governments, or by cooperative organizations. The important thing is that ownership and management be placed in the hands of either public or cooperative agencies.

The Regina Manifesto provides for social ownership in the following terms: "Socialization (Dominion, Provincial or Municipal) of transportation, communications, electric power and all other industries and services essential to social planning, and their operation under the general direction of the Planning Commission by competent managements freed from day to day political interference."[8]

One of the first questions to be faced is the choice of industries for initial attention. As in the British Labour Party, the CCF anticipates that socialization should take place over a period of time. Should L.S.R. standards be used, the party would choose Canadian industries for early socialization according to their key importance, monopolistic role, demonstrated inefficiency, and control over natural resources. The "First Term Program" of 1948 called for immediate socialization of transportation,

[8] Regina Manifesto, plank 3.

the manufacture of iron and steel, the farm implement industry, meat packing, and fuel and power enterprises.

In addition to the fields specifically mentioned in the Manifesto, Canadian industries which would probably qualify for early national action are the manufacture of aluminum and nickel, and petroleum exploration and refining of the raw product. The smaller manufacturing and distributing concerns might well be left for the time being in private hands, provided that their functioning did not involve exploitation or antisocial tendencies, that they operated efficiently, and that they were loyal to the national plan.

Business enterprise under national or provincial ownership would not be operated under a single type of overhead organization. Modern governments have found several forms suitable for the management of socialized industries. Among the leading possibilities are (1) the public corporation idea and (2) the joint-stock company.

The public corporation plan as utilized in the United Kingdom calls for the establishment of a directing board for a particular socialized industry. Such a board, although appointed by the appropriate minister, has a large measure of autonomy in the management of the industry which it directs. This scheme has the advantage of preserving the operative independence enjoyed by private business, but it eliminates private profits and makes central planning possible. Examples of public corporations already in operation were the Canadian Broadcasting Corporation, the Hydroelectric Power Commission of Ontario, and the London Passenger Transport Board. Presumably, such public corporations would be established by act of Parliament or chartered by act of provincial legislative assemblies.

The joint-stock company, or mixed enterprise plan, is a scheme through which the government may acquire control of an existing concern without changing materially its form of organization. The government might purchase 51 per cent of the stock of a company over which it desired control and then permit the company to continue operations under policy dictated by the government. It is often suggested that the government could legitimately use the device of a holding company in order to bring scattered operating concerns under a unified control. Since 1936, the Bank of Canada has been controlled by the government through acquisition of 51 per cent of its stock.

A large measure of autonomy and a considerable sphere of action would be left to existing cooperative enterprises and others subsequently formed. More than any other of the labor parties in the British Commonwealth of Nations, the CCF reserves a place in its plans for a national economy for cooperative enterprises. Party policy calls for a vast extension of cooperation.

The CCF has also come to grips with the knotty problem of compensation of the former owners of socialized industries. One of the principal controversies in the Regina conference centered around this question. Left-wing delegates opposed the scheme proposed by the National Council on the grounds that it was too conciliatory toward the owners of private stocks and bonds. In the end, the National Council drafted a compromise proposal and it was adopted. It declares that no policy of outright confiscation is proposed. The broad principles are laid down that community welfare is paramount to private wealth. Some compensation for individuals and institutions whose need is great is recognized. It warns, however, that a CCF government will not rescue bankrupt concerns for the benefit of security holders nor build up a great debt in order to compensate "a functionless owner class."[9]

Agriculture.—It was perhaps inevitable that the Regina Manifesto, drafted in the depths of the great depression, should dwell upon the security of the farmer and place great stress upon cures for the sickness of Canadian agriculture. The plank on agriculture reads: "Security of tenure for the farmer upon his farm on conditions to be laid down by individual provinces; insurance against unavoidable crop failure; removal of the tariff burden from the operations of agriculture; encouragement of producers' and consumers' cooperatives; the restoration and maintenance of an equitable relationship between prices of agricultural products and those of other commodities and services; and improving the efficiency of export trade in farm products."[10]

Perhaps the most surprising feature of this item of the program, both to doctrinaire socialists and to hostile newspaper editors, was the absence of a declaration for the nationalization of land. Opponents of the CCF had anticipated the gift of a club with which to beat down farmers' support for the new party. Denied this effective weapon, the opposition newspapers cried out long and hard against this deviation from traditional socialist policy. CCF leaders have repeatedly pointed out that nationalization of the land may be a desirable step in an old country in which concentration of ownership has developed to an extreme degree. Indeed, the CCF government in Saskatchewan has turned some attention toward

[9] *Ibid.*
[10] Regina Manifesto, plank 4.

the possibilities of improving the lot of depressed farmers by means of cooperative farms. In general, however, sentiment within the party is strongly opposed to any deviation from the ideal of family ownership and operation of the farm, secure from mortgage foreclosure and capricious agricultural prices.

Stress is placed throughout on "security of tenure." Presumably, this would require easy credit facilities and extraordinary precautions against foreclosures. The severe plight of the Canadian farmer of 1933 was to be relieved in part by the rejuvenation of the purchasing power of the Canadian consumer through import-export boards and other devices.

The role of farmers' cooperative enterprises was to be expanded under CCF auspices. This would include both consumers' cooperatives which would permit the farmer to purchase farm and home supplies on most favorable terms, and marketing and processing cooperatives which would eliminate some of the too numerous barriers between the farmer and the ultimate consumer.

As the years have gone by, the CCF has placed more and more emphasis upon marketing schemes which require the planning of production and the payment of a guaranteed price for major products. The farmer would be protected against crop failures by low-premium crop insurance. He would be made secure against farm implement monopolies through cooperative or state-owned implement plants. He would benefit from modern conservation practices as applied to soil, water, and forests. As a result of the Saskatchewan experience, it may be assumed that great stress will be placed upon the farmer's security on the land and upon better farm living through modernized farm homes and improved domestic facilities.

Foreign Trade.—Since much of Canada's products must be sold in world markets, the declaration of the CCF on external trade—that there is to be "regulation in accordance with the National plan of external trade through import and export boards"[11]—is particularly important.

The panacea proposed is control of foreign trade through import and export restriction or selection. Since 1935 the CCF has received the benefits of reports on the experience of the New Zealand labor government with export-import controls. In that sister dominion, the government has effectively brought under public monopoly the export of butter and cheese. In general, the results were reported as favorable, and it was not difficult to confirm the CCF convictions that the old-fashioned methods of dealing with tariff problems required extensive revision. Accordingly, the policy of the CCF concerning export-import controls differs materially from the reciprocity policy cultivated by the Mackenzie King government since 1935. Under their trade agreements, both Canada and the United States have enjoyed a lively trade to the mutual advantage of both parties, although there are some on both sides of the border who have been adversely affected.

The CCF manifesto for the 1945 election gave added emphasis to the regulatory aspects of foreign trade. It advocates import and export boards to regulate and expand trade and to stabilize export prices. It proposes agreements for bulk sale and purchase in the interests of "stability of trade," "lowering of consumer prices," and removing "barriers to international trade." This sounds like the old story of having one's cake and consuming it

[11] Regina Manifesto, plank 5.

276 The Third Force in Canada

too. Neither a system of absolutely free trade nor a completely controlled import-export plan seems likely to prevail in Canada. If Canada had the choice of one or the other, however, it would be well advised for its own and the world's prosperity to choose freedom of trade. Should a CCF government in the Dominion carry out protection through tariffs and import licensing to the extent done in the U.S.S.R. or even in New Zealand, there would likely be an immediate lowering of the standard of living.

The Liberals, especially the late J. W. Dafoe of the Winnipeg *Free Press*, have repeatedly labeled the CCF hostile to the free movement of trade. There are good reasons to doubt the soundness of CCF trade policy, but it has thus far remained general enough to permit differing interpretations. It would be reasonable to have two policies: one, to be applied so long as world economic conditions permit, providing free movement of trade through low tariffs and reciprocal trade agreements with most-favored-nation clauses; the other, to be used should Canada be faced with a world hobbled by trade restrictions, providing the most advantageous trade relations through import selection, bulk sales, preferences, and other restrictive devices. The latter alternative will surely mean a living standard below that which would prevail under the former. Canada is a great trading nation, and her prosperity depends on the freedom and volume of the flow of her imports and exports.

Cooperative Enterprises.—CCF plans for the expansion of cooperative enterprises are restated throughout the party's policy declarations. In pledging itself to "the encouragement by the public authority of both producers' and consumers' cooperative institutions," the CCF adopts no policy unique to Canadian governments. Existing laws in the Dominion and in most of the provinces provide favorable terms under which cooperative enterprises may be launched, and in some provinces have provided financial assistance as well. Farmers' marketing cooperatives are already well established in the prairies. Credit unions have large memberships throughout most of Canada. Consumers' and fishermen's cooperatives are now flourishing in the Maritimes. It appears that the CCF may find its greatest field for expansion of cooperatives in the consumers' field, both retail and wholesale. The assignment of the major responsibility for the distribution of consumers' goods might conceivably be made to wholesale and retail consumers' cooperative societies.

OF SOCIAL SIGNIFICANCE

Labor and Social Security.—The CCF pronouncements in labor and social fields are of importance both to industrial workers and to the general public. The Manifesto declared for "a National Labor Code to secure for the worker maximum income and leisure, insurance covering illness, accident, old age, and unemployment, freedom of association and effective participation in the management of his industry or profession."[12]

The National Labor Code anticipated by the plank would, if adopted, bring Canada to the forefront among the nations, in labor and social security legislation. Canada has been particularly backward in these fields because of the difficulties which have been encountered in the interpretation of the British North America Act. Primary jurisdiction over labor legislation lies in the hands of the provinces. The National Labor Code anticipated by the CCF could not be validly enacted under

[12] Regina Manifesto, plank 7.

existing interpretations of the Canadian Constitution; hence, a constitutional amendment assigning to the Dominion government full powers over labor and social legislation is a necessary prerequisite to effective action.

The proposed code would guarantee to all who are able and willing to work the right to work at suitable employment. Should such employment not be available, the Dominion government would be obligated to provide maintenance. Maintenance might be supplied either through unemployment insurance or other means. This idea of the right to work or the right to maintenance was contained in the declarations and writings of J. S. Woodsworth throughout his long public career.

The steps toward social security include not only unemployment insurance, but also plans for protection against the hazards of sickness, death, accident, and old age. The party declares for the limitation of hours of work, but does not state any specific number as desirable.

Collective bargaining in Canada has a rather uncertain status because the provinces have primary jurisdiction in this field. The CCF would foster the organization of trade unions and guarantee absolutely the right of the freedom of association. The Regina Manifesto speaks of collective agreements and works councils as leading to worker participation in the management of industry. This would appear to be a gesture toward allaying trade union apprehension that there would be no workers' voice in the management of socialized industry. This item has raised an acute controversy within the British Labour Party, and may yet prove a highly debatable question if and when the CCF controls the government of Canada.

Health Services.—The CCF program for health services is set forth in rather vague terms. The Regina Manifesto merely declares in favor of publicly organized health, hospital, and medical service. CCF literature tells the story of inadequate medical care, but the precise solutions for the problem are to be found mainly in the remarkable record of the party in Saskatchewan. Unquestionably, the party would greatly extend public health services, especially in the field of preventive medicine. The national party has refrained from committing itself to any particular solution to the health problem. It has neither embraced state medicine nor declared in favor of a health insurance scheme.

An index to the CCF's approach to the health problem may be obtained by observing the program of the CCF government in Saskatchewan. Medical services in Saskatchewan have already been socialized to a greater extent than in any other of the Canadian provinces or in any American state. The province has long provided special hospitals for victims of tuberculosis and cancer. General hospitals are, for the most part, owned and operated by public bodies and charge low rates. For many years the rural municipalities of Saskatchewan have been authorized to employ municipal physicians, who provide free medical services to the residents of these units of government. In spite of the extent of these services, however, there remained in Saskatchewan acute health problems. A significant proportion of the people received almost no medical services, mainly because of poverty. A contributory health insurance scheme is often proposed as the solution for a situation like this. Health insurance, however, would provide coverage for only a small portion of the people of Saskatchewan who need medical services. A contributory scheme of this kind is designed especially for industrial wage earners for whom contributions may be handled as a pay-roll tax. In a prairie province like Saskatchewan, most of the gainfully employed work in agriculture, and it would be exceedingly difficult to devise a contributory arrangement as simple as that involved in the pay-roll tax.

Education.—Education is now, and is likely to remain, under the jurisdiction of the Canadian provinces. Therefore, educational matters are not dealt with in specific terms in the Regina Manifesto or in the policy resolutions of successive CCF national conventions. On the other hand, for CCF governments in the provinces, education will constitute one of the outstanding fields for achievement.

Because a large number of CCF leaders both in the Dominion Parliament and in provincial legislatures are teachers by profession, the educational policies of the CCF have been stated as effectively as policies on any other subject. Perhaps the most common demand the CCF makes with respect to educational services is for more expenditures. Additional money can provide more nearly adequate teachers' salaries, better buildings, improved instructional materials, school lunches, and additional health services.

Beyond these things which can be purchased with added appropriations, there is much stress in the CCF policies upon reworking the emphasis in the schools and examining the fundamentals of the character and purpose of education. Some of the earliest attacks upon the CCF government in Saskatchewan in 1944 were made on the basis of "alleged CCF intentions of indoctrinating [for] socialism in the schools." What the CCF has argued for is not a chance to indoctrinate anyone in a particular philosophy, but to open the minds of youth to the total picture of society so that students will be able to make up their own minds intelligently and be somewhat liberated from the environmental influences of the past.

GOVERNMENT AND MAN

The Canadian Constitution.—The CCF recognizes that its ambitious program cannot be achieved through Dominion legislation without amendments to the British North America Act. The Regina Manifesto provides for "the amendment of the Canadian Constitution, without infringing upon racial or religious minority rights or upon legitimate provincial claims to autonomy, so as to give the Dominion Government adequate powers to deal effectively with urgent economic problems which are essentially national in scope; the abolition of the Canadian Senate."[13]

The British North America Act, as interpreted by the Judicial Committee of the Privy Council, does not provide powers by means of which the federal government might deal adequately with the great social and economic problems of the present day. The limitations on Dominion powers were reëmphasized in the experience of the Bennett government (1930–1935) with its belated "new deal." Although there is much general sentiment in Canada for a reallocation of powers between the Dominion and provincial governments, the specific amendments required and the methods for securing their adoption are matters of controversy. Since 1932, CCF sentiment has mainly favored national action in key fields, social and economic. As the CCF gains control over provincial governments, however, emphasis may shift to some advocacy by it of provincial rights.

---

[13] Regina Manifesto, plank 9.

After the publication of the Rowell-Sirois report on federal-provincial relations, a special conference of the CCF was assembled to discuss the whole question thus raised. The National Council meeting at which the policy of the CCF with respect to the report was formulated was held in Regina in February, 1941. Members of the National Council agreed that the Dominion government must take the initiative in calling another Dominion-Provincial Conference.[14]

There was general support for the major recommendations of the Rowell-Sirois report, including the recommendation that the federal government should have sole responsibility for unemployment relief and social services (excluding education).

Another fundamental change likely to be effected by a CCF government of the Dominion, if not before, is the forbidding of further civil appeals from the Canadian courts to the Judicial Committee of the Privy Council in London. The Supreme Court of Canada has already given an advisory opinion that such appeals may properly be forbidden by statute of the Canadian Parliament. CCF sentiment is overwhelmingly for eliminating them. Early in 1949 it became clear that the policy of the Liberal Party ran in the same groove. French Canada is, however, opposed.

Abolition of the Senate.—The CCF faces a barrier in the Canadian Senate, which is far more formidable than ever was or now is the British House of Lords to the Labour Party. A Labour government can advise the King to create new peers in numbers sufficient to enact the party's legislative program. If this drastic step appears inadvisable, the House of Lords can be abolished in two

---

[14] National Council meeting, Regina, February 9, 1941, pp. 1–2.

sessions in one year by ordinary legislation passed by the House of Commons alone. A CCF government, on the other hand, would have power only to fill vacancies in the Canadian Senate up to the normal number of ninety-six, plus a maximum of eight additional members as provided under Section 26 of the British North America Act. Since the term of office in the Senate is life, it might take two decades for the CCF to obtain appointments enough to get control of that House. Nothing could be transacted governmentally in the meantime save in the limited field of consent.

The CCF stands flatly for abolition of the Senate. It is difficult to see how this can be accomplished under existing constitutional procedures. Amendments to the British North America Act require approval of both the House of Commons and the Senate and final enactment by the British Parliament. Probably the CCF would introduce early in its regime legislation calling for revision of the amending process of the B.N.A. Act. The Senate, entirely Liberal and Conservative, will no doubt decline to agree to any changes that would reduce its power over constitutional amendments. It is not surprising, therefore, that the conservative interests of Canada have come to look upon the Senate as the eventual bulwark of support for private property should the CCF gain power.

In *Social Planning for Canada* it is proposed that an amendment of the British North America Act to abolish the Senate might be introduced after the Senate has blocked some major piece of legislation. On defeat in the Senate, the government can either call an election on the issue "Abolish the Senate," or proceed to ask the British Parliament to amend the B.N.A. Act without

Senate concurrence.[15] The Constitution was amended in 1875 on request of the Cabinet alone. One additional power possessed by a government is the authority (B.N.A. Act, Sec. 26, referred to above) to appoint eight additional senators if a deadlock between the two houses occurs; but eight would be a divisory number as compared with the solid phalanx of Liberals and Conservatives already in possession.

Taxation and Public Finance.—Like other socialist parties, the CCF would use the power of taxation to accomplish social ends as well as to raise revenue. The original declaration of the Regina Manifesto was for "a new taxation policy designed not only to raise public revenues but also to lessen the glaring inequalities of income and to provide funds for social services and the socialization of industry; the cessation of the debt-creating system of Public Finance."[16]

The existing taxation system in Canada is alleged by the CCF to be excessively regressive. Because the larger proportion of Canadian revenue is, in normal times, obtained from customs duties and excise and sales taxes, the revenue system is said to place a disproportionately heavy burden on those whose capacity to pay is least. In place of the old policy, the CCF would substitute a progressive tax policy, involving high income and inheritance taxes, graduated according to ability to pay. With the background of experience in public finance obtained during World War II, the CCF would retain the stiff personal income and corporation tax rates, and remove, so far as possible, taxes which fall upon articles of general consumption.

---

[15] *Social Planning for Canada,* p. 510.
[16] Regina Manifesto, plank 11.

The CCF does not promise lower taxes for the people of Canada. In the transitional period, its ambitious social and economic program will cost a great deal of money. The party does look forward, however, to a time when taxation may be eliminated entirely in a substantially socialist economy.

The party has not looked favorably upon those recent theories concerning debt and public finance which have emanated from New Deal economists in the United States. The idea that a rather heavy burden of public debt may be used to secure a measure of stability in the economic system is repugnant to the socialist theory that such debt perpetuates the "parasitic interest-receiving class." It is at this point that the Regina Manifesto makes a gesture to the followers of Major Douglas by declaring that public works "should be financed by the issuance of credit based upon the national wealth of Canada."

Lewis and Scott, in *Make This Your Canada,* estimated that carrying out the CCF program might require $2,500,000 a year in the initial stages, as follows: for social security, $1,000,000; housing, $500,000; rural electrification, $300,000; other purposes, $700,000. These sums appear small after the huge expenditures of World War II, and cannot be regarded as adequate at the present purchasing level of the dollar. From time to time the capital levy has been proposed as a revenue-raising and a social device, but it has never been incorporated in the official policy of the party.

Civil Liberties.—Although its opponents condemn the CCF as "national socialist" enemies of freedom, the party has, from the beginning, been preoccupied with defending the rights of individual citizens. Its original policy declarations on this subject were framed to demand "freedom of speech and assembly for all; repeal of Section 98 of the Criminal Code; amendment of the Immigration Act to prevent the present inhuman policy of deportation; equal treatment before the law of all residents of Canada irrespective of race, nationality, or religious or political beliefs."[17]

According to the CCF analysis, freedom of speech and assembly have repeatedly been denied to persons whose political and social views differ from those of the government of the day. During World War II, the CCF was particularly on the alert to protect the rights of numerous minority groups. The party sought the elimination of the government's ban on the Communist Party, certainly one of the CCF's greatest enemies, and has defended the free-speech rights of Jehovah's Witnesses and of Technocrats.[18]

The party has also committed itself in favor of an amendment to the B.N.A. Act providing a formal bill of rights somewhat comparable to that of the American Constitution. After December, 1941, the CCF stood almost alone among political groups in Canada willing to defend the rights of Japanese-Canadians. CCF liberality with respect to religious freedom may prove a definite political asset in the western provinces where the Doukhobors, Mennonites, and other peculiar sects have considerable voting strength.

Formation of a CCF Government.—If the CCF should win a majority of the seats in the House of Commons in a federal general election, the Governnor-General would be obliged to send for the leader of the party and ask him to form a government. This duty Coldwell or his suc-

[17] Regina Manifesto, plank 12.
[18] Report of the 1942 convention, p. 18.

cessor would undertake. He would choose the members of the cabinet after consulting with the appropriate bodies within the party. The national constitution of the CCF does not require any elaborate consultation or caucus action like that found in some of the provincial CCF's and in the labor parties of Australia and New Zealand.

Should the CCF win a plurality (i.e., the largest number of seats but not a majority), the Governor-General presumably would be bound to send for the CCF leader, who might attempt to form a government. The CCF is not committed to any particular tactics should this situation occur. Much would depend upon the exact circumstances. If the election took place in a summer or fall several months before the time for Parliament's normal opening, Coldwell might form a government which would hold office until the opening of Parliament. At that time the CCF government would introduce socialist legislation or otherwise precipitate a vote of confidence. It is to be expected that the government, lacking a majority, would go down to defeat. The Prime Minister might then either (1) ask the Governor-General to dissolve the House of Commons and set another general election date, or (2) resign. The Governor-General might refuse to dissolve Parliament under these circumstances. There are on record in the British Commonwealth fifty-one refusals to dissolve, including one involving the Dominon of Canada in 1926.[19]

Should the CCF government resign, it is assumed that the Conservatives and the Liberals would form a coalition government. The CCF has long predicted the eventual coalition of the two old parties in opposition to its social-

---

[19] Eugene Forsey, "The Crown, the Constitution, and the C.C.F.," *Canadian Forum*, 23 (June, 1943): 54–56.

ist policies. CCF participation in a coalition with the Liberals or Conservatives or other nonsocialist party is forbidden under the terms of convention decisions. The proposal for CCF participation in a national government was defeated at the 1942 CCF convention by an overwhelming majority.[20]

EXTERNAL AFFAIRS

Early Policy.—It is in the field of international relations that the program of the CCF has undergone the most noteworthy transformation during the past fifteen years. The Regina Manifesto called for "a Foreign Policy designed to obtain international economic cooperation and to promote disarmament and world peace."[21]

Leaders of the CCF point with pride to this declaration and claim with some degree of accuracy that the basic principles of external relations have not changed. On the other hand, world conditions have undergone revolutionary changes; and only the fact that the goal of world peace, security, and economic cooperation was stated in the most general terms makes the Regina declaration applicable today.

In 1933 the CCF declared its support of international cooperation through the League of Nations and the International Labor Organization. The League was recognized, however, as having become "a League of capitalist great powers." The external affairs plank in the Regina Manifesto ended with a ringing declaration that Canada must refuse to become involved in any more wars fought to make the world safe for capitalism.

Isolationist Period.—The CCF was not alone in failing

[20] Report of the 1942 convention, p. 15.
[21] Regina Manifesto, plank 10.

to take a strong stand on matters of foreign policy. Neither the Liberal nor the Conservative Party did much in the late 1920's and early 1930's to formulate guiding principles for Canada in international affairs. In common with the peoples of several other countries which had been involved in World War I, Canadians were disillusioned with the results and reacted strongly against the idea of being drawn into another European war.

During 1933 and 1934 the *Canadian Forum* carried a number of articles on foreign policy in which the issues were clearly stated. At a time when confidence in the League of Nations was at an extremely low ebb, Escott Reid showed that Canada, if a collective security system were lacking, might have to choose between (1) continued membership in a new centralized British Empire and (2) a North American alliance.[22]

CCF leaders doubtless read with much interest the analysis made by Reid, who is now an official in the Department of External Affairs. The economic advantages of the British tie were enumerated and balanced against the disadvantage of acquiring a moral obligation to fight if Britain should become involved in war. If, on the other hand, Canada should choose to rely mainly on collaboration with the United States, the export market for wheat might be lost but danger of involvement in war could be reduced. Throughout his series of articles, Reid advocated the formulation of a foreign policy in peacetime in order that there should be the fullest possible parliamentary and public advance understanding of all obligations and commitments.[23]

---

[22] Escott Reid, "Canada and This Next War," *Canadian Forum,* 14 (March, 1934): 207–209.

[23] Escott Reid, "A Foreign Policy for Canada," *Canadian Forum,* 14 (July, 1934): 379–382, and "Can the League Be Saved?" *ibid.* (April, 1934), pp. 348–351.

In the 1934 national convention, held in Winnipeg, a manifesto on immediate policy was drafted. It contained declarations that "the CCF is unalterably opposed to war."[24] If the capitalist nations should become involved in war, Canada should observe strict neutrality. Further, Canada must refuse military assistance to the League of Nations "as at present constituted."

League Sanctions.—In the latter half of 1935, the Italian invasion of Ethiopia precipitated an attempt by the League of Nations to use for the first time its authority to invoke economic sanctions against an aggressor nation. The CCF was divided over the issue. Two national councilors, Irvine and Taylor, supported both economic and military sanctions.[25] They were ruled out of order by the chairman on the grounds that their proposal conflicted with the 1934 convention declarations which had declared against the application of sanctions in the League's present condition and had demanded reorganization of the League. Graham Spry favored economic sanctions, subject to the limitation that Canadian men and munitions should not participate in a European war. Evidently Woodsworth's position prevailed, that sanctions should not be employed unless disarmament and League reorganization preceded.

A House of Commons debate over the League followed the introduction of a resolution by T. C. Douglas in March, 1936. Although it urged the government to fulfill its obligation to the League, especially in regard to economic sanctions, the motion recognized the "danger and futility of sanctions unless collectively imposed."[26]

---

[24] Frank H. Underhill, "The C.C.F. Convention and After," *Canadian Forum*, 14 (September, 1934): 463–465.

[25] Minutes of the National Council, Winnipeg, November 30–December 1, 1935, p. 12.

[26] House of Commons, *Debates*, session 1936, I: 667.

The resolution listed conditions which must be met before Canada would participate in any foreign war. They included reduction in armaments, open diplomacy, and revision of treaties.

Canadian Neutrality.—The 1936 national convention adopted a declaration on foreign policy which stated more fully the position of the CCF with respect to external relations. It condemned the imperialist powers for betraying the principles of the League and preparing for war.[27] It listed as the principal causes of war the struggle for raw materials and competition for markets; these factors were designated essential attributes of the capitalist system. Again a good word was said for a properly organized League of Nations, but the heart of the declaration was that Canada should remain strictly neutral should war eventuate. The 1937 convention qualified the word "war" with the adjective "imperialist."

Early in 1937, Mr. Woodsworth proposed a resolution in the House of Commons calling for strict neutrality in the event of war abroad.[28] Prime Minister King in the course of the debate declared that Parliament would be called should a war situation arise and assured the members that no commitments existed which would require Canada's participation in war. Although his motion was defeated by a combination of Liberals and Conservatives, Woodsworth's resolution produced the fullest discussion of foreign policy in the House of Commons since 1919.[29]

Although CCF foreign policy declarations were becoming increasingly isolationist in tone, the party was not

[27] R. A. MacKay and E. B. Rogers, *Canada Looks Abroad* (Toronto: Oxford University Press, 1938), pp. 387–388.

[28] House of Commons, *Debates*, session 1937, I: 237–249.

[29] F. H. Underhill, "The Debate on Foreign Policy," *Canadian Forum*, 16 (March, 1937): 8–10.

callous to the need of adjusting Canadian practices to handicap aggressors. In a statement issued to the Canadian press on September 14, 1935, the National Executive called upon the government to apply neutrality legislation to the Sino-Japanese conflict. The statement drew attention to the fact that Canadian exports of metals in 1936–37 were four times those of the previous year. Not long afterward, the National Council authorized the sending of a cable to C. R. Attlee, leader of the British Labour Party, condemning developments in British foreign policy and asking for more attention to the interests of the Dominions.[30]

Declaration of War.—Following the German invasion of Poland on September 1, 1939, Great Britain and the Dominions, except Ireland, declared war against Germany. Canada was the last of the Dominions to enter the war. In keeping with his pledge made earlier to Parliament, Mackenzie King delayed action until full consultation with Parliament could take place. An emergency CCF National Council meeting was held the first week in September, 1939. The Council decided without difficulty that the CCF should not enter a union or national government. A committee was appointed to draw up a statement of policy toward the European war.[31] The statement was approved by a vote of 13 to 9; subsequently, G. H. Williams (Saskatchewan) and Stanley Knowles (Manitoba) withdrew their opposition, and the final vote was recorded as 15 to 7.

This declaration was entitled, "CCF Statement on Canada and the Present Crisis," and was issued September 9, 1939. It reaffirmed the CCF conviction that this

---

[30] Minutes of the National Council, Ottawa, February 26–27, 1938, p. 3.
[31] Emergency meeting of the National Council, September 6–8, 1939, pp. 2–4.

war, like the last one, was caused by a struggle for trade supremacy and political domination. The statement pointed out that the Canadian people had had no voice in the foreign policies of Europe which led to war. The Canadian government was denounced for its failure to take steps to secure for Canada full powers in foreign affairs, in order to avoid automatic involvement in war.

The Council was willing, however, to concede that the struggle might involve the survival of democratic institutions, and that in part, at least, the people of Britain and France were waging a war against aggression. In view of these factors, the CCF called for a policy based upon the national interests of the Canadian people. Canadian participation should be limited to the defense of Canada's shores and to economic aid, but must not include conscription or overseas expeditionary forces. A demand was made for tax policies and economic controls that would result in equality of sacrifice.[32]

At the time of the declarations of war, CCF M.P.'s stood with a small group of French-Canadian isolationists in opposition to the use of troops overseas. They were defeated in the House of Commons by a vote of 151 to 16.[33] Woodsworth took a pacifist view of the war, and from this point onward M. J. Coldwell appeared as the chief spokesman of the CCF in matters of foreign relations.

Conscription of Wealth.—As the events of the war unfolded, in the years 1939–1941, the CCF developed an attitude toward the war which was quite different from

---

[32] The text of the September 9 statement is appended to a pamphlet, "Canada and the War—The C.C.F. Position" (Ottawa: CCF National Office, 1939).

[33] F. H. Soward, *Canada in World Affairs: The Pre-war Years* (Toronto: Oxford University Press, 1941), p. 161.

its policy declarations of a few years before. It reaffirmed its opposition to an expeditionary force in Europe, but, once this force was sent, the CCF members felt it necessary to vote the soldiers supplies. Increasingly, the CCF leaders utilized wartime conditions to justify some of the steps toward nationalization of industry, long a part of its peacetime program. At first, the attitude of the CCF toward the war did not win a particularly favorable response from the electorate. The disappointing results of the federal general election of 1940 may be explained, to an important degree, in terms of a lack of public support for the semipacifist stand of the party.

The general outlook of the CCF changed considerably during 1941. In December, 1941, however, the Japanese attack on Pearl Harbor and the entry of the United States into the war made it possible for the CCF to adopt a new and successful approach to the problems of a nationalist war. In CCF circles it was said after December, 1941, that this would have been the logical time for Canada to enter the war as a fully united nation. Prior to this time, North America had not appeared sufficiently in danger to warrant action on European or Asiatic battle fronts. After Pearl Harbor, both the United States and Canada had a clear stake in World War II because their own security was threatened. This new support for the Canadian war effort did not constitute an all-out endorsement of the Liberal government's conduct of the war. The CCF did not retract its previous opposition to conscription for overseas service, but stoutly maintained that the conscription of wealth must take place before, or simultaneously with, the conscription of man power.

In April, 1942, Prime Minister King submitted to the voters of Canada in a national plebiscite the question of freeing the government from its 1940 election pledge not to draft men for overseas service. The CCF National Council decided to recommend a "Yes" vote on the plebiscite. It did so because of its conviction that, in the critical situation then existing, the Canadian government should be free to act in the best interests of Canada and her allies. During the plebiscite campaign, the CCF stated openly that when the plebiscite was over the party would devote its efforts to securing equal sacrifice, including the conscription of wealth.[34]

After the plebiscite was completed, the returns showed that a strong majority of the voters in every province except Quebec favored the release of the government from the pledge against conscription for overseas service. The Premier then proposed in the House of Commons a bill which would permit the government to proceed with ordering conscripts to overseas duty at such time as the government should require their services. In the epic debate which followed, in June, 1942, the CCF exploited to the maximum the propaganda value of its unique position. The party, having supported a "Yes" vote in the plebiscite, now opposed the legislation which would permit the government to carry out the results of the plebiscite. There were two principal grounds for this stand. The first pertained to the form of the legislation, which empowered the government to take action in its own time rather than to establish a general policy which should go immediately into effect. The second and more fundamental objective was the call for equal sacrifices through conscription of wealth. Dissatisfied with the government's gestures in this direction through increased taxes, the

---

[34] M. J. Coldwell, "Go to the Polls—Address on the Issues of the Plebiscite" (Ottawa: Director of Public Information, 1942), pp. 1–8.

CCF National Council called for government ownership or control of war industries, nationalization of financial institutions, limitation of profits to 4 per cent, and limitation of total earnings to a flat maximum.

Wartime Policies.—Concerned over certain undemocratic tendencies in the conduct of the war and the administration of liberated territories, the National Council in September, 1943, adopted a resolution summarizing CCF views on some of the problems of the war and immediate postwar period.[35]

Its first point stressed as a necessity that the Western democracies must work with the Soviet Union both during and after the war. The CCF condemned Allied military governments in Africa and Italy for what it regarded as a willingness to work with Fascists. Support was given to De Gaulle's Committee of Liberation as the true representative of the French nation. As a general policy for dealing with liberated peoples of Europe, the CCF favored local self-government, trade union and cooperative sponsorship, freedom of speech and assembly, and economic rehabilitation. Finally, Canada's responsibility and leadership in international affairs was stressed. Her qualification for such a role was defined as freedom from imperialistic ambitions and the important contributions she had made to the war effort of the United Nations.

Postwar Policy.—The CCF policy statement entitled "For Victory and Reconstruction" was adopted by the national convention in July, 1942.[36] Most of this declaration is concerned with domestic problems, but an important part concerns world reconstruction. The CCF

---

[35] This statement is reprinted in the *New Commonwealth*, October 14, 1943.

[36] "For Victory and Reconstruction," policy statement adopted July 29, 1942 (Ottawa: CCF National Office, 1942).

recognized that national reconstruction is contingent upon the building of a "democratic world order." Canada and other nations must forswear economic imperialism and devote their resources to achieving the abundant life.

The 1942 statement called for the establishment of an international body to plan the rehabilitation of peoples and areas devastated by war. The establishment of the United Nations Relief and Rehabilitation Administration, in which Canada participated, temporarily filled the need for an agency in this field. The second principal demand of the CCF on the international front was for a commission to make plans for a new "world association of nations." At first this commission would be representative of the wartime allies alone, but other nations would be admitted as they were liberated from Axis control. The new association of nations would construct a permanent system of collective security. Ultimately, membership would be open to all nations willing to accept the obligations and responsibilities. Instead of hedging on the question of national sovereignty, the CCF makes a forthright declaration that national sovereignty must be subordinated to the authority of the collective system in order to secure international peace and justice.

In keeping with its emphasis on economic motivation and factors, the CCF stresses the importance of raising living standards throughout the world by effective utilization of economic resources. An advanced view is taken by the CCF with respect to security against aggression. International authority, according to the 1942 statement, must have power not only to settle disputes but also to enforce its decisions by means of an international police force under its control. There is a flat declaration for the "abolition of national armaments."

The statement disposes of the knotty problem of colonial areas with the declaration that all colonial peoples must attain self-government, but it gives no indication of how long this process would take or the means by which it should be achieved. Likewise, the declaration that minorities must be protected is not implemented by any explanation of the methods of attaining this laudable end.

In general, the CCF has only recently begun to think deeply on matters of external relations. The party has to a large degree purged itself of isolationist and pacifist thought. Its recent policy declarations on foreign affairs have been thoughtful and reasonable. During 1948 and 1949 the party pledged its support to the European Recovery Program, the Western union in Europe, and to the North Atlantic Security Pact proposal.

THE UNITED NATIONS

The next phase of CCF policy with respect to external relations concerns the United Nations. M. J. Coldwell was a delegate to the San Francisco conference at which the U. N. organization was born. The Charter of the United Nations contained many of the provisions suggested in "For Victory and Reconstruction." The differences between Coldwell and Mackenzie King over the various issues raised at the conference were certainly less than those between Canada on one side and the Big Four on the other. The two party leaders differed on minor matters such as the admission of Argentina and the representation of trade unions, but they stood together as exponents of the "middle power" point of view.

The United Nations is, by CCF standards, an imperfect instrument. It does not go far enough in curbing national sovereignty; the great powers have too much control over enforcement machinery. The field in which Coldwell, as a Canadian delegate, had a distinct influence on the Charter, was in social and economic cooperation. Partly as a result of Canadian insistence, the United Nations Economic and Social Council (UNESCO) was made a "principal" agency of the U. N. and its duties were expanded.

In the 1946 CCF national convention, pacifist proposals were defeated by overwhelming votes and the leadership of Coldwell, Knowles, Lewis, and the National Executive was followed. An influential minority in the CCF favors crusading for world government. On this point the differences are mainly in tactics rather than in policy. Most majority spokesmen would concede that world federation is a desirable ultimate goal, but argue that the U. N. must be supported now in order to achieve an improved organization later.

THE BRITISH COMMONWEALTH

Sentiment in the CCF is in favor of retaining Canada's connection with the British Commonwealth of Nations. In addition to all the other ties that unite Canadians with the British, CCF leadership is, to an important degree, of British birth. Maintenance of the ties of the Commonwealth, however, does not mean that the same relationships that existed in the past between Canada and the United Kingdom will be retained intact. The CCF is strongly in favor of acquiring for Canada the power to amend its own constitution and autonomy in the conduct of its foreign relations. CCF faith in the British Commonwealth of Nations as a force for good in the world has been reaffirmed by the growing influence of labor governments, as in Great Britain, Australia, and New Zealand, in Commonwealth affairs. On the other hand, the CCF is perhaps the most nationalistic of the three leading political parties of Canada. It contends that Canada should make its own foreign policy, not blindly follow London or Washington. There is strong support for reciprocal trade relations with the United States and other nations. Sentiment for exclusive economic arrangements within the British Empire is difficult to find within the CCF. The party is opposed to the carrying of judicial appeals to the Privy Council in London, and is not in favor of formalizing the organization of the British Commonwealth through creation of a secretariat. Alone among Canadian parties, the CCF advocates Canadian membership in the Organization of American States.

CHAPTER IX

Looking Forward

PRESIDENT CONANT of Harvard several years ago called for a native American radicalism as the best means of combating totalitarianism of the left or right. Léon Blum of France and other Continental leaders of democracy put their hope and faith in the "third force," a united front that can stave off the attacks of both Communists and reactionaries. The British Labour government, like those of Australia and New Zealand, seeks amid difficulties to follow the road to a socialist economy using a vehicle of democratic and parliamentary politics. These are the opposite numbers of the Canadian CCF.

The CCF shares with its overseas social-democratic colleagues many policies and tactics and much in structure and problems. It entered a party system in which the traditional parties had become substantially alike in principles and platforms. The new Canadian party produced leadership that was dynamic, able, and devoted. It brought forward a comprehensive economic program that involved drastic departures. The CCF built a party organization in the country on the firm foundation of an individual dues-paying membership and with party machinery highly responsive to popular controls.

SIGNIFICANCE OF THE MOVEMENT

Granted that there are many similarities between the CCF and other democratic socialist parties, what are the unique features of the Canadian party? Three new de-

partures appear important enough to warrant special
consideration: (1) the reconciliation of farm and labor
interests in a common political movement; (2) adaptation
of socialist ideology to North American conditions and
problems; and (3) restoration of some pluralist content to
contemporary socialist practice.

Farm-Labor Unity.—The original conception of the
CCF, already partially realized, was a federal union of
agricultural and labor interests. The party had its origin
at Calgary in 1932 when representatives of urban labor
and rural farmers convened to build a common program.
No elaborate philosophy has been devised to explain or
justify this alliance, which would appear passing strange
in France, Britain, or in contemporary America. In the
depression it was obvious that the several aspects of the
economy of the country were so interdependent that
neither workingman nor farmer could regain prosperity
unless the other did also. The man who works on the
land buys the product and services of the man who works
in the mill or shop; the industrial worker consumes the
produce of the agriculturalist. Of course, one may gain
some temporary advantage over the other by a set of
"natural" circumstances such as a crop failure or world
economic adversity. The more divisive situation is found,
however, when one group manages to outgrab the other
in "artificial" benefits, such as a tariff that keeps farmers
poor but produces high wages for labor and high profits
for business.

Since 1944, the main testing ground in this field has
been in Saskatchewan. There, a legislative majority composed mainly of farmers and representatives of rural
districts enacted the most advanced labor and social
legislation in Canada. Labor men representing urban

constituencies worked and voted for farm security and other legislation of importance to rural areas. Whether this mutual respect and tolerance will last cannot be predicted now. The 1948 Saskatchewan provincial election returns suggest that the CCF is gaining more support in the cities and declining slightly in the countryside. Some critics of the CCF see in these returns a tendency for the party to become a labor party, as it is substantially in both Ontario and Nova Scotia.

The saving element may prove to be the ingenuity of the leadership in representing both labor and farm viewpoints on major issues, and especially in including the largest possible sector of the population among the beneficiaries of social legislation. For example, instead of following the stereotype of Bismarckian health insurance for wage earners only, the Saskatchewan government sponsored a plan that permits the people of each region to decide what services they wish. Where, as in the Swift Current area, a comprehensive prepaid health service was desired, the coverage was the whole population.

Perhaps the best assurance of labor-farm unity within the CCF flows from the constant contact of representatives of these two great interests in party bodies. It was the participation of farm folk in early CCF conventions that prevented the scheduling of land for eventual nationalization, a plank included in most socialist platforms. Had land nationalization been advocated, much rural support would have been alienated at the outset. Instead, the Regina Manifesto and subsequent policy declarations have attracted farmers with their forthright statements against the alleged exploiters of agrarian Canada—the grain exchange, farm implement manufacturers, middlemen, and speculators.

Farm-labor unity appears to be entirely feasible if certain conditions are present. Each group must use self-restraint, avoiding the excessive demands that inevitably arouse either ill feeling or counterdemands, or both. Consultation must be regular and frank; the party machinery in the constituencies, the provinces, the nation, and in Parliament offers abundant opportunities for this. Party policy must be kept balanced, and proposed social services as broad in coverage as possible. Given these conditions, it is likely that the movement can hold farm and labor elements together despite the terrific propaganda barrage leveled against it by business and other interests that have much to gain by the disunity of the two elements.

Socialism in North America.—In its seventeen years of existence the CCF clearly has won the most support and achieved the greatest success of any avowedly socialist party in the history of North America. Eugene V. Debs, even in 1912, his best year as Socialist candidate for President of the United States, won only 16 per cent of the total popular vote. In the 1945 general federal election the CCF polled more than 15½ per cent of the total votes cast, and in the Canadian Institute of Public Opinion polls it had stood to win more than 25 per cent. This remarkable record has been made possible in part because the CCF has been able to adapt successfully to North American conditions its socialist ideology.

Socialist thought in Europe has appealed primarily to people in substandard economic circumstances and in a class system which offers little chance of advancement. In Canada and the United States the quantity of natural resources and the effectiveness of industrial development have minimized the size of this chronically depressed class. The newness of the country and the opportunity offered by the frontier has made for rapidly shifting fortunes, a far cry from the stable class-stratification found in Britain and continental Europe. Both Canada and her great neighbor developed free public education, which helped to ensure a larger measure of occupational mobility.

Because of these differing factors it has been necessary for the CCF to devise new approaches in converting Canadians to its cause. The case for central economic planning must be made, not as an alternative to collapsing private enterprise, but as a justifiable extension of controls over a rather prosperous and productive economy. The case for nationalization or provincialization of an industry may have to be made in terms of greater efficiency or better service, not as an appeal for a doctrinaire response to a well-learned catechism. The typical common man of North America has tasted some of the fruits of property ownership and has enjoyed a few luxuries and conveniences beyond the minimum level of subsistence. Being a practical fellow, he wants to be sure he will not lose the bird in the hand while prospecting one in the bush.

Consequently, the CCF has advanced proposals that would appeal positively to an essentially practical and nondoctrinaire voting public. One of the most effective appeals has been the promise of expanded social and educational services, which are traditional objects of progressive programming. During the first decade of CCF history, both old parties were lagging behind the public appetite for developments in this field. Into this breach the CCF pushed its social program and won a reputation as the party of social progress. The old parties, confronted with this potent threat, began to propose social legislation which, a short time before, they had regarded as unwarranted. Being in national office, the Liberals were able to enact the family allowance system and health grants to the provinces, but they were sharply rivaled by the aggressive social program of the CCF government in Saskatchewan.

In addition to the social services appeal, the CCF has advanced in popular esteem by its espousal of specific socialization projects for which the need is obvious to many. This tactic is not unlike that used a generation ago by "Bull Moose" Progressives in the United States, who were not averse to public ownership of monopoly utilities in which abuses existed. The party also has demonstrated its ability, particularly in the prairie provinces, to choose issues of regional interest like the Hudson Bay route for wheat exports, lower farm implement prices, and mortgage moratorium legislation.

Socialization Is More than Nationalization.—In the long run, the CCF's most distinctive contribution to socialist theory and practice may be its concept that socialization is broader than nationalization and can take the form of provincial, municipal, or cooperative endeavor, whichever is deemed most appropriate. In Great Britain and New Zealand, labor parties in office have placed heavy reliance upon nationalization. Canadian CCF thought, without fanfare or open controversy, has taken on a pluralist and guild socialist strain. Some nationalization projects involve the creation of huge public corporations or departments, the control of which is far removed from both the people served by the public enterprise and the employees who operate it. Partly because of the scattered pattern of Canadian population and partly because of strong traditions of self-help and home rule developed throughout that young country, straight national state socialism does not evoke much enthusiasm in CCF circles.

Where it is possible and practical, CCF planners prefer to keep economic undertakings close to the people. Obviously, socialization of the Canadian Pacific Railway would mean nationalization, but the greater number of regional and local enterprises that were scheduled for socialization could be better handled, CCF leaders believe, through provincial, municipal, or cooperative ownership and operation.

This plural approach to socialization helps to reassure many who have legitimate fears of an all-powerful national government, and it may serve to take the wind out of the bellows of those who proclaim that socialism, however much democratic forms are maintained, will lead to totalitarianism. The socialist will continue to demand a central planning agency with real powers of direction and coordination, but the diffusion of ownership and control will be some guarantee against undue centralization of economic power in a single level of government.

Assets

The rise of the CCF to a position of national influence during the last decade and a half has not been a story of consistent and unbroken successes, but of a gradual increase of strength with many setbacks and recurring problems. The time has come to take stock, to assess the assets and liabilities of the movement, and to try to see in what direction it is headed.

A Democratic Organization.—The CCF organization is as democratic in form and spirit as one is apt to find in the free world. Party structure is built, like a pyramid, from the foundation course upward. Throughout the organization, party officers and bodies are ultimately answerable to the rank-and-file membership. In political party affairs it often happens that the form is democratic but the spirit becomes autocratic. This has not yet occurred in the CCF. The membership has coveted and exercised its prerogative of holding its party officials strictly accountable. Even in Saskatchewan, where the CCF government is well into its second term of office, party organization has remained responsive to the membership.

Another crucial test of democracy in party organization is the basis of financing party campaigns and activities. Popular control can be frustrated by overreliance upon contributions from vested interests. Like the British Labour Party, the CCF from its beginning has based its financing on the dues and gifts of the many rather than the few. Every member of the party helps to carry the cost of operation. The broad base of party finance keeps the party free from obligation to special contributors who seek favors to serve their own selfish interests.

One of the most creditable features of CCF organization is the way in which it avoided in earlier and difficult years the temptation to hand over control of the party organization to trade unions in exchange for support. While full credit should be given to those leaders who saw early the problems involved in trade union domination, the fact is that the unions were not ready for that measure of political activity during the formative 'thirties. When the industrial groups did begin affiliating in considerable numbers, from 1942 on, the party gave them appropriate though modest representation in party conventions. It studiously avoided the unfortunate features of British trade union affiliation to the Labour Party: proxy voting, union domination of national party affairs, and the inevitable charges of external control. Wisely, the CCF has provided for trade union affiliation, with the exception of the United Mine Workers, District 26, directly with provincial rather than with the national organization. Far from being dominated by trade unions, the CCF still has some difficulty in engaging the active interest and participation it would like to have from affiliated unions.

Able Leadership.—Reference has been made several times to the extraordinarily able and devoted leadership of the CCF. In the late J. S. Woodsworth it had a veritable saint and one of the most respected men in the land. In M. J. Coldwell and T. C. Douglas the party has two of the most attractive leaders in Canadian public life. Beyond these are two dozen or more men and women who not only make the CCF their lifework, but who also possess the qualities that make them top-rank leaders in provincial parties and legislatures, in Parliament and in the national office. They are the persons who have built the organization, and they are the ones who have guided it with rare devotion in spite of many opportunities for personal preferment by compromising or going over to a rival camp for a snug consideration.

In addition to those who man the party machinery and represent the CCF in public office, some of the ablest academic men of Canada have associated themselves with the CCF, occasionally at some risk to their professional careers. In the formative years of the CCF the League for Social Reconstruction hammered out background materials on which the party program could be based. In common with the British Labour Party, but unlike those of New Zealand and Australia, the CCF has given great responsibilities to intellectuals. This has helped to assure thoroughness of preparation in policy matters. It has posed certain other problems, too.

A Good Record.—Reviewing the record of sixteen years, an unprejudiced observer assigned to appraise the effectiveness with which the CCF has built a new party and conducted itself in provincial and national legislatures must render the verdict, "Well done." In a country in which personal scandal occasionally upsets political careers of both individuals and parties, the CCF has not one serious blot on its escutcheon. Party affairs have been reported with frankness; even in the field of party funds the record has been published for all to see. Several defections have taken place, both to left and to right, but the conduct of the CCF in dealing with the M.P.'s, M.L.A.'s, and others who have left the party has been marked with singular patience and evenhanded justice.

It is, of course, the record in public office that will be most decisive in the attitude of the public mind toward the CCF. As has been seen in earlier chapters, the CCF has earned a deserved reputation in the Dominion Parliament and in provincial legislatures for hard work and great vigilance. If one grants the validity of the CCF's concept of the interests of the common man, he must record that its M.P.'s and M.L.A.'s and local councilors have striven to serve them faithfully. The CCF representatives have fought consistently for the privileges of the cooperative movement, the rights of labor, civil liberties, and farm security and prosperity. They have opposed special favors to business interests and have sought expansion of public controls over industry and commerce.

LIABILITIES

Excluding the matters of program and policy, the principal liabilities of the CCF appear to be: (1) deficiency of money with which to publicize policies and to combat attacks; (2) failure to develop a strong mass following and to make a potent appeal to the masses; (3) inability, thus far, to build a fully national party; and (4) an unfavorable world situation.

Lack of Money.—Although the CCF today is in a much better financial situation than it was in earlier years, the party cannot match the large sums that are raised by opponents to vilify it. Of course, the CCF can get along well on substantially smaller budgets than its opponents, because it has so much volunteer assistance in performing party work. The principal need for large funds is to answer the propaganda campaigns directed against the CCF movement. Since these have been carried through the media of newspapers, radio, and pamphlets, the same channels probably should be utilized in replying.

It is difficult to see how the party can raise funds large enough to do this job. The most promising approach to added revenue is expansion of the dues-paying membership. If Ontario, Manitoba, Alberta, British Columbia, and Nova Scotia had as large an individual membership, proportionately, as Saskatchewan, the financial picture would be vastly improved. Enlargement of membership would mean more than added resources; it would augment that chorus of devoted voices which by passing ideas along by word of mouth probably exceeds in effectiveness all the modern mass media of communication.

Lack of Mass Support.—A stranger in the midst of CCF supporters is impressed by the great earnestness with which they approach politics. It is perhaps true that the party could not have advanced so far without thorough and serious conviction on the part of its inner core of leaders. On the other hand, the time has now arrived for making an effective appeal to the great majority of voters in the country, many of whom are either not capable of understanding the fundamental philosophy of the party or are not interested in doing so. Some are wedded to one of the old parties by family or regional tradition and can be persuaded to change allegiance only by the most glittering approach. Some have a protective coating of inertia and sales resistance; their consciousness can be penetrated only by the unusual and the spectacularly attractive. With few exceptions, CCF campaigns and activities have been drab affairs, utterly lacking in the flash and glamour which can bring brightness into the lives of people for whom the most logical arguments fall flat when presented by the conventional public address or through literature. The party badly needs to learn to utilize such fields of expression as motion pictures, drama, dance, and music. The time has come for a bit of Barnum with social significance.

All this does not imply that the intellectuals ought to be demoted from places of responsibility. They have played an important role in the party, and ought to continue so to do. It does mean, however, that the political and economic thought on which the CCF has based its program should be presented to the Canadian people in terms that the common man can grasp. The intellectual has his uses, but this is a task in which the public relations counsel, the advertising man, the documentary film expert, and the "practical" politician have an outstanding part to play. A campaign that is made as meaningful as possible to the mass of the voters should include stratified electioneering which makes a distinctive appeal to each of the major elements in the electorate. Stratification of appeal does not necessarily mean that different groups are recipients of opposite stories and contradictory promises. Quite aside from the moral aspects, no party could long get away with such duplicity. Correctly conceived, stratification involves making a special effort to reach a group with the aspect of the program in which that group has greatest interest. Some such special appeals have been used in the past, but they require further refinement and additional consideration of appropriate channels of communication. As an example of this technique, in the next federal election, the story of Saskatchewan farm security legislation ought to be brought to every farmer in Canada through farm journals and radio stations serving predominantly rural areas. The CCF fight in Parliament for price controls might be brought to housewives through advertising in women's magazines and daytime radio broadcasts. Obviously, such approaches cost a great deal of money and their full use cannot be expected until the financial situation is much improved.

Nonnational Coverage.—Although the CCF is a national party both in the sense that it has some organization and candidates from coast to coast and that it engages vigorously in national politics, it must concede that thus far it has not penetrated deeply into some geographic areas which are vital. The most conspicuous deficiency in strength is found in Quebec, where the surface has barely been scratched. Without some foothold in French Canada, CCF aspirations to a House of Commons majority appear unlikely to be satisfied. After a decade and a half of thought and work on the problem of Quebec there is an almost total absence of progress. Hope persists, however, that a change may come suddenly, as when the province of Quebec a half century ago moved from the Conservative to the Liberal side. The CCF is also miserably weak in New Brunswick, where the 1948 provincial election showed the party weaker than in 1945. Prince Edward Island, the smallest province, is substantially unorganized. In Alberta the CCF is still unable to make headway against its Social Credit rival. Newfoundland, the new and tenth province, should have been a fertile field for the CCF, but the party failed utterly in the provincial and federal elections of 1949.

Unfavorable World Situation.—The political situation of the world since 1945 places the CCF in an unsatisfactory position. The emergence of mighty Russia as a superpower and as a potential enemy of the Western countries has cast a pall of suspicion over all left-of-center movements. While the CCF has been very careful to disavow Communist support, to exclude Communists from its membership, and to take its stand squarely with Britain and America, many opponents of the CCF have sought to paint the party and its leaders in red hues. Name-calling can be an exceptionally effective propaganda device in a period of hysteria. Critics of the CCF dwell upon the "similarity" of economic planning as practiced by the U.S.S.R. and that advocated for Canada by the CCF. When the Labor-Progressives ostentatiously "supported" CCF candidates in the Saskatchewan provincial election of 1948, the *de facto* union of Communists and socialists was proclaimed by enemies of the CCF. As a matter of fact, the Communists supported the Liberal government in the 1945 federal election, and have reserved their bitterest attacks for the CCF both in the trade union movements and in much of their political activity; but that is not going to be admitted, certainly not emphasized, by old-line party propagandists.

IMPACT

The rise of the CCF has already brought great changes to the Canadian party system and to the great interest groups of the Dominion. Let us summarize the impact of the new party first with reference to the other political parties, and then to organized pressure groups.

Changes in Parties.—The Liberal Party, which has been in power nationally since 1935, commenced belatedly around 1939 to adapt its program to meet the CCF challenge. The strategy was obvious: propose and enact piecemeal a number of new social services. First, the British North America Act was amended to empower the federal government to establish a plan of unemployment insurance. Next, the national family allowance system was set up. Later, a federal health act was passed, granting large sums to provinces for hospitals and health services. The Liberal Party national organization, with no national convention between 1919 and 1948 and with little "grass roots" party activity during most of the same period, was able to win two general-election victories in wartime, a decisive one in 1940 and a close one in 1945. The reluctance of the Liberal leadership to yield to popular desires for reform might have led to defeat had not the elections been called at the politically most favorable junctures by the canny Mr. King. With the handwriting clearly on the wall, the government began to move cautiously toward the left in policy. Unable to win over the CCF's Coldwell when seeking a leader to succeed King, the Liberals have followed the sound tactic of borrowing some of the more respectable planks from the CCF platform. Under the leadership of Louis St. Laurent, King's successor, the Liberals may be expected to cling rather closely to the middle of the road or even veer somewhat to the right.

The Conservative Party has undergone a bewildering number of changes of leadership and program since the CCF was born. Throughout most of the reign of Mackenzie King, the Conservatives were fumbling for an opening. Although the core of the Conservative leadership is right-of-center on domestic and imperial matters, it recognizes the difficulty of winning independent votes without some show of progressivism. Under the leadership of John Bracken, 1942–1948, the Conservatives did recoup some of their losses, but it is difficult to see how the country can support two major parties that are essentially conservative in outlook. The existence of the CCF may have been a factor in Bracken's selection as national Conservative leader, but its chief contribution probably has been to supply a scapegoat for Tory orators. Only in Ontario have the Conservatives been able to maintain enough strength to form a government. Actually, the presence of the CCF, a potent challenger of the essentially conservative Liberal Party, may doom the Conservatives to slow decline, especially now that a strong rightist, George Drew, has been chosen as national leader.

Social Credit is still a factor to be reckoned with in Canadian politics, and it constitutes a formidable opponent of the CCF. Its firm hold on Alberta was demonstrated again in the overwhelming provincial election victory of 1948. On the other hand, the presence of the CCF has been a major factor in minimizing Social Credit strength in other prairie provinces. Circumstantial evidence indicates that Social Credit in Alberta is now considered by conservative and business interests as a bulwark against radicalism. The sole consolation of the CCF is that most Albertan voters have not returned to old-party allegiances, but are, by whatever name, third-party followers.

The impact of the CCF on the Labor-Progressive Party has been the most interesting of all. Ever since 1932 the Communists have been handicapped by the existence of a well-organized non-Communist movement of the left. Unable to develop a large following themselves, the Labor-Progessives have tried to affiliate with the CCF but have been rejected decisively on each application. From time to time the Labor-Progressives' groping for a successful tactic has led them to endorse the Liberals. Occasionally the CCF has been embarrassed by Labor-Progressive support, not asked for but loudly proclaimed. On the industrial front, Communists bore from within and often rise to high office in trade unions. Their influence is thrown in such a way as to prevent union affiliation with the CCF. On the political front, the presence of the CCF has operated to expose individual Communists to public scrutiny and to prevent the development of a united front in which Communists might predominate.

Interest Groups.—The rise of the CCF has spread alarm in business and financial circles. Naturally, reactions have been uneven, but the typical business group displays fear and business as a whole has been aroused so far as to raise large sums of money in order to combat the menace. The CCF threat has unified business interests that previously were not in a cooperative mood. The campaign against the "socialist menace" has provided employment for public relations counsel and others. Whether it has induced greater direct financial support for the Liberal and Conservative parties, it is difficult to judge; certainly the big-business offensive against the CCF has benefited the old parties indirectly, so far as the fears aroused drive voters toward "safe and sane" standards and "reliable" men.

The CCF impact on the trade unions is already felt and will become stronger. Finding in the CCF a party that consistently represents the side of organized labor in Parliament and provincial legislatures, the unions have moved from the old A. F. of L. tactic of nonpartisan, limited participation in politics toward the United Kingdom tradition of full support for a single party. Both C.C.L. and T. and L. C. unions have entered the party and increasingly regard it as their political instrument.

FUTURE OF THE CCF

Since the course of politics rarely runs smooth, no man can foretell the future with precision. One can, however, assemble pertinent facts and use them as a basis for making qualified forecasts.

Political Prospects.—In the first place, it appears that there is no possibility that the CCF will form a coalition with one of the old parties or otherwise lose its separate identity. A few individuals may be tempted by the prospect of sharing power with the Liberals, but the rank and file would surely disown them as rapidly as the British Labour Party ousted Ramsay MacDonald in 1931. Others might like to do business with the Labor-Progressive Party, in the interests of working-class unity, but any form of union with Communists would do the CCF more harm than good. Some kind of electoral agreement with French nationalists in Quebec might be within the realm of possibility, but it would require the greatest patience in cultivation and meticulous care to avoid compromising on principles. Social Credit advances in Quebec and the continuing strength of that movement in Alberta might possibly warrant some negotiations, but the eventual break-up of a party so feebly based and superficial seems certain.

Electoral Prospects.—A series of provincial elections in 1948–49 served as a prologue to the 1949 federal election; and the year 1949 was one of the bleakest and most discouraging of recent CCF history. Having rewon power in Saskatchewan and the opposition role in Ontario, in 1948, the party expected important gains in the provincial elections of other provinces and in the federal general election that would be held by mid-1950. In rapid succession, June elections were scheduled in Nova Scotia, British Columbia, and the Dominion. Although reëlecting its two M.L.A.'s in Nova Scotia, the CCF lost its opposition role to the Conservatives and dropped in popular vote from 14 per cent in 1945 to 9.5 in 1949.

In British Columbia the results were even more disappointing. Only six CCF M.L.A.'s were returned, as against ten in 1945 and fourteen in 1941. In popular vote the CCF dropped from 38 per cent in 1945 to 35 per cent in 1949. Although the old parties remain in coalition and their votes are not available separately, the CCF probably continues to be the largest single party in B.C.

The federal general election of 1949 represents the first actual reduction in the popular vote received by the CCF in a national poll. The CCF proportion of the total vote was cut from 15.6 per cent in 1945 to 13.6 in 1949; and the number of M.P.'s elected, from 28 in 1945 to 13 in 1949. The CCF parliamentary caucus still includes, however, most of the top national leaders of the party.

Numerous explanations have been given for the setbacks of 1949. Perhaps the chief factor in the national defeat lay in the major party alignment: moderately progressive voters so feared a Conservative victory that they threw their support to the Liberals. Indeed, the campaign of the CCF itself did much to develop public apprehension over the alleged Drew-Duplessis-Houde "axis." Both Liberal and CCF campaigners concentrated attacks upon what they called a conspiracy of reaction and isolation.

Once the possibility of voting Conservative had been eliminated from an elector's mind, he had a choice, in most constituencies, between a Liberal candidate standing on a platform of gradual change and a CCF candidate advocating far-reaching social and economic reform. Because the CCF had practically no chance of gaining a parliamentary majority, the Liberals constituted the only possible group that could win. In the roles of Prime Minister and party leader, Louis St. Laurent inspired confidence in his middle-of-the-road program and in the government he headed. The result was a landslide victory for the Liberals.

A party of the left must expect scare attacks at election time. The CCF had its share in 1949. There was the usual attempt to associate the party with Communism. Opponents gave wide publicity to the failure of the B. C. provincial convention to support the North Atlantic Pact, to the stand of some Manitoba CCF members against the Pact, and to the playing of the "Red Flag," a traditional British labor song, at a British Columbia CCF rally.

Of great importance was the Liberals' success at winning to their side the moderate progressive vote. The Liberal spokesmen put forward a program of modest expansion in the social services, promising medical care, improved old-age pensions, and other advances. A decade earlier the CCF was almost unique in advocating a comprehensive system of social security for Canada. By 1949 both old parties were making pledges in that field, and the Liberals could point to a record of legislation already enacted.

The occupational breakdown of voters by the Canadian Institute of Public Opinion confirms the impression that the CCF is more of a labor party than a farm party: 34 per cent of union laborers polled, and 13 per cent of farmers, declared their support of the CCF. Notwithstanding that organized labor still supports the Liberals more strongly than it does the CCF, antilabor voters may be frightened away from the CCF by the fact that unions are affiliated with it.

Seriously weakened both in the House of Commons and in the British Columbia legislature, the CCF faces a very heavy task of rebuilding electoral support. The severe blows it sustained will not mean its collapse, as many opponents predicted. The events of 1949 do indicate, however, that the road ahead is a difficult one, and that success on the national political scene must await fuller organizing and educational achievements, or a major business depression, or both.

On the federal front, probably the most the CCF can hope for at the next election is an indecisive result, with no party securing a majority and the CCF securing the largest number of seats. This might enable the party to govern for a few months and to choose the time and issues of the following election. The prestige of the CCF, after having governed for even a brief period, would likely be so much augmented that the old parties would be forced into some form of electoral unity with each other. Of course, there is always an outside chance that a major depression might speed the process of political conversion and place the CCF in control of the government much sooner than could be anticipated through the ordinary process of growth.

Given a rather uneventful period of years ahead, the rise of the CCF to national power may be delayed an election or two by the merger of the Liberal and Conservative parties. There are many degrees of unity that are possible between the old parties, ranging from free competition at election time with coalition government afterward, through electoral agreement assigning constituencies between the parties, to a formal merger of organizations and all. The mildest form would not be so likely to harm the CCF at the polls, but either of the other two might result in a serious setback, for many CCF M.P.'s win their seats by a plurality, not a majority vote. Until, however, the old parties are convinced that there is no other way to stop the CCF, they are likely to continue going their separate ways. At this stage both Liberals and Conservatives are so preoccupied with hopes of winning power in their own right that it will take another CCF scare, comparable to that of 1943 in Ontario, to make the spirit of unity prevail.

Policy Frontiers.—On the whole, CCF policy is well stated and well conceived. National domestic policy, as proposed in the "First Term" program adopted by the 1948 convention, probably goes beyond the realm of practicality in scheduling the commercial banks for early nationalization. No other labor government in the British Commonwealth has yet carried out full socialization of banks. After four years of power, British Labour has nationalized only the central bank. In fourteen years in office, New Zealand Labour has taken over the central bank and about half the trading-bank facilities. Australia's Labour government has passed a bank nationalization bill, but it has been declared unconstitutional in the High Court, and that decision has been confirmed by the Judicial Committee of the Privy Council in London.

The 1948 CCF program also includes iron and steel among the early objects of socialization, yet this aspect of heavy industry has only now begun to be envisioned, and was undertaken by British Labour only after four years of power.

Before the assumption of national power, some hard thinking ought to be done on the problem of incentives. After full employment and a full measure of social security have been achieved, as in New Zealand, the task of getting people to work to keep production high is an acute one. Likewise, the management of socialized industry ought to be studied thoroughly, under such headings as: Should employees have representation on governing boards? What degree of control by government and Parliament ought to be exerted over a public enterprise? It is questions of this type that arise as socialization plans mature and are put into force. Unless they are studied in advance and satisfactory answers are found, a case may be made for deëmphasizing nationalization and perhaps even provincialization.

Insufficient thought has been given to the foreign trade aspect of the controlled economy. Under the devices proposed in the 1945 manifesto, a CCF government might be held guilty of discriminatory trade practices as defined by the International Trade Organization.

On the international front, after a period in which iso-lationist-pacifist convictions predominated, the party has moved far along the road to a belief in collective security, and now stands in favor of a United Nations with real power to enforce peace and root out the causes of war.

Conclusion.—This, then, is the CCF: a new progressive party, democratic in organization and aspiration, socialist in policy, and pragmatic in tactics. Born on the Canadian prairies in the depression of the 1930's, the new party has suffered the inevitable attacks and ills that beset a young movement. Having survived to the age of seventeen without being absorbed into one of the old parties, or merged with either, the CCF now appears headed for its majority, surely in years and perhaps in votes.

Even at this tender age the CCF has great significance for North Americans. Canada has often been seen as a link between the United States and Great Britain, combining her ties of sentiment in the British Commonwealth and those of location on the North American continent. The CCF is demonstrating how the British Labour Party idea may be adapted to the American environment. Canada and her great neighbor are so much alike socially, politically, and economically that a program which serves as good medicine to one may at least suggest a tonic to the other.

In each of these North American democracies third party movements have been rising and falling for generations. Canada's basic major party alignment has remained the same since early post-Confederation days. The United States last gave birth to a major political party in 1856, when the Republican Party was launched. Some of the third parties have possessed attractive leadership, others popular programs, and still others a measure of staying power. A few have combined two of these elements for a while, but none has achieved all three sufficiently to acquire major party status. It is no exaggeration to say that the CCF has the best prospect, in three-quarters of a century of North American history, of displacing a major party. At present the Canadian party system is in a fluid condition. Both old parties have new leaders, both have suffered recent losses, yet neither is willing to give up hope of winning power to govern the Dominion on a one-party basis. Meanwhile, Canadian politics has become a many-sided affair, with five different parties holding power in the several provinces and two coalition provincial governments. The time for decision in the matter of old-party coalition may come suddenly, when the results of the next federal election are available. A national Liberal-Conservative merger or coalition might delay the CCF's rise to federal office, but it would probably hasten the day when the new party will win the support of an electoral majority in the country in its own right.

Bibliography

GOVERNMENT PUBLICATIONS

Canada. Department of External Affairs. *Report of the Secretary of State for External Affairs* (Ottawa: King's Printer, annual).
—— Department of Labour. *Report on Labour Organization in Canada* (Ottawa: King's Printer, annual).
—— —— *The Labour Gazette* (Ottawa: King's Printer, monthly).
—— Department of Trade and Commerce. Dominion Bureau of Statistics. *Canada* ... (Ottawa: King's Printer, annual).
—— —— —— *Financial Statistics of Provincial Governments in Canada, 1945* (Ottawa: King's Printer, 1947).
—— House of Commons. *Debates*, 1932–1948.
—— Royal Commission on Co-operatives. *Report* ... (Ottawa: King's Printer, 1945).
—— Royal Commission on Dominion-Provincial Relations. *Report* ... (3 vols.; Ottawa: King's Printer, 1940).

Alberta. Legislative Assembly. Agricultural Committee. *The Douglas System of Social Credit* ... (Edmonton: King's Printer, 1934).
—— —— *First Interim Report on the Possibility of the Application of Social Credit Principles to the Province of Alberta* (Edmonton: King's Printer, 1935).

Saskatchewan. *The Dominion-Provincial Conference on Reconstruction, 1945–46: The Reply of the Saskatchewan Government to the Proposals Submitted to the Conference by the Dominion on August 6, 1945* (Regina: Bureau of Publications, 1946).
—— *The New North: Saskatchewan's Northern Development Program, 1945–1948* (Regina: Bureau of Publications, 1948).
—— *Progress Report from Your Government* (Regina: Bureau of Publications, 1948).
—— *Saskatchewan and Reconstruction* (Regina: Bureau of Publications, 1945).
—— *Social Welfare in Saskatchewan* (Regina: Bureau of Publications, n.d.).
—— *Toward Health Security* (Regina: Bureau of Publications, 1948).

Bibliography

Unpublished Manuscripts

C.C.F. National Office, 301 Metcalfe Street, Ottawa. Minutes of meetings and conferences, 1932–1948, including:

"Conference Resulting in the Formation of the Cooperative Commonwealth Federation held in the Labour Temple, Calgary, Alberta, August 1, 1932."

Reports of national conventions, variously titled, for 1933, 1934, 1936, 1937, and 1938. Subsequent convention reports available in mimeographed or printed form.

Minutes of National Council meetings.

Minutes of National Executive meetings.

Minutes of various special and extraordinary meetings.

C.C.F. Alberta Section, 10010 102d Street, Edmonton. Minutes of meetings and conventions, 1937 to date.

C.C.F. Saskatchewan Section, 510 Kerr Building, Regina. Minutes of meetings and conventions, 1932 to date.

University of California Library, Berkeley 4, California

Taylor, Malcolm G. "The Social Credit Party in Alberta." Unpublished M.A. thesis, 1943.

—— "The Organization and Administration of the Saskatchewan Hospital Services Plan." Unpublished Ph.D. dissertation, 1948.

University of California Library, Los Angeles 24, California

Rusch, Thomas A. "The Political Thought of the Cooperative Commonwealth Federation." Unpublished M.A. thesis, 1948.

University of Michigan Library, Ann Arbor, Michigan

Lederle, John W. "The National Organization of the Liberal and Conservative Parties in Canada." Unpublished Ph.D dissertation, 1942.

Organizational Publications

C.C.F. National Office. *Report of the . . . National Convention . . .* (Ottawa: C.C.F., biennial). Mimeographed, 1940, 1942, and 1944; printed, 1946 and 1948. Earlier reports are variously titled and contained in national office minute books.

—— *The First Ten Years—1932–42, Commemorating the 10th Anniversary of the C.C.F. . . . .* (Ottawa: C.C.F., 1942).

—— *C.C.F. Handbook* (Ottawa: C.C.F., 1948). A manual for members.

—— *News Comment* (Ottawa: C.C.F., twice monthly). A research bulletin.

—— *Across Canada* (Ottawa: C.C.F., monthly). National membership bulletin.

—— *Horizon* (Ottawa: C.C.F., monthly). National Cooperative Commonwealth Youth Movement magazine.

—— Various leaflets, pamphlets, posters, and other materials issued occasionally. Some of these, of more enduring value, have been listed under the authors' names in the section "Books and Pamphlets," below.

C.C.F. Alberta Section. *People's Weekly* (Edmonton: Alberta C.C.F., weekly).

C.C.F. British Columbia and Yukon Section. *Report of the . . . Provincial Convention* (Vancouver: B. C. and Yukon C.C.F., annual). Printed, 1946 and 1947; mimeographed, 1948.

—— *CCF News* (Vancouver: Federationist Publishing Co., weekly).

C.C.F. Manitoba Section. *Manitoba Commonwealth* (Winnipeg: Manitoba C.C.F., twice monthly).

C.C.F. New Brunswick Section. *True Democracy* (Fredericton: New Brunswick C.C.F., monthly).

C.C.F. Nova Scotia Section. *The Maritime Commonwealth* (Halifax: Nova Scotia C.C.F., twice monthly).

C.C.F. Ontario Section. *Report of the Annual Provincial Convention . . .* (Toronto: Ontario C.C.F., annual).

—— *Planning for Freedom: Sixteen Lectures on the CCF, Its Policies and Program* (Toronto: Ontario C.C.F., 1944).

—— *CCF News* (Toronto: Ontario C.C.F., monthly).

C.C.F. Quebec Section. *Le Canada Nouveau* (Montreal: Quebec C.C.F., monthly).

C.C.F. Saskatchewan Section. *Delegates' Handbook . . . Annual C.C.F. Provincial Convention* (Regina: Saskatchewan C.C.F., annual).

—— *The Commonwealth* (Regina: C.C.F. Publishing & Printing Co., weekly).

Canadian Congress of Labour. *Proceedings of the ; . . Annual Convention . . .* (Ottawa: Canadian Congress of Labour, annual since 1940).

Labor-Progressive Party. *Manifesto of Unity, Victory and Prosperity* (Toronto: Labor-Progressive Party, 1943).

—— *Constitution and Bylaws . . .* (Toronto: Labor-Progressive Party, n.d.).

—— *Program . . .* (Toronto: Labor-Progressive Party, n.d.).

Progressive Conservative Party. *Policy of the Progressive Conservative Party . . . 1942* (Ottawa: Progressive Conservative Party, n.d.).

Progressive Conservative Party. *Public Opinion* (Ottawa: Progressive Conservative Party, monthly).
Trades and Labour Congress. *Report of the Proceedings of the ... Annual Convention* ... (Ottawa: Trades and Labour Congress, annual since 1886).

BOOKS AND PAMPHLETS

Andras, A. *Labor Unions in Canada* (Ottawa: Woodsworth House, 1948).
Brady, Alexander. *Canada* (New York: Scribner's, 1932).
Buck, Solon J. *The Granger Movement* (Cambridge: Harvard University Press, 1913).
Canadian Parliamentary Guide, ed. G. P. Normandin (Ottawa: the editor, annual).
Cassidy, Harry M. *Social Security and Reconstruction in Canada* (Toronto: Ryerson, 1943).
Claspy, Everett M. *Canadian Section of Atlas of Parliamentary Government* (Dowagiac, Michigan: the author, 1939).
Clokie, Hugh McD. *Canadian Government and Politics* (Toronto: Longmans, Green, 1944).
Coady, M. M. *Masters of Their Own Destiny* (New York: Harpers, 1939).
Cohen, J. L. *Collective Bargaining in Canada* (Toronto: Steel Workers Organizing Committee, 1941).
Coldwell, M. J. *Left Turn, Canada* (New York: Duell, Sloan & Pearce, 1945).
Cragg, R. Cecil. *Canadian Democracy and the Economic Settlement* (Toronto: Ryerson, 1947).
Dawson, R. MacGregor. *The Government of Canada* (Toronto: University of Toronto Press, 1947).
Fowler, Bertram B. *The Lord Helps Those ... How the People of Nova Scotia Are Solving Their Problems through Co-operation* (New York: Vanguard, 1938).
Irvine, William. *Co-operative Government* (Ottawa: Mutual Press, 1930).
———— *The Farmers in Politics* (Toronto: McClelland & Stewart, 1920).
League for Social Reconstruction. *Social Planning for Canada* (Toronto: Nelson, 1935).
Lewis, David, and F. R. Scott. *Make This Your Canada* (Toronto: Central Canada Publishing Co., 1943).

Logan, Harold A. *Trade Unions in Canada* (Toronto: Macmillan, 1948).

King, Carlyle. *What Is Democratic Socialism?* (Ottawa: National C.C.F., 1943).

Mackintosh, W. A. *Economic Problems of the Prairie Provinces* (Toronto: Macmillan, 1935).

McCollum, Watt H. *Who Owns Canada?* (Ottawa: Woodsworth House, 1947).

Mooney, George S. *Co-operatives Today and Tomorrow: A Canadian Survey* (Montreal: prepared for the Survey Committee, 1938).

Reid, Escott M. *Canadian Political Parties: A Study of the Economic and Racial Bases of Conservatism and Liberalism in 1930* (Toronto: University of Toronto Press, 1933). Also in *Contributions to Canadian Economics*, 6 (1933): 7–39.

Scott, F. R. *Canada Today: A Study of Her National Interests and National Policy* (2d ed.; New York: Oxford University Press, 1939).

Staples, Melville H. (ed.). *The Challenge of Agriculture: The Story of the United Farmers of Ontario* (Toronto: Morang, 1921).

Wood, Louis A. *A History of Farmers' Movements in Canada* (Toronto: Ryerson, 1924).

Woodsworth, J. S. *Toward Socialism: Selections from the Writings of J. S. Woodsworth*, ed. Edith Fowke (Toronto: Ontario Woodsworth Memorial Foundation, 1948).

Yates, S. W. *The Saskatchewan Wheat Pool: Its Origins, Organization and Progress, 1924–1935*, ed. A. S. Morton (Saskatoon: United Farmers of Canada, 1947).

ARTICLES

Alexander, Robert. "The Socialist International," *Canadian Forum*, 25 (January, 1946): 235–237.

Andras, A. "The Government of a Central Labour Body," *Canadian Journal of Economics and Political Science* (hereafter *C.J.E.P.S.*), 13 (November, 1947): 572–580.

Anon. "Socialism Is Nearer than We Think," *Magazine Digest*, 37 (September, 1948): 29–35.

Argue, Hazen R. "Canadian Wheat Policy," *Canadian Forum*, 26 (October, 1946): 151–153.

Beder, E. A. "What Is a Socialist Economy?" *Canadian Forum*, 27 (April, 1947): 10–12.

Bothwell, J. R. "Libraries in Saskatchewan Today," *Canadian Forum,* 26 (January, 1947): 231.

Britnell, G. E. "Alberta, Economic and Political, II. The Elliott-Walker Report, Alberta Review," *C.J.E.P.S.,* 2 (November, 1936): 524–532.

Brockington, Hugh. "Can Socialism Be Democratic?" *Canadian Forum,* 23 (July, 1943): 83–85.

Brown, P. M. "Must Socialism Include Farm Land?" *Canadian Forum,* 24 (August, 1944): 103–104.

Burnet, Jean. "Town-Country Relations and the Problem of Rural Leadership," *C.J.E.P.S.,* 13 (August, 1947): 395–409.

Cameron, Colin. "Aspects of a Socialist Economy," *Canadian Forum,* 27 (June, 1947): 57–59.

Carroll, Margaret. "Doctors in Saskatchewan," *Canadian Forum,* 27 (September, 1947): 127–128.

Clark, S. D. "The Canadian Manufacturers' Association," *C.J.E.P.S.,* 4 (November, 1938): 505–523.

Coe, V. F. "Dated Stamp Scrip in Alberta," *C.J.E.P.S.,* 4 (February, 1938): 60–91.

Crouch, Winston W. "Alberta Tries Consolidation," *National Municipal Review,* 32 (January, 1943): 21–25.

Crowe, H. S. "The Winnipeg Citizen: First Co-op. Newspaper," *Canadian Forum,* 27 (March, 1948): 273–274.

Duncan, Lewis. "Towards a Canadian Foreign Policy," *Canadian Forum,* 27 (September, 1947): 130–132 and (October, 1947) 158–159.

Eagleton, Clyde. "The Share of Canada in the Making of the United Nations," *University of Toronto Law Journal,* 7 (Lent Term, 1948): 385–394.

Eggleston, Wilfrid. "Dominion-Provincial Relations," *Annals of the American Academy,* 253 (September, 1947): 40–43.

———— "The Future of the C.C.F.," *Saturday Night* (Toronto), 63 (August 28, 1948): 4.

Ferguson, G. V. "Parties of Protest," *Annals of the American Academy,* 253 (September, 1947): 32–39.

Forsey, Eugene. "Appointment of Extra Senators under Section 26 of the British North America Act," *C.J.E.P.S.,* 12 (May, 1946): 159–167.

———— "The Crown, the Constitution and the C.C.F.," *Canadian Forum,* 23 (June, 1943): 54–56.

———— "Disallowance of Provincial Acts, Reservation of Provincial Bills and Refusal of Assent of Lieutenant-Governors since 1867," *C.J.E.P.S.,* 4 (February, 1938): 47–59.

—— "Disallowance of Provincial Acts, Reservation of Provincial Bills and Refusal of Assent of Lieutenant-Governors, 1937–1947," *C.J.E.P.S.*, 14 (February, 1948): 94–97.

—— "Planning from the Bottom—Can It Be Done?" *Canadian Forum*, 24 (March, 1945): 277–279.

Gordon, J. King. "Prairie Socialism," *The Nation*, 163 (August 17, 1946): 180–183 and (August 24, 1946): 207–209.

Grube, G. M. A. "British Foreign Policy," *Canadian Forum*, 26 (August, 1946): 103–107.

—— "The Ontario Election," *Canadian Forum*, 28 (July, 1948): 83.

—— "Socialism and Freedom," *Canadian Forum*, 27 (September, 1947): 128–130.

Hanson, Frank G. "Civil Servants and Politics," *Canadian Forum*, 27 (June, 1947): 61–62.

Irving, John A. "The Evolution of the Social Credit Movement in Alberta," *Canadian Journal of Psychology*, 1 (March, 1947): 17–27, (June, 1947) 75–86, (September, 1947) 127–140.

Laing, Lionel H. "The Nature of Canada's Parliamentary Representation," *C.J.E.P.S.*, 12 (November, 1946): 509–516.

—— "The Pattern of Canadian Politics: The Elections of 1945," *American Political Science Review*, 40 (August, 1946): 760–765.

Lalande, Leon. "The Status of Organized Labour," *Canadian Bar Review*, 19 (November, 1941): 638–681.

Lederle, John W. "National Party Conventions: Canada Shows the Way," *Southwestern Social Science Quarterly*, 25 (September, 1944): 118–133.

Lewis, David. "Canada Swings Left," *The Nation*, 158 (June 10, 1944): 671–673.

—— "Farmer-Labor Unity: The Experience of the C.C.F.," *Antioch Review*, 4 (June, 1944): 166–176.

Lipset, S. M. "Political Participation and the Organization of the Cooperative Commonwealth Federation in Saskatchewan," *C.J.E.P.S.*, 14 (May, 1948): 191–208.

—— "The Rural Community and Political Leadership in Saskatchewan," *C.J.E.P.S.*, 13 (August, 1947): 410–428.

MacMillan, Isabel. "Albertan Politics," *Canadian Forum*, 27 (November, 1947): 178–179.

McGoun, A. F. "Alberta, Economic and Political, I. Social Credit Legislation: A Survey," *C.J.E.P.S.*, 2 (November, 1936): 512–524.

Mallory, J. R. "Disallowance and the National Interest," *C.J.E.P.S.*, 14 (August, 1948): 342–357.

Morrison, J. J. "Parties and Platforms," *Canadian Forum*, 5 (August, 1925): 330–331.

Bibliography

Morrison, J. J. "Political Future of the U.F.O.," *Canadian Forum*, 7 (February, 1927): 138–140.
Morton, W. L. "The Western Progressive Movement, 1919–1921," in Canadian Historical Association, *Report of the Annual Meeting ... 1946* (Toronto: University of Toronto Press, 1946), pp. 41–55.
Reid, Escott. "Can the League Be Saved?" *Canadian Forum*, 14 (April, 1934): 348–351.
——— "Canada and This Next War," *Canadian Forum*, 14 (March, 1934): 207–209.
——— "A Foreign Policy for Canada," *Canadian Forum*, 14 (July, 1934): 379–382.
——— "The Saskatchewan Liberal Machine before 1929," *C.J.E.-P.S.*, 2 (February, 1936): 27–40.
Scott, F. R. "Constitutional Adaptations to Changing Functions of Government," *C.J.E.P.S.*, 11 (August, 1945): 329–341.
——— "The End of Dominion Status," *Canadian Bar Review*, 23 (December, 1945): 724–749.
——— "Socialism in the Commonwealth," *International Journal*, 1 (Winter, 1945–46): 22–30.
Shumiatcher, Morris C. "Alberta Election," *Canadian Forum*, 24 (September, 1944): 127–128.
——— "Hospitals: Saskatchewan's New Public Utility," *Canadian Forum*, 26 (January, 1947): 226–228.
——— "Saskatchewan Socialism Works," *Canadian Forum*, 26 (June, 1946): 54–56.
Underhill, F. H. "The Debate on Foreign Policy," *Canadian Forum*, 16 (March, 1937): 8–10.
——— "The Development of National Parties in Canada," *Canadian Historical Review*, 16 (December, 1945): 367–387.
——— "Canadian Party System in Transition," *C.J.E.P.S.*, 9 (August, 1943): 300–316.
——— "Random Remarks on Socialism and Freedom," *Canadian Forum*, 27 (August, 1947): 110–111.
——— "Some Reflections on the Liberal Tradition in Canada," in Canadian Historical Association, *Report of the Annual Meeting ... 1946* (Toronto: University of Toronto Press, 1946), pp. 5–17.
Ward, Norman. "Parliamentary Representation in Canada," *C.J.-E.P.S.*, 13 (August, 1947): 447–464.
Woodsworth, J. S. "The Labor Movement in the West," *Canadian Forum*, 2 (April, 1922): 585–587.
Young, Fred M. "Maritime Political Trends," *Canadian Forum*, 27 (February, 1948): 247–249.

Index

Aberhart, William, 126, 127, 128, 147–148, 210

Across Canada, 45, 54

Action Libérale Nationale, 170–171

Affiliations to CCF: incomplete U.F.A., 45, 64–65; C.B.R.E., on provincial basis, 46, 47; applications of cooperative commonwealth groups, 46–47; national, discouraged for most applicants, 47, 309; provincial, 47, 49, 74–75, 84, 99, 103, and rules for, 49–50, 84; national, desired for nation-wide economic groups, 47; importance of U.M.W., 47–48, 99, 309; fear of external domination through, 48–49, 308; National Executive provisions for trade union, 49–50; question of representation for affiliates, 50–51; fees, 51–52; of U. F. of C. and local labor parties end, 63; Communist Party request refused, 119; National Council resolution against alliances with other political parties, 119; Labor-Progressive Party's application rejected, 121–122, and again, 133, 317

Agriculture: in provinces, 4, 8–9, British Columbia, 138, Alberta, 144, Manitoba, 153, 156, Ontario, 161, Quebec, 168, Maritimes, 173

    CCF program for: cooperative enterprises, 108–109, 274, 277; security of land tenure, 273, 274; no nationalization of land, 273–274, 303; cooperative farms, 274; marketing schemes and guaranteed price, 274. *See also* Canadian Federation of Agriculture; Farmers' movements; United Farmers of Canada; Wheat

Alberta: agriculture, 4, 8–9, 144; farmers' groups, 10, 11; U.F.A., 10–11, 13, 45–46; cooperative elevators, 11; resources, 144–145; during depression, 145, 147; politics, 145–148

    CCF in: relations with U.F.A., 45, 64–65; organizational situation, 64 ff.; Calgary central council of CCF clubs, 66; Canadian Labour Party controversy, 66–67; unified since 1942, 67; conventions, 74, 75; provincial board, 76, 79, 84; constituencies, 85, 87; finances, 92; press, 93; educational program, 97; cooperatives, 110; CCF electoral strength in, 148–149, 152; CCF handicapped by preferential voting system in, 149; task, 152. *See also* United Farmers of Canada

Alexander, W. H., 24, 26, 42

All-Canadian Congress of Labor: organized, 19; national unions, 19; industrial over craft type of organization, 19; C.I.O. unions unite to form C.C.L., 20, 100; C. F. of L. split from, 21. *See also* Canadian Congress of Labor

American Federation of Labor (A. F. of L.): formed in United States, 18–19; conflict with Knights of Labor, 19; entry into Canada, 19; international unions affiliated with, 19

Banking and finance, Regina Manifesto plan for, 28, 268 ff.; socialization of financial machinery, 28, 109, 268–269, 322–323; proposed control over

[335]

Elections *(Continued)*
  local CCF units, 87–89; national, 134 ff.; Liberal victories, 134; Conservative voters, 134; CCF progress, 135–136; prospects for CCF, 178 ff.; 1949 federal, 319
Elevator companies, grain: grievances against, 9; provincial ownership legislation, 11; cooperative, 11

Farm Security Act, 234, 235, 259–260
Farmer-Labor Group: convention, 67, 220; becomes CCF, 67–68, 220
Farmers' Association of Ontario (F.A.O.): platform, 12; merged with Grange, 12
Farmers' movements: flourish during economic depressions, 4; in western provinces, 4–5; Grange, 5–7; Patrons of Industry, 7–8; Grain Growers' Association, 8–11; United Farmers movements, 11–15; National Progressive Party, 15–17. *See also* Progressive Party; United Farmers of Canada
Farmers' Union, amalgamated with Grain Growers' Association to form U. F. of C., 208
Federated Labour Party (British Columbia), 64
Federated Trade Unions Act of 1872, 21
Ferguson, G. V., 117–118
Finance, national CCF: full statement read at conventions, 35; national office expenses, 44; affiliation fees and contributions, 51; reports of receipts and disbursements, 51; contributions of federal M.P.'s, 52, 189; dues from provincial organizations (quotas), 52, 53; 1946 adoption of national membership fee, 53, 308; expenses, 54, 58; budget, 54; problem of support, 54–55, 311; labor support, 55; few direct individual contributions, 55; election deposit rule, 55–56; problem of financing by-elections, 56; problem of general elections campaign funds, 57–58; needs, 58–59, 311
  provincial, 89–92; receipts from "Victory Fund," 90; from individual gifts, 91; from special fund-raising campaigns, 91; expenditures, 91; financing Saskatchewan socialism, 260
Fines, C. M., 24, 25, 215, 216, 219, 222, 223, 224, 240, 260
Foreign policy, CCF: change in program, 288; Regina 1933 Manifesto for disarmament and world peace, 288; international cooperation, 288; League of Nations, 288, 290, 291; isolationist period, 288–290, 291; *Canadian Forum* articles, 289; economic sanctions, 290; neutrality, 291; condemns British, 292; statement that World War II caused by struggle for trade supremacy and political domination, 293; wartime policies, 296; postwar "For Victory and Reconstruction," 296, 298; for rehabilitation, 297; for new "world association of nations," 297; self-government for all colonial peoples, 298; protection of minorities, 298; pacifist proposals defeated in 1946 convention, 299; supports United Nations, 298–299, 324; connection with British Commonwealth of Nations, 299–300; support for reciprocal trade relations, 300; advocates membership in Organization of American States, 300; British Columbia fails to support North Atlantic Pact, 320

Ontario, CCF in (*Continued*)

with, 70; Communist influence, 71; section abolished in 1932 and new provincial body, 71; local groups, 71; 1935 defeat, 71; largely a labor movement, 72, 167; conventions, 74, 75; provincial council, 77, 78, 80, 82, 83; "Woodsworth House," 80; constituency associations, 85, 87; federal constituency basic unit, 87; financial strength, 89–92 *passim;* nominating convention, 94–95; educational program, 96; electoral strength, 166; fluctuation in vote, 166; reasons for decline, 166; strength in urban and industrial centers, 167. *See also* U. F. of C.

Opposition party, CCF as, 200–201; techniques of opposition, 203 ff.; device of moving amendment to Address in Reply to Speech from Throne, 204–205

Organization, CCF national: party founded, 23–30, 161, 302; democratic, 31, 81–82, 188, 307–309; supported by provincial and local organizations, 32; convention, 32–39; National Council, 39–41; national office, 41–45; affiliations, 45–51; finance, 51–59; rigidity of party system, 101; offices, 188; leader of parliamentary group is president of national party, 188, 192; role of M.P.'s in, 201–203; officers accountable, 308. *See also* Affiliations; Leadership; National Council; National Executive; National office; Origin; Parliamentary group; Provincial organization

Organization of American States, CCF favors Canadian membership in, 300

Origin of CCF: merger of farm and labor movements in 1932, 23, 99, 302; League for Social Reconstruction, 23; plan for "Commonwealth Party," 23-24; Western Conference at Calgary 1932, 24–25, 63; name, 25–26; officers, 26; broad policies, 26–27; organizing campaign, 27; first national convention at Regina adopts policy declaration, 27–29, and frames constitution, 27, 29–30. *See also* Policies; Regina Manifesto

Parker, R. J. M., 233

Parliamentary group, CCF: relation with party machinery, 80–81, 187–188, 202–203; caucus, 181–184, 319; 1945 group, 184–185; caucus committees, 186–187; meetings, 188; future problems, 189; leadership, 189–192, 195–198, 205, 319; standing committees, 193; special committees, 193; procedure on floor, 194–195; personnel 1945–1949, 198–200; role of opposition party, 200–203; resolutions for cooperative commonwealth, 203–204; fight for price controls, 313; caucus includes national leaders, 319

Partridge, E. A., 11

Patrons of Industry (P. of I.), 7–8; spreads from Michigan into Ontario, 7; in Manitoba, 7, 8; political policies, 7, 8; opposes protective tariff, 7, 8; influence wanes, 7, 163; 1894 election in Ontario, 8, 163

Patterson, W. J., 209, 211, 212, 214

Pattullo, T. D., 140

Peart, Helen, 45

Phelps, J. L., 215, 218

Poale Zion (Ukrainian Labor), 47

Tariff, protective: Conservative policy, 2; Grange supports in early days, 6; farmers' concern over, after 1890, 6; Patrons of Industry oppose, 7, 8

Taylor, J. S., 182, 290

Technocrats, 286

Thomson, Watson, 258

Tolmie, Simon F., 140

Trade Union Act of 1944, Saskatchewan, 254

Trade union movement. *See* Labor movement

Trades and Labour Congress of Canada (T. and L. C.), 7; most influential central organization of Canadian unionism, 18; excludes unions of conflicting jurisdiction, 19; expels C.I.O. unions, 20, 100; need for direct representation in parliament and local offices, 22; approves Canadian Labour Party, 22; composed of international unions affiliated with A. F. of L., 99; craft unionism, 99; skilled craftsmen, 99; refers disputes to U. S. body, 101; trend toward more political action, 101–103; alleged growing influence of Communists, 103; affiliations, 103; Winnipeg general strike, 158, 160; Dominion Labour Party formed under, 159; signs of regarding CCF as its political instrument, 318

Trestrail, B. A., 125, 166

Tucker, Walter, 218

Uhrich, J. M., 233

Ukrainian Labor organization, 47

Underhill, Frank H., cited on formation of Canadian parties, 2

Union Nationale: Conservative support in Quebec, 115; extremist leaders and policies, 115; electoral victory in 1935, 170-171; social legislation, 171; attacks on international unions, 171; 1944 victory, 171

United Civil Servants of Canada, 255

United Farmers of Canada: 1910–1919 movement in most provinces, 12; U.F.A. formed, 10–11, 13, political action, 13, controls Government of Alberta 1921–1935, 13, "economic class idea" to promote agrarian interests, 13, delegates to Western Conference, 25, relations with CCF, 45–46, 64, 65–66, 99, abandons politics, 45, 46, 99, 106; U.F.O. successor to F.A.O., 12, platform, 12, policy toward conscription, 12, majority, 1919–1923, 12–13, 161, and reforms, 12, Drury-Morrison clash on tactics, 13, delegates to Winnipeg conference, 15, loses identity in Federation of Agriculture, 70, 106; Saskatchewan Section, 14, cooperative enterprises, 208–209, educational work, 208, pressure politics, 208, 209, for marketing legislation and mortgage moratoriums, 209, joins with I.L.P., 209; U.F.M. organized, 14, member of Progressive Coalition, 14, launches Bracken on career, 14, affiliation with I.L.P., 46; U.F.B.C., 14; of Nova Scotia, 14–15; U.F.N.B., 15 f.; of Quebec, 15

United Mine Workers (U.M.W.): affiliates with CCF, 47–48, 99, 100; in C.C.L., 101

United Nations, CCF policy toward, 298–299, 324

Veterans, rehabilitation (Saskatchewan), 263–264

CPSIA information can be obtained
at www.ICGtesting.com
Printed in the USA
BVHW042258160822
644779BV00006B/20

9 780520 373075